AMERICA'S DECLARATION OF FINANCIAL INDEPENDENCE

Robert H. Schuller and Paul David Dunn

Rutledge Hill Press

Nashville, Tennessee

Published in Nashville, Tennessee, by Rutledge Hill Press, 211 Seventh Avenue North, Nashville, Tennessee 37219.

Distributed in Canada by H. B. Fenn & Company, Ltd., 152a Park Street Lane, Park Street, St. Albans, Hertfordshire AL2 2AU.

Typography by E. T. Lowe, Nashville, Tennessee

Library of Congress Cataloging-in-Publication Data

Schuller, Robert Harold.
    Eliminating the national debt is—: America's declaration of financial
independence / Robert H. Schuller and Paul David Dunn.
      p. cm.
    Includes bibliographical references.
    ISBN 1-55853-376-1 (HC)
    1. Debts, Public—United States.   I. Dunn, Paul David.
  II. Title
  HJ8119.S44   1995
  336.3'4'0973—dc20

95-44330
CIP

Printed in the United States of America
1 2 3 4 5 6 7 8 9—99 98 97 96 95

CONTENTS

Dedicated to Jennifer, Stephanie, and David, and all the nation's other children and grandchildren whose future will shine brighter with a debt-free America

ACKNOWLEDGMENTS

We would like to thank Dr. Milton Friedman, Dr. Gary Schilling, Dr. Arthur Laffer, Dr. Beurt SerVaas, John Templeton, John Crean, J. Peter Grace, and Dr. Martin Feldstein for their valuable contributions to this book. We also extend our gratitude to Lawrence M. Stone, president of Rutledge Hill Press, for believing in this dream for more than ten years. And special thanks to Jeanne Dunn for her love, encouragement, and countless hours of tirelessly organizing, typing, and editing this manuscript.

INTRODUCTION
Robert H. Schuller

It was Monday, February 13, 1995. Abraham Lincoln's birthday was being celebrated this day because the twelfth fell on a Sunday. I was alone commemorating his birthday in his bedroom in the White House, sitting behind his desk, reading the Emancipation Proclamation written in his own hand. Lincoln's one bold commitment had set free four million Americans from slavery. America, not yet one hundred years old, did not have a problem. It simply had a decision that needed to be made. That decision would be painful. It would erupt into civil war. But the decision Lincoln made to set slaves free was the right decision. Abraham Lincoln did not surrender leadership to pressures that would promise painless peace at the price of immorality.

Now, at the invitation of President Bill Clinton, I was spending the afternoon behind Lincoln's desk. Later I would sleep in Lincoln's bed and in the morning have breakfast in the second floor of the White House. A few hours earlier, when I had walked with President Clinton to this historic bedroom, I had given him a copy of a book I had written with Paul Dunn ten years earlier, *The Power of Being Debt Free*. The president and I had prayer, and I watched him walk out of the door to go to his own bedroom down the hall. I prayed he would read the book. The next morning I stepped out of my door just as he came out of his bedroom. We met at the elevator. I was pleased to see him still carrying the book as he left to take Air Force One on an official engagement.

As I watched President Clinton leave, I wondered again—as

I frequently did when Paul and I wrote the *The Power of Being Debt Free*—how many Americans are enslaved to financial debt. I wondered how many presidents of the United States, because of our national debt, have lost their freedom to lay out creative, constructive, inspiring budgets—budgets that would build great cities, underwrite cures for deadly diseases, and inspire and motivate children to develop their potential. How many presidents in the future will be enslaved to a national debt that will demand so much money to pay the interest that neither the president nor Congress can dream great dreams for an incredibly beautiful, bold, and exciting future?

America needs another Abraham Lincoln! We need a leader who can dare to envision a great dream that will break the country free from the tyranny of this awesome, merciless federal debt. No person escapes the penalty of the debt. The debt keeps the poor from having the opportunity to discover—much less develop—their potential. The rich watch while a large portion of their taxes goes just to pay the $260 billion annual interest on the debt. No one escapes. We cannot vote on whether or not we would like to pay the interest; we do not have that freedom. Because of the debt, we do not have the freedom to choose where we want to channel our energies and our resources. Interest on the debt is not a choice. It is a demand.

Senators, representatives, and presidents all have surrendered their leadership to this profound force that heartlessly and greedily grasps the first money that comes to the federal government from the hard-working American citizens who—more than they know—have become the serfs to an economic despotism. We call out, hoping some visionary American will set the people of the United States free by announcing America's declaration of financial independence, just as Abraham Lincoln set free the slaves by announcing the Emancipation Proclamation.

In the summer of 1995, we celebrated the fiftieth anniversary of the end of World War II—the defeat of Adolph Hitler and, later, victory over Japan. The twentieth century has been a century of conflict: two world wars, the Korean conflict, Vietnam, and the Persian Gulf War. But we have one last great war to fight—the war to eliminate the national debt and provide economic freedom for our children and grandchildren.

I'll never forget the evening I spent alone in Lincoln's bedroom. That night, before I went to sleep, I knelt at Lincoln's bed to pray. I prayed for my children. I prayed for my friends. I prayed for my family, and I named each of my seventeen grandchildren. I prayed for their future, for their faith, for their families, and for their friends.

It was also while I was in the Lincoln bedroom that I realized that although the book President Clinton took with him to read on Air Force One issued a warning America desperately needed to hear, it was written ten years too early. In 1985, Americans were not ready to do battle with the debt, the enemy that would do more damage to future generations than to us. But in 1995, I believe we are ready to fight that fight. Therefore, Paul Dunn and I revised our earlier book. We have brought the statistics up to date and added some current illustrations, but we have kept those parts of the earlier book that so clearly called all of us to join in the battle to eliminate the national debt. Only by eliminating the debt can we build a strong future for ourselves and our children, thereby announcing America's declaration of financial independence.

I need to mention that when you encounter the pronoun "I" in this book, you can assume that it is Robert Schuller speaking. When you encounter the pronoun "we," you can assume it is the joint expression of the co-authors. Our ideas have mutually blended so much that it is frequently difficult, I must admit, to know what words came from which pen. The interfacing has been quite remarkable.

The goal of being a debt-free nation is possible! And the power it can release for the future is awesome! If you are ready to think bigger than you have ever thought before—then read on!

Robert H. Schuller

INTRODUCTION
Paul David Dunn

I first began thinking about the national debt when a newspaper headline caught my eye as I was sitting in an Arab coffee shop in East Jerusalem: "U.S. Budget Deficit Approaches $35 Billion." The amount seemed insignificant as I thought about the strength of my country. America did not have the turbulent political problems of the Middle East, where I was living. The United States was, in my mind, an endless power source and stronghold. I tossed the newspaper aside, unconcerned.

While I was living in the Middle East, however, I began to see what debt can do to a country's economy and way of life. I encountered devalued currency and runaway inflation. When I returned to the United States in the mid-eighties, I learned that our deficits had grown to more than $100 billion a year and our national debt was approaching $2 trillion.

Alarmed by the problem, Dr. Robert Schuller, one of the great motivational leaders in America, and I addressed the issue in *The Power of Being Debt Free,* a book that proved to be uncannily accurate in foretelling the magnitude of the problem. Ten years have passed and the national debt now stands at nearly $5 trillion with annual interest payments of $260 billion.

Today America faces a crisis brought on by an excessive burden of debt. We are living on borrowed money. We are stealing from our children and borrowing massive amounts of money that has accumulated into an alarming federal debt. Our currency, once the backbone of the world's economy, now remains humbly weak against most other currencies, including the Japanese yen, the British pound, the German mark, and the Swiss franc.

The United States is still the leading economic, military, and philosophical power in the world. However, our weakness is our debt. Never before in history has a debtor nation led the world economically. In order for America's philosophical and political ideas to continue to have influence and value, they ultimately must rest on a solid economic foundation, for who would follow the lead of a country standing at the door of bankruptcy?

Bankruptcy? Not a nation as strong as the United States, you might say. But we are facing a debt so monumental that some claim it can never be repaid. The debt is so out of control that it is equal to more than 70 percent of our gross domestic product.

It is time to throw off the shackles of this debt. It is time to proclaim America's declaration of financial independence. We can do it. It will take ordinary people who are willing to make an extraordinary effort to imagine the possibilities of a debt-free America. But history is made by people who believe in a dream so intensely that they are willing to commit themselves totally to the realization of that dream.

America's Declaration of Financial Independence was written with the hope that it will create an awareness of the financial crisis facing America and that it will rally people behind the dream of making America stronger than it has ever been before. It is my hope that Americans will continue to demonstrate the qualities of freedom and democracy that have made our nation great. The real wealth of America is not in our financial statement but in the great ideas of our people, and the concept of a debt-free country is a powerful idea that can change the course of America forever. We are committed to the realization of that dream. We Americans must take leadership back into our own hands and solemnly commit to balance the budget and pay off the national debt.

It is my sincere hope and prayer that you will share in this commitment. Together it is possible. Together we can make it happen for ourselves and for our children.

Paul David Dunn

America's Declaration of Financial Independence

1 STEALING FROM OUR CHILDREN

The young father bounded silently up the deserted stairway to the third floor of the hospital maternity ward. His tennis shoes squeaked on the top step. He waited breathlessly. Had he been heard? Visiting hours were not until 9:00 A.M. He glanced at his watch. It was only 6:30 A.M., but he had to see his wife and tell her the good news. He opened the door, moved quickly through the hallway, and slipped into his wife's room.

"Honey, I had to see you. You'll never believe what happened! Last night I got a $700 bonus from my boss. I bought a new crib, blankets, and some toys, and I even paid off the rest of the medical bills not covered by insurance. We don't owe anything!" he declared excitedly.

"How wonderful!" the young mother said and smiled with a sense of relief. Just then the head nurse entered the room with a scolding but forgiving look. She allowed the excited father to stay.

Today was the joyous event the proud parents had long awaited as they prepared to take their newborn son home. The nurse helped the mother into the wheelchair. "It's regulations that you must ride down to the front door," she said as she placed the little bundle of new life wrapped in a blanket in the mother's arms. "Oh, and you'll want to take these home," she added as she handed the father a bundle of cards and a vase of flowers.

As they rode down the elevator the father proudly boasted, "It's all paid for, you know. We don't owe anything."

"Really?" the nurse said with a look of admiration. "This child is privileged indeed to have parents who have planned ahead. I am sure he will have a very bright future."

"Well, we worked hard," the young man replied. "After seven years we were able to save $15,000 for a down payment on our condo, and now that we can handle the payments, we wanted to start our family."

The elevator door opened, and as the nurse said good-bye, the father wheeled his wife and new son to the front door. As the mother stood carefully so that she would not disturb the sleeping child, a uniformed official hurried to meet them.

"Congratulations!" he stated enthusiastically as he pushed back the blanket to take a peek at the tiny face. "Welcome to America," he said, speaking directly to the child. "Here is your inheritance from your country." He tucked a small envelope under the child's blanket and turned and walked briskly away.

Puzzled, the father reached down to take the letter. He read the official notice aloud to his wife.

"As a newborn citizen you are entitled to all of the privileges of being a citizen of the United States including 'life, liberty, and the pursuit of happiness,' and great opportunities for personal development. The price you are charged for these privileges is $22,950.[1] You are not required to pay this until you begin earning money, at which time it will be deducted from your paychecks in the form of taxes and inflationary prices. By the time you earn your first paycheck, it is estimated that the $22,950 will compound at the current 11 percent interest to $150,000."

The father's face tightened with anger as he spoke the final figure. "$150,000! He will never be able to afford a college education. What about a down payment for a home? They can't do that to my child! It's not fair! It's not fair!"

Ten Years Later

The preceding illustration introduced our book, *The Power of Being Debt Free,* in 1985. It dramatically illustrates the profound impact of our country's financial situation on the lives of every citizen. Although America did not respond to the warning of the danger of a huge national debt a decade ago, today we are beginning to face the challenge. The national media finally seem to have accepted the responsibility of communicating this situation to the public. Hardly a day goes by when the evening news does not discuss the potential economic catastrophe caused by our national debt.

It is truly frightening how much worse our country's economic situation has grown in just ten years. Let's visit the same family at the birth of another child ten years later.

A ten-year-old boy accompanies his father to visit his mother and newborn sister in the maternity ward. He watches proudly as his mother signs the paper that confirms the date and time of his sister's birth. The hospital registrar smiles warmly and offers further assistance. "After I file the birth certificate, would you also like me to apply for your daughter's social security number?"

"Oh, yes," the mother agrees. "That would be great! I'll be needing it for our tax return in a few months."

The hospital registrar hands the parents the application. It reads:

Thank you for your application. Due to increased public pressure, we are obligated to inform you that while you will be paying taxes and social security wages until your retirement, there are insufficient funds in our social security system for you to ever make a claim.

Additionally, you are responsible for the U.S. public debt of $5 trillion. Off-budget liabilities and commitments bring the total to more than $17 trillion.[2] Your share of this $5 trillion financial obligation is $43,500. At an average 9 percent interest, it will be $205,320 at age eighteen. This is due and payable upon your first paycheck.

The little boy notices a look of despair on his mother's face. "What's wrong, Mommy? You look so worried."

"I am, honey," his mother admits. "You and your sister are going to owe a lot of money when you grow up. The government spent more money than it had to take care of people like Grandma and Grandpa."

The boy looks puzzled, frowns, and then stamps his foot. "Well, that's not fair. They can't do that to my sister. They can't do that to me!"

Stealing from Our Children

It is not fair, but the sad truth is that all children born in the United States today are met with a burden they cannot begin to shoulder, a burden they did not ask to bear. That burden is the mounting federal debt caused by the federal deficits. When we, the current generation of Americans, spend money that we expect the next generation to pay back or to pay interest on, we are stealing from the disposable income of our children.

It is not fair because we have severely limited our children's number one birthright as Americans—the freedom to grow into healthy and happy individuals in a stable economic society dedicated to the principles of freedom and justice for all. Not only are we stealing income from our children, but we are robbing them of economic freedom. The debt we have incurred and are willfully passing on to our children will greatly impair their personal liberty. This is not just unfair; it is irresponsible, unjust, and immoral.

The founders of our country considered freedom to be of utmost importance. Their dream was for a country in which all people could choose their own faith, speak their own views, vote and elect officials to enact laws to ensure each person's rights, and have freedom to achieve financial security through the free enterprise system.

Today all children born in the United States still have these opportunities, but nothing looms more threatening to limit their economic freedom than the growing national debt. Our founding fathers warned us two hundred years ago that there was no threat to our freedom greater than the shattering of our economic base. Thomas Jefferson said it best:

> I place economy among the first and most important virtues and public debt as the greatest of dangers to be feared. . . . To preserve our independence, we must not let our rulers load us with public debt . . . we must make our choice between economy and liberty or confusion and servitude. . . .

> If we run into such debts, we must be taxed in our meat and drink, in our necessities and comforts, in our labor and in our amusements. . . . If we can prevent the government from wasting the labor of the people, under the pretense of caring for them, they will be happy.[3]

Today babies are born in Alaska, New Hampshire, Michigan, Hawaii, Nevada, Florida, New York, and California. They are being born throughout our country as citizens of the United States of America. They are our greatest national resource. The strength of our nation tomorrow depends to a large degree on the health and strength of our next generation. Consider what the future of America would be if all babies were born with a genetic condition that would shorten their life span, limit their learning ability, and affect the development of their potential. If this condition perpetuated itself through the following generations, what would be the future of our country? The future of America depends on the health of the next generation. We can do something about it. Later on we will give ten possible solutions to the problem of the national debt and also spell out ten things you can do. But before looking at the solutions, we must clearly outline the problem.

Currently, our economy is infected with a dangerous cancer that threatens not only our children's future but also our own future. Nothing can destroy our freedom more quickly than our federal debt of $5 trillion and our yearly deficits of $200 billion.

How Serious Is Our Debt Today?

In 1985, we asked, "How serious is our debt?" The answer then was "serious." The answer today is that the United States is about to be hit with a tidal wave of debt that threatens to flood the economic fruits of the past two hundred years.

In 1985, we called for immediate action to reduce and eventually eliminate our still manageable debt of $1.8 trillion and $165 billion annual deficits. We projected that if nothing was done, we would soon face financial debacle.

Unfortunately, our warning and similar warnings of others went unheeded. The public awareness just was not there. The various administrations and politicians were not concerned. Today America's financial house is on the verge of collapsing inward. Our debt load is more than 70 percent of our gross domestic product (GDP). Interest of $260 billion on the debt consumes almost 20 percent of our federal budget and is the fourth largest budget expenditure behind social security and Medicare (35 percent), defense (24 percent), and social programs (17 percent). Whereas other budget items provide needed services, interest on the debt produces nothing.

In their informative book *Bankruptcy 1995,* authors Harry E. Figgie, Jr., and Dr. Gerald J. Swanson warn that the size of the national debt will accelerate due to the compounding interest on it.[4] They plotted the figures of the current and projected debt load

Debt versus GDP

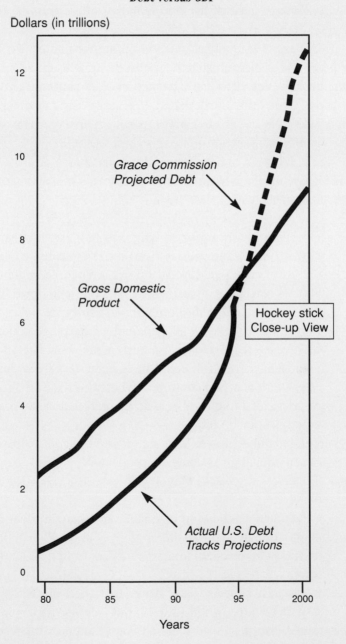

Dollars (in trillions)

Grace Commission
Projected Debt

Gross Domestic
Product

Hockey stick
Close-up View

Actual U.S. Debt
Tracks Projections

Years

onto the chart on page 7. This "hockey stick" chart demonstrates the accelerating speed of the compounding interest on the debt. We are currently at the elbow of the hockey stick.

We are now at a critical junction before the interest expense compounds so rapidly that the debt climbs straight up the handle of the hockey stick. This has happened in other countries and has resulted in hyperinflation, deflation, or a credit crisis in which the country defaults on its obligations, resulting in a currency collapse or some other catastrophic economic event.

The tidal wave of debt approaching the shores of our country is almost unbelievable, almost unthinkable, almost unmanageable, almost unsolvable. Here's why:

- Government has grown so large and bureaucratic that the cost of maintaining it has risen astronomically. In 1995, the government employed 18.6 million people, more than all manufacturing industries in America combined. It is growing faster than the computer and software industries.
- Forty-one percent of all personal income tax collected each year goes just to pay interest on the debt. That means your personal tax bill could have been 41 percent less if the government had controlled its credit spending.
- Nearly $260 billion will be paid in interest alone on the national debt in 1996.
- The federal debt is so large that it is more than 70 percent of our annual gross domestic product.
- Taxpayers work until May 3 each year just to pay for their taxes.
- Government borrowing to finance the national debt consumes 70 percent of all credit activity in the U.S. Without such a huge demand, interest rates could be substantially lower.
- In the last sixteen years, America went from being the largest creditor nation to the largest debtor nation in the world. Never in history has a debtor nation maintained its

position of prominence and power among the world's nations.

- For the past ten years, our national debt has continued to exceed our country's growth rate. The debt is currently growing at $1 billion a day. That breaks down to $41.7 million per hour, $694,444 per minute, or $11,574 per second.
- The personal savings rate in the U.S. is among the lowest of the industrialized nations in the world. Americans save 2 to 3 percent of their income compared with Germans, who save 15 percent, and Japanese, who save 16 percent.
- Our currency has devalued against the world's major currencies as our debt has accelerated and our trade deficits have widened. These drops have been sharp, almost panic driven, and are closely linked with economic news reports of trade deficits and other significant economic developments.

A Burden Too Heavy to Bear

We need to clarify the distinction between the *deficit* and the *debt*. The *deficit* is the amount in a single year that the federal government spends more than it receives from taxes and other revenues. In fiscal year 1995, for instance, the United States government spent nearly $200 billion more than it took in—up from the $165 billion it spent more than it received in 1984. Although this $200 billion deficit is more than the deficit in 1984, it is a significant decrease over 1991, when the deficit was $270 billion; 1992, when it was $290 billion; or 1993, when it was $255 billion. The *debt* is the accumulation of all of the deficits in our entire history. Much has been said about balancing the budget, which would eliminate the *deficits*. But balancing the budget will be difficult to do because of our *debt*. In 1984, the Congressional Budget Office said that $114 billion was paid in interest on the national debt of $1.836 trillion. In fiscal 1995, 18 percent of the

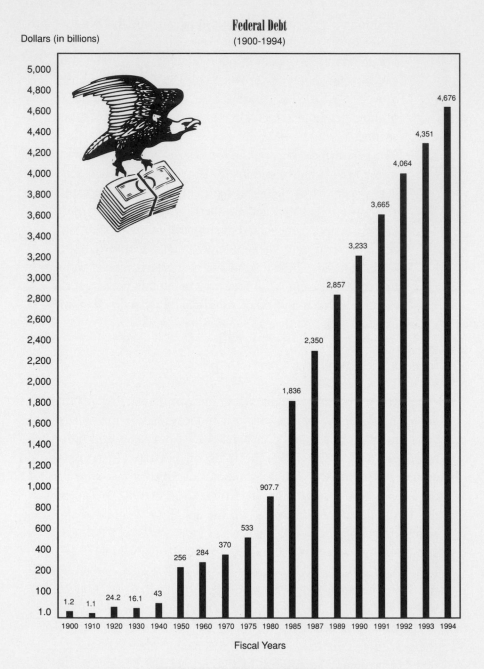

Dollars (in billions)

Federal Debt
(1900-1994)

Fiscal Years

Source: U.S. Bureau of Public Debt, U.S. Dept. of the Treasury

Federal Debt—per Capita
(1900-1994)

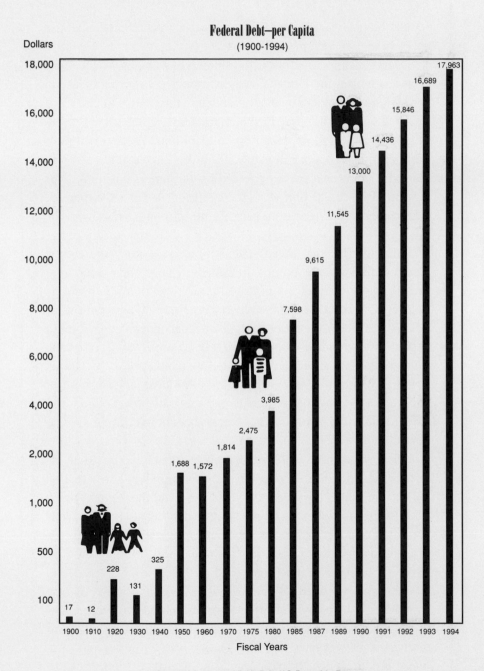

Dollars

Fiscal Years

Source: U.S. Bureau of Public Debt, U.S. Dept. of the Treasury

federal budget was allocated just to pay the interest on the debt— up from the 14 percent in 1984.

Most people think of the national debt as being financed by Americans. But the United States is indebted to foreign nations for more dollars than any other country in the world. The amount of debt owned by foreigners, which the United States Treasury is obligated to pay, is approaching $592 billion. While the deficit has grown from $165 billion to $200 billion in eleven years, it is cause for alarm that the debt owned by foreigners has more than doubled from $220 billion to $592 billion in the same period. This represents a significant shift in the economic framework of the world.

For decades, the United States was an economic superpower, lending money to countries in order to spur their economic growth. Now for the first time in history, the situation has dramatically reversed. The United States continues to lend billions of dollars to foreign countries, but we are dependent upon foreign capital inflow simply to pay the interest on our debt. This saps money out of other countries' economies and makes the United States the largest debtor in the world. We have stolen from our children the legacy of a powerful, economically free country and given them in its place a country whose economic future may be controlled by others.

Without an inflow of foreign money financing our deficit, interest rates could be substantially higher, possibly three to five percentage points above the current rates. And the higher the interest rates, the higher the interest on the debt would be. The Congressional Budget Office estimates that by the year 2000, for every one percentage point rise in rates, $50 billion would be added to the interest on the debt.

Because we need the money, we encourage foreign ownership of our country by promising to pay high rates of return to nations that invest their money to support our rising deficits. We offer high interest rates to attract their money with the hope that future production of our nation will be able to pay them back. To

Gross Public Debt

as Percentages of GDP as of December 31, 1991

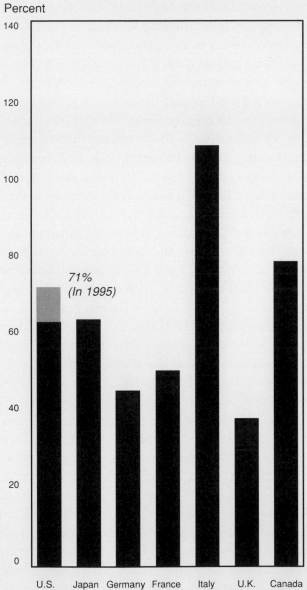

Sources: OMB; Organization for Economic Cooperation and Development

encourage investors, Congress passed a law in July of 1984 removing a long-standing 30 percent withholding tax on bonds owned by foreigners.

In an article in the *Los Angeles Times,* Robert M. Dunn, Jr., professor of international economics at George Washington University, pointed out the severity of this situation: "Advanced nations are supposed to contribute capital to the rest of the world. That is how we help developing countries grow. But the United States has turned this role upside down. We've become a net drain on the scarce capital resources of the world." In the same article, a chief lending officer of one of America's largest banks lending money to developing nations said, "If I were rating the United States as I do other countries, I would put it in the highest of high risk categories."[5]

The rest of our federal deficit is financed by Americans who have invested in their country. The federal government is obliged to pay interest rates ranging from 3 to 18 percent for money invested in the form of bonds, Treasury bills, and other financial instruments.

In light of our current astronomical deficit of $200 billion, it is easy to think of deficit spending as a normal government practice. But the truth is that out of the 203 budgets our government has had, it has successfully balanced 100 of them. The deficits we have incurred have averaged less than 2 percent of the GDP of goods and services that our nation produces each year.[6] Until recently, the deficit had exceeded 4 percent of our GDP only four times in history.[7] The first was at the formation of our republic and the three others were during the Civil War, World War I, and World War II. But since 1984, our deficits have ranged from 3 percent to almost 5 percent of our GDP. These deficits are larger as a percentage of GDP than any of the deficits during the wartime crises in our nation's history. The alarming reality behind these statistics is that these deficits are taking place in peaceful times that include booming stock markets and robust economies.

Perhaps these good times easily blind us to the real danger of the encroaching calamity of financial disaster.

In the jungles of Java near Djakarta stands an archaeological wonder. Borobudur is one of the greatest monuments ever erected to Buddha. Built in the ninth century, it covers nearly ten acres, and three miles of bas-relief commemorating historic events in the life of Buddha cover its walls. When it was finished, Borobudur must have appeared to be stronger than the jungle, immune to decay. But as years passed and it was left unattended, the jungle began to encroach upon the edge of the monument. Beautiful green vines growing slowly upon the rock surfaces soon found soft spots and minuscule cracks in which to take their first hold. Surely, the vines must have looked attractive and harmless as they curled along the ridge of the monument. But soon, like a giant octopus, the vines overtook it. The quiet, slow-growing jungle overtook the seemingly indestructible temple. Years later, archaeologists cut the jungle back and began to rebuild the broken temple so that it could once again stand as an inspiration to all people.

Our national debt is not unlike the jungle. It keeps growing slowly and quietly with little or no attention given to it. But unless the debt is eliminated, it will eventually engulf our society and strangle our economy. Every man, woman, and child, rich or poor, will pay a higher and higher price for the debt as it continues to grow. The national debt must be dealt with in the strongest and most responsible terms because it threatens to engulf our nation.

2 THE LAST GREAT WAR

How could the national debt have grown so large? How could it have become so out of control? In the course of our two hundred years, we Americans have faced many crises that justified and necessitated borrowing money. In fact, many times we were forced to borrow funds because our freedom and the economic strength of our nation were at stake.

A child born in 1776, the year our great nation was born, would witness in his lifetime two wars that would pull the country into debt. In the War of 1812, American soldiers went into battle while the new nation borrowed to finance their weaponry. Over the next twenty-three years the country completely paid off this debt, but by age eighty-four, that child would watch the young republic split apart in the ghastly Civil War. When the gut-wrenching battles were finished, the United States dug deep into the pockets of its citizens to reconstruct itself so that in 1876, it could celebrate its first centennial birthday.

At slightly more than one hundred years old, America was hit with the depression of the 1890s. We recovered in time only to witness the greatest war the world had yet known—World War I. There were some who felt we should isolate ourselves from the conflict, but under the leadership of Woodrow Wilson, Americans decided to do their part. We wanted to make the world "safe for democracy," as President Wilson phrased it. And so again we borrowed and prayed and believed that this was the war to end all wars. When peace was finally at hand, prosperity exploded. Great hopes and expectations allowed us to believe the bubble would never break.

But the bubble burst with a deafening noise during the Great Depression. Voices shouted forth, declaring that capitalism was dead. Masses became enthralled with the revolution that had occurred less than twenty-five years earlier in the Soviet Union, a revolution that promised economic equality to all. Franklin Delano Roosevelt courageously led our country out of this depression. The people voted to borrow the money to create jobs and preserve our free enterprise system. Once again the debt was increased.

Prior to that time our debt was tied to the gold standard. But by an act of Congress in 1934, it was agreed that all printed money would be backed with the collateral of the people's deposits. No longer could we back up our paper currency with gold.

As the debt increased, America faced a second world war. We had been through the War of 1812, the Civil War, the Spanish-American War, and World War I. We couldn't afford another war! But Pearl Harbor gave us no choice. Our survival as a nation was at stake. With Hawaii still smoldering from Japan's surprise air raid, Americans were urged to take their money out of savings accounts and loan it to their country. War bonds promised to return 3 percent interest on the money that the government borrowed to buy the necessary defensive equipment and finance the military forces used to defeat the Axis powers.

With the unconditional surrender of the enemy, we continued to borrow billions of dollars to carry out the Marshall Plan, which encouraged us, as a noble and civilized country, not to abandon the defeated nations but to help rebuild them. We lent money to European countries and to Japan to launch their new economic and productive recoveries. Where did we get this money to rebuild these other nations? We borrowed it, of course. We increased our federal debt.

World War II was hardly over when we faced an expansionist international Communist threat. The Korean War engaged us, and then the Vietnam War drew upon our resources. After a defeat in Asia, our nation was in debt greater than anyone could have envisioned. Not only did we leave Southeast Asia with thousands of lost lives, but we pulled out with an enormous debt.

Our current $5 trillion debt is due not only to wars to preserve our own freedom and that of others but is due also to wars on poverty in our own country. We believe that the dignity of the individual is a nonnegotiable human value. Most Americans are willing to share their wealth to keep children and older people from starvation, to provide employment opportunities to all who are able to work, and to offer a high quality education to all young Americans.

In the early 1960s, John F. Kennedy started the Peace Corps to promote world peace and friendship. Peace Corps volunteers still share their technical knowledge with people in less developed nations. Later, Lyndon Johnson promoted the Great Society, a package of social programs that included Medicare, federal aid for primary and secondary school education, the Model Cities Act, the War on Poverty, and various consumer protection and anticrime programs.

America has come through a revolution, a civil war, and two world wars. We have enabled many nations to choose freely their own form of government. We have sought to provide economic equality for all our people. We have survived, but only by borrowing and therefore increasing our national debt.

We must make no apologies for this debt. Not to be in debt today would be at the expense of our conscience and our freedom. How honorable would our prosperity be if we did not share it with the less fortunate? How noble would our liberty be if we had turned our backs on the injustices of Hitler? How honorable would our freedom be if we had turned a deaf ear to the cry from weaker nations threatened by oppressive powers? Let us credit our past administrations for building up a debt that is essentially honorable. We gave our best sons and daughters and incurred an incredible debt to help other people who spoke different languages, lived in diverse cultures, and embraced religions alien to our own.

The necessity and obligation of incurring our debt, however noble the intent may be, do not negate our responsibility to set in motion a plan for repaying it. One factor in the continuing deficit is the obviously wasteful spending, mismanagement, and inefficiency our federal government has established as its trademark since the early 1930s. This government waste is not the primary cause of the debt, but it has contributed greatly to it and is one of the most obvious areas where change can occur. Many efforts have been made to streamline the government, but mismanagement and inefficiencies continue.

In 1981, for instance, President Reagan appointed a special commission, paid for by the private sector, to undertake a comprehensive, monumental task of assimilating data on wasteful government expenditures, program mismanagement, system failures, and overall inefficiency. After its three-year study, the commission produced nearly twenty-five hundred cost-cutting, revenue-enhancing recommendations that would save $424 billion in the first three years of implementation and would rise to more than $1.9 trillion each year by the year 2000.[1]

In a personal letter to the president, the late J. Peter Grace, the head of the commission, said, "If the American people realized how rapidly government spending is likely to grow under existing legislative programs, I am convinced they would compel their elected representatives to 'get government off their backs.' "[2]

The letter to the president continued, "The project was structured and staffed to effect enduring improvement so that our children and grandchildren would not inherit a situation that would be devastating to them and on the values of our economic and social system."[3]

President Clinton has also worked to make the government more efficient and cost-effective. Under his direction, Vice President Gore is working to "reinvent government" through the efforts of the National Performance Review, begun in the fall of 1993.

Several watchdog groups have led the way in pinpointing government waste and mismanagement, and they have kept the public informed. Groups such as the National Taxpayers Union have increased public awareness. But in spite of all these efforts, there have not been significant changes in the lavish spending habits and mismanagement of Congress.

The facts are real and frightening as we come to understand the enormous burden the federal debt and deficits place upon our economy. The thought of what might face our children is even more frightening. We have been called the richest country in the world, a world economic leader. But we must ask ourselves if we are really so rich. If we are that wealthy, it is only because we are spending the money that rightly belongs to our children, grand-children, and great-grandchildren. In reality we are poor. Our national debt threatens to impose a taxation without representation on future generations. Concerned citizens, including you, can make a difference, and we will show you how.

The Last Great War

We predict that the twentieth century will be remembered as the century of the great wars. World War I, World War II, the Cold War—all will be recorded as major events in the annals of human history. When World War II ended, Americans helped to rebuild our enemies' countries from the rubble of war.

But while we were successful in clearing up the rubble of the wars in foreign lands, we focused less attention on the rubble in our own back yard. Today the rubble takes the form of decaying and crumbling infrastructures, schools, and roads and bridges that need to be completely rebuilt. Classrooms need to be upgraded and outfitted with computers, textbooks, and special education programs. Families are buried in poverty in our inner cities.

We need to clean up the rubble in our own towns. But we

cannot because the money that should be spent on valuable social programs instead must be paid as interest on our national debt. We still have not paid for the bullets, the bombs, and the fuel used by our jets and tanks. War is not finished and it is not really won if we do not pay the bills and if we continue to roll over the debt. In so doing we deprive our children of the opportunities they should have.

We fought the War of Independence and the War of 1812. We incurred debt to fight the Civil War and the Spanish-American War. In this century, World War I and World War II added to our debt, as did the Korean War and the Vietnam War. Our nation had a wartime economy from 1941 until July 1991, when we witnessed the end of the Cold War. Now that we are finally at peace, America has its biggest fight on its hands—the Last Great War!

The Last Great War is one we must commit to fight and we must commit to win! The Last Great War to pay off the national debt is a noble and just cause that will require leadership, commitment, and sacrifice. But the payoff is freedom: freedom for our children, freedom for our grandchildren, and freedom for our nation's economic future.

When we fight this Last Great War, there will have to be sacrifices. We all will need to be prepared to suffer. Everyone will be affected by the actions necessary when we make paying off the national debt a priority. But when we willingly sacrificed to fight the battles of World War I and World War II, we knew that turning our backs was not an option. The vision set by America's leaders today must be based on the realization that the problems caused by the huge national debt will not go away but will get worse until we tackle them. We have no choice but to go to war again. To continue to increase the debt is no longer an option.

Imagine that you are a young parent of a family with great financial needs. You have children who need to be fed, clothed, and educated. Housing and transportation are expensive. Your job does not pay as well as you would like. You are allowed to go into debt to pay for the lifestyle you desire, but there is one hitch:

under no circumstances can you ever go bankrupt. If your personal debt becomes too much, rather than file for bankruptcy—which would eliminate all your debt—your debt would continue to grow, compounding the interest already owed on it, only to be passed on to your children and, if they could not pay it, to their children. Rather than inherit only your assets, your children could inherit all of your liabilities also. That sounds frightening, doesn't it? This situation exists today. There is a family that lives under this hardship. It is our great family—our nation of the United States of America.

Interest on the debt claims the first cash received by the federal government. The interest on the debt demands to be paid before we can help people who are dying, before cancer research, before funding any of the services that we hold to be honorable, valuable, and essential. Before the government can pay educators, health providers, members of the armed forces, or medical researchers, it must satisfy the holder of its mortgage, who demands, "I get paid first!"

While we applaud the move toward a balanced budget, we do not hear many in the House or the Senate or local politicians suggesting that we eliminate and liquidate the item that dominates the budget: the interest on the national debt.

A balanced budget is not a balanced budget if it does not include a plan to eliminate the national debt!

This call to eliminate the national debt is simply an idea, an idea that must give birth to a plan. We need a plan that has as its long-term goal to wipe out the debt.

Who Are We to Speak Up?

Why, you might ask, are a Protestant minister and a businessman writing a book about the federal debt? What credentials in economics can we marshal to gain credibility in dealing with this subject?

We believed that the economy was too important to be left to the economists. And so in 1984, we set out to bring attention to the national debt, at the time a little-known and little-discussed subject. To be sure, deficit reduction and deficit spending were in the news, but not to the extent that they are in 1995. Although *The Power of Being Debt Free* became a bestseller, most of what we called for was ten years too early. It has taken nearly a decade of huge deficits and mounting federal debt to awaken the public consciousness to this alarming threat. Now is the time to accept the challenge of eliminating the national debt before it is too late.

Finally, the American people are stirring. The tide of public opinion is rising. The overwhelming majority of Americans favor a balanced budget. We must seize the moment!

In 1984, our nation's debt stood at $1.836 trillion. We predicted that if nothing was done by the year 2005, the debt would grow to $13 trillion and the nation would feel severe economic hardship. Eleven years later, in 1995, we must report that we are more than one-third of the way there with a debt of $5 trillion.

Many times over the last ten years we have wrestled with the need to motivate the American people to face this economic challenge. Perhaps we could do what economists and politicians have not been able to do. In recent visits with Newt Gingrich and President Clinton, I expressed the need to view the national debt as a moral issue that is worthy of our nonpartisan efforts. We should combine all of our ingenuity, experience, and fortitude to solve this crisis.

The economic future of America is too important to be left to the economists and politicians. Responsibility for the future of the American economy ultimately falls on the shoulders of the electorate. The people decide who will represent them and what issues are important, and they look to their elected leaders to carry out their will.

But the will of the people must be inspired and challenged. We must be motivated to believe that we can make a difference. We recall the words of Paul's high school basketball coach, "Don't let anyone tell you you're not qualified." His motto read, "We the unqualified led by the unwilling have been doing the unbelievable so long with so little that we now attempt the impossible with nothing." The challenge of eliminating the national debt can be met head-on. But it cannot be done by leaving the solution to economists and politicians. You and I must become involved.

Some years ago I retained the noted architect Philip Johnson to design the Crystal Cathedral. His first set of drawings left me unenthused. He noticed the conspicuous lack of excitement within me. "Is something wrong?" he asked warily.

"Who am I to question the man who is the leading architect of our time?" I asked cautiously. I remember the scene vividly. His slender body was silhouetted against the east window of his thirty-fifth-floor office of the Seagram Building on Park Avenue in New York City.

His eyes focused firmly on mine as he admonished me, "Let's understand something right now, Dr. Schuller. Architecture is too important to leave to architects."

Encouraged and disarmed, I blurted out my honest feelings. I said, "I love the glass roof in your plan, but the walls should be glass, too."

He accepted my suggestion and went on to design a cathedral with glass walls as well as a glass ceiling. In retrospect I have come to believe that Philip Johnson was articulating a universal principle. Architecture is too important to leave to the architects. Likewise, religion is too important to leave to the theologians; science is too important to leave to the scientists; government is too important to leave to the politicians; peace is too important to leave to the diplomats; and economics is too important to leave to the economists.

Ultimately, all disciplines must take into account the nature of the human being. Human values cannot be disregarded in any subject. Possibility thinking is the study of human development.

It is intensely relevant to the subject of the national economy, for possibility thinking motivates human beings to tackle great problems with a positive mental attitude.

Possibility thinking asks challenging questions, such as, What goals would you set for yourself if you knew you could not fail? And what decisions would you make if there were no outside forces to limit you? Possibility thinking believes in managing by objectives. Creative leadership rather than crisis management naturally follows.

What the United States needs right now is possibility-thinking leadership to tackle the economic problems that face us today and will surely engulf us tomorrow.

Let us never forget that in a democracy, leadership is in the hands of the electorate. Leadership is the force that sets the goals. In a democracy, that force is offered to the people. The people, who will have to pay the bills and live with the results of the economic climate, must not surrender leadership of the economic situation to the economists. Ultimately, if our country dies from economic mismanagement or thrives with economic prosperity, the blame or credit will rest upon neither politicians nor economists but upon the consensus of the majority expressed at the ballot box. Therefore, we call upon all citizens of America to rise up and take command by demanding that our elected officials set goals that will guarantee the economic freedom of our unborn children and their children's children.

The time has come for the people of the United States of America to call for a declaration of financial independence. Let's unite to pay off the national debt ourselves and give our children and grandchildren the opportunity of enjoying the fruits of their labor and creativity.

How Can Anything Be Done?

How will we do it? Exactly the way we tackle and solve all other problems: By getting down to the ABCs of mountain-moving, problem-solving, success-generating possibility thinking. And what are these basics?

A—Attitude

Everything starts with an attitude. A negative attitude is certain to produce negative results. A positive attitude is certain to produce positive results.

Social philosopher George Herbert Mead suggested that attitude constitutes "the beginning of an act." He said,

> If one approaches a distant object, he approaches it with reference to what he is going to do when he arrives there. If one approaches a hammer he is muscularly ready to seize the handle of the hammer. The latter stages of the act are present in the early stages . . . in the same sense that they serve to control and process itself.[4]

According to Mead, an attitude is not simply a point of view, a static state of mind. It is an integral part of action, a determinant of the course and outcome of any human act. Your attitude governs the way you act, the way the action will unfold, and the consequences of action. What can come about from a positive attitude is clearly exciting!

The financial crisis facing our country demands that, as citizens, we should examine our personal attitudes toward the situation because it is our money the government is spending.

B—Belief

Impossible situations change permanently when a positive attitude evolves into belief. Negative thinkers say, "I've got to see it before I believe it." The error in that attitude is obvious. The truth is, we've got to believe it before we see it. In every situation we have the freedom to choose what dreams we will believe in. Again and again the history of individuals, institutions, and nations proves the thesis that what we achieve depends on what we choose to believe.

C—Commitment

Possibility thinking moves mountains when a positive attitude produces a positive belief that evolves into a concrete commitment. Again and again in sports, in politics, in war and peace, success does not necessarily go to the most talented or to the wealthiest, but to those who are the most committed. There are no great people. The difference between the so-called great persons and nations and those of lesser rank is a matter of commitment. Great people simply make commitments to greater goals. They dream nobler dreams. The greatest people in history are average people who have the commitment to tackle bigger problems than anyone else before them. The greatness of any generation will be molded and measured by the mountains it chooses to conquer.

D—Decisions

Possibility thinking works wonders because it is such a practical philosophy for creative decision making. In reality, problems are only decisions waiting to be made. I have counseled troubled persons with this honest evaluation: "You don't have a problem to solve; you simply have a decision to make!"

For more than forty-five years I have applied the principles of possibility thinking to every conceivable problem short of erasing the national debt. Possibility thinkers are decisive leaders. Never do we surrender leadership to problems. We always let the positive, undeveloped possibilities call the shots. Never, then, do we let the problem-solving phase move into the decision-making phase. We make the right decisions simply because they are the right decisions, even if they appear to be impossible to carry out.

Again and again we see the miracle unfold. When the right decision is made in the face of impossible problems, the waters separate. Moses marches across the dry bottom of the Red Sea to the astonishment of the enemy behind him. The first step to paying off the national debt is to make a decision.

We can regain our true wealth as a nation only with a concentrated and deliberate commitment and decision to liquidate the debt we have accumulated during our first two hundred years.

Our Dream for America

We can be a debt-free nation! To be debt free would give us real wealth and real power: power to maintain our middle class; power to wipe out poverty; power to educate all citizens; power to expand our human values worldwide. Underdeveloped countries could have their potential developed through low-interest loans and investments from America. No longer a debtor, our country would become a lender once more at low interest rates to struggling people worldwide. The money that now goes to pay off the interest on the debt of the past two hundred years would instead spur economies around the world. Our children would know the power that comes with economic freedom.

As a nation, we have reached a time when we must grow up and face our responsibilities to pay off the federal debt. Then in 2026, when we celebrate our 250th anniversary, the writers of history will declare that the greatest battle ever fought in our first 250 years was not the War of 1812, the Civil War, World War I, or World War II. The greatest battle ever fought and won was the battle of the twenty-first century when the people of the United States of America waged an all-out war to eliminate the federal debt and liberate future generations!

They Did It in New Zealand

Do you doubt that this is really possible? We know it is possible because the South Pacific country of New Zealand did it. Isolated from the world's thoroughfares, coming out of a socialistic the-government-should-take-care-of-me attitude, New Zealanders have set a new course for their country's fiscal future. They have decided to take hold of their most pressing problem, their national debt.

In 1991, the national debt of New Zealand stood at 51 percent of its GDP. The New Zealand government made the tough choice to balance its budget with the long-term goal of repaying the debt. In 1992, 1993, 1994, and 1995, the country enjoyed strong economic growth with large fiscal surpluses. Because of their commitment to repay the debt, New Zealanders were able to withstand the pressures and temptations to use the excess cash on social spending. They made paying down their debt their number one priority. So far, they have reduced their debt to 33.6 percent of New Zealand's GDP, with a target of 20.0 percent by 1997. "This will be a major step in saving our children from a huge debt burden," announced Bill Birch, finance minister, in his last budget speech. "Furthermore, by holding the current course we can anticipate a number of reductions of tax rates over the next few years. New Zealanders simply pay too much tax."[5]

If you don't believe it is possible to pay off the debt, we suggest it is time you doubt your doubts and instead dream of a debt-free America—for our sake, for our children's sake, and for the sake of our children's children!

3 THERE'S A CRACK IN THE LIBERTY BELL

In one form or another, debt reaches into the home of each person on earth, whether it is the international bank conglomerates transferring money via satellite from Zurich, Switzerland, to Johannesburg, South Africa, or the nomadic Bedouin shepherd in the Sinai desert trading goat skins for the promise of water rights from an oasis.

Carefully managed debt is essential to trade and commerce. From the very basic level to the most sophisticated technological currency transactions, debt is a part of everyday life. Whenever there is a transfer of goods and services to someone who agrees to pay in exchange for them, debt is incurred.

The flow of your earnings finances the debt on your house. In a similar way, the flow of the government's earnings through tax revenues and sales of Treasury bonds, bills, and other financial instruments finances the federal debt.

Debt is an integral and vital part of our world's economic system. Much of the expansion the United States has enjoyed in the last two hundred years has been because our nation, corporations, and individuals have had the freedom and ability to borrow against their future productivity.

Few people will disagree that there are many times when it is moral, honorable, and smart to incur debt, both individually and institutionally. Few of us, for instance, have the ability to pay cash for our homes, and so we borrow the money and plan to pay the debt from future earnings.

However, the practice of financing our wants and needs through borrowed funds has become a national habit. We borrow to purchase our homes, our cars, our appliances, even our college educations. Many enterprises and individuals correctly calculate that the cash flow derived from the sale of their goods and services can finance long-term, fixed-rate mortgages and still return a profit.

Many prudent investors and speculators have borrowed money to invest in prime parcels of land and have seen the value of their investments increase. Others borrowed to buy gold when it was $35 an ounce. When gold skyrocketed to more than $800 an ounce, some investors received their investment back twenty times, more than enough to pay the interest on the borrowed money. However, this points up the danger of debt as well. Many investors borrowed money to buy gold when it was $800 an ounce, expecting its price to go even higher. When the price declined to $400 an ounce, they were left not only with gold that was worth half what they paid for it but also with interest and principal to pay on the debt.

It also makes sense to go in debt if you come across a once-in-a-lifetime opportunity. If you have a limited number of days, months, or years in which to take advantage of a passing opportunity and you have the cash flow to finance a mortgage, then you would be smart and responsible to incur a debt.

Many economists believe that debt is necessary and advantageous. For instance, our country suffered a terrible shock following that fateful day in October 1929 when the floor of the New York Stock Exchange was littered with worthless sell orders silently testifying to the unexpected crash of the stock market. Banks and private investors lost billions of dollars. Food lines and homeless people were common scenes in America's cities and countrysides. The jobless rate soared to crippling proportions. It was one of the darkest times in our nation's history.

But the theories of John Maynard Keynes were credited with pulling our nation out of this period of depression. He said it would be advantageous for our nation to go in debt in order to create jobs and opportunities. His basic credit-supply theory worked. America struggled to its feet by borrowing the money against future productivity.

But Keynes also formulated specific guidelines in the implementation of his theory that have gone unheeded by our nation: (1) never run a deficit in an expanding economy, and (2) repay the debt during a productive cycle. According to Keynes, to disregard either of these economic rules would bring on hyperinflation, recession, or depression.

Managed properly, debt can be a positive means to growth and productivity. But excessive debt and the resulting interest payments can be a strangling, crippling, restricting force. Debt can be draining not only financially but also emotionally.

I will never forget watching my father struggle under the heavy burden of debt he incurred.

Work was tough in northwest Iowa in the early 1900s. As a teenager, Anthony Schuller could find only a job as a hired hand doing manual farm chores. But he managed to save a dollar here and there until finally, he took a chance on his dream. With all the courage he could muster, my father stepped into the office of the local banker. Land prices in the area had been rising steadily. As far as Dad could see, the value of an Iowa farm could only go up. The bankers thought so, too. However, it was only a few short months before the Great Depression hit. Land prices plummeted. Dad looked back later and knew he "bought high," but he knew he could always draw from the soul of the earth to repay his mortgage.

Then the dust bowl years came. Suffering from the relentless drought, crops were wiped out. The raw produce Dad took to market was hardly enough to make the interest payments on his debt. He hoped and prayed for times to change, for miraculous record crops and all-time-high market prices for his eggs, milk, and hogs. Dad held on to his dream, knowing that in a few short years the payment of the principal on his mortgage would be due.

Then another disaster hit.

It was late one summer when I was home from college. The clouds grew dark as the noise of thunder rumbled in the distance. Suddenly, a long, balloonlike cloud seemed to stretch out into a twisting snake. It was unmistakably a tornado.

"We're going to have to make a run for it, and fast!" Dad shouted. We quickly climbed into the car and headed out of the path of the tornado. From several miles away we watched the twisting funnel make its path across our farm.

After it had gone, we headed back down the familiar country roads. As we crested a small hill, we couldn't see the top of the barn that usually landmarked our farm. All nine farm buildings were gone. There was no rubble, only clean white foundation lines where the buildings once stood. The pedigree breeding bull walked dazed in the deserted farmyard. Somehow he survived even though the barn was dropped in splintered pieces a mile downwind. All of the horses were dead. The pigs were dead. The machinery was gone. The crops were cut off at the roots. Besides the bull, only the milk cows survived since they grazed in pastures outside the direct path of the tornado.

My father's hand drew into a tight fist, and he beat the steering wheel and cried in agony to his wife. "It's all gone, Jennie. It's all gone!" The farm he nurtured, cultivated, and cared for all those years was sucked up in a matter of seconds. And the heavy mortgage he acquired years before would fall due in only three years. Everything he worked for was totally wiped out.

The insurance paid only $3,500. Sparing only a few hundred dollars, Dad took the money to the bank. "Sir," he said to the banker, "I want to make a payment on my mortgage. It falls due in three years, you know. I counted on a good crop this year, but now that is gone. But I want you to know that I plan to pay off my debt. I can't lose my farm."

The banker was visibly impressed, especially when my father

mapped out how he planned to keep farming without buildings or machinery. With $50 of the insurance money, Dad bought a dilapidated four-story house. Piece by piece, nail by nail, board by board, we dismantled it and rebuilt our house. We even made a makeshift barn to protect the animals. The house was tiny and far less attractive than the one that was lost, but I'll never forget when my father said, "Well, at least the buildings are paid for!"

With renewed confidence the bankers extended my father's loan for another ten years. It was a moving moment when Dad came home that night and at the dinner table prayed, thanking God that he did not lose the farm.

I learned my first lesson about economics that summer. Debt is an oppressive burden when times are tough. And interest on the debt is the toughest and most thankless bill to pay.

Years later my father saved enough money so that he not only paid off his mortgage but also bought a small "luxury" house in the nearby town of Alton, Iowa. There he enjoyed the last years of life with the freedom that comes from being debt free. It is amazing how liberating that feeling was to my parents and is to those who experience it today. That freedom can be ours as a nation. Later we shall see how our society would be different and our standard of living improved if, as a nation, we would discover the power of being debt free.

The destructive force of excessive debt is not limited to individuals or corporations. The emotional and financial drain of being in debt is also felt at the national level.

Monumental debt has virtually destroyed the economies of many Latin American countries. Their outstanding debt to United States banks is more than $1 trillion, most of which has been written off, never to be collected by the American banks that loaned your and my money. In 1982, the inability of the Latin American countries to pay their interest payments sent shock waves through the financial communities.[1] American bankers kept saying, "Countries don't go bankrupt, do they?" And they lent more billions of dollars to the countries so that they could meet their interest payments.

In 1995, when Mexico defaulted on its obligation to make interest payments, the United States government stepped in with a $20 billion aid package. Nonetheless, the peso still devalued more than 60 percent within days, and controversy surrounded the proposal to lend more money to the debt-ridden country.

The harsh reality is that the excessive debt of the Latin American countries has crippled their economies and financially strapped the United States as well. As long as a person or a country is indebted, that entity is enslaved to the consequences of economic swings, such as when oil prices go down at a time they are expected to go up. The responsibility of paying off the debt remains.

Financial crisis caused by excessive debt is not limited to foreign countries. In 1975, New York City ran out of money, effectively defaulted on its financial obligations, and was for all intents and purposes bankrupt. The city had built up a monumental debt of $13.6 billion! The day of reckoning finally came when interest payments on New York City's debt obligations could not be paid.

Major United States banks refused to underwrite and purchase New York City bonds, which financed the city's debt. Mayor Abraham Beame appealed to the federal government's sense of loyalty for a bailout. He asked, "Would the French disown Paris? Would the Soviets abandon Moscow?" But the government could not establish a precedent on which other cities might rely in the future. President Ford declared, "If we go on spending more than we have, providing more benefits and more services than we can pay, then a day of reckoning will come to Washington and the whole country as it has to New York City. . . . When that day of reckoning comes, who will bail out the United States?"[2]

More recently, in 1995, Orange County, California, went bankrupt investing in heavily leveraged complex financial instruments known as derivatives. These complex financial instruments were nothing more than a highly speculative, debt-burdened leveraged bet made on interest rates using massive amounts of borrowed money (debt).

Using taxpayer money, the Orange County treasurer speculated interest rates would continue to fall. However, interest rates rose unexpectedly and the small equity portion of the treasurer's bet was immediately wiped out. The highly leveraged debt continued to grow, depleting the treasury balance, causing Orange County to default on its bonds. Institutional money managers have already written off the value of these bonds in their portfolios under the assumption they never will be repaid.

Recently, a ballot initiative was presented to Orange County voters, asking them to raise the sales tax in order to pay for this debt-induced fault. The voters soundly rejected this proposal. It is still unclear how Orange County will work itself out of this bankruptcy. Perhaps the state or federal government will bail it out. But the bigger question is, who will then bail out the federal government?

Debt holds hostage both the debtor and the creditor. Could the United States with its $5 trillion debt and yearly budget deficit of $200 billion be headed down the same path as many Latin American countries, New York City, and Orange County?

In 1972, when the national debt was $427 billion, the deficit was $23 billion, and interest payments on the debt were $21 billion, the *Los Angeles Times* printed an article suggesting ways to pay off the national debt. It was to be taken as a sophisticated joke because everyone knew the debt would take care of itself. People laughed. But now no one is laughing. In less than twenty-five years, a $427 billion debt has grown to $5 trillion, a $23 billion deficit has grown to $200 billion, and interest on the debt of $21 billion a year has grown to $260 billion a year. Unconcerned smiles have been replaced by shocked, blank stares. How did it happen? How could the debt have grown so deep and so fast?

Some economists say the bulk of the debt is caused by excessive government spending. In the past twenty years, government spending has increased dramatically. Others say a shortfall in

Government Expenditures Compared to
Gross National Product
(1929-1994)

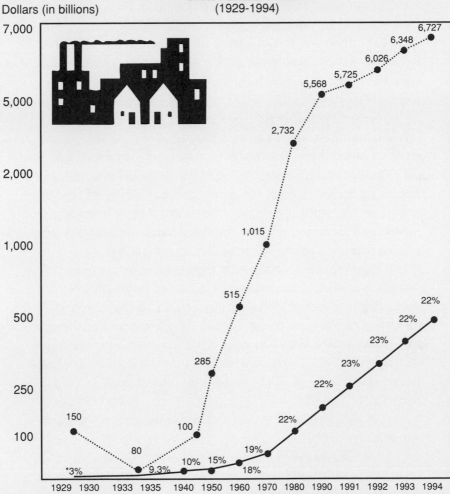

Dollars (in billions)

Fiscal Years

GNP ....
GOVT. OUTLAYS* _____

Source for GNP: U.S. Dept. of Commerce, Bureau of Economic Analysis
Source for Expenditures: U.S. Treasury Dept; Annual Statement as taken from *World Almanac–1984*

*Expenditures as Percentage of GNP

tax revenues is the cause. Mismanagement and inefficiency are also considered to be causes. But one of the most important elements contributing to the rise in the federal debt is the *interest on the debt itself*. In 1984, the Congressional Budget Office reported that $114 billion was paid in interest on the debt. Today interest on the debt is $260 billion. President Clinton recently complained, "I would have had a balanced budget if it weren't for the interest payments on the debt."

Interest is the ultimate entitlement. It must always be paid, and it is the most unproductive outlay of money in the government's budget. It produces nothing.

For a nonprofit institution, such as the government, paying interest on borrowed money is not as advantageous as it is for the private sector, which can borrow funds and deduct interest payments from income taxes. The federal government does not pay income taxes and therefore cannot deduct the interest.

The government's borrowing to pay the interest on the debt reminds me of the one time when I had to borrow money for something that literally went up in smoke! In September 1950 I took my first job as pastor of a small church in Ivanhoe, Illinois. In addition to my $200-a-month salary, the church provided me with a parsonage. We had just moved in when I received a call from a church deacon. "Bob, I think you should order your coal."

"Coal?" I asked.

"Yes," he explained. "Your furnace in the parsonage is coal burning."

Then I remembered that I was responsible for all of my utilities. So I went to the local lumberyard where I was told I could order the coal. The manager greeted me enthusiastically and seemed to know exactly how much coal I needed: five tons at a total cost of $77.50.

"When can you deliver?" I asked.

"Tomorrow afternoon, if that is okay."

"That sounds great!" I said as I turned around to leave, my order complete.

"Oh, Reverend!" the manager called after me. "That will be $77.50, please!"

I stopped in my tracks. I assumed he would bill me. "But I don't have any money with me. Can't you bill me? I'd like to open a charge account anyway."

The decision was written all over the manager's face even before he spoke. "Sorry, Reverend. But we don't deliver any coal unless it is paid for in advance." He went on to explain, "Your coal bin is in the basement, right? Well, if we deliver the coal and dump it in the basement, and you don't pay the bill, it's a heck of a job trying to haul it out. If you want a loan, you'll have to go to the bank."

Somewhat taken aback, I left the lumberyard and headed straight to the First National Bank. The manager greeted me warmly, saying he had heard good things about me. Finally, he leaned back in his chair and asked, "What can I do for you, Reverend?"

"I am here to borrow $75, sir," I said unashamedly.

"What do you want to borrow the money for? Whether I lend it to you or not depends on what you plan to do with it."

I knew I had an unbeatable cause. My needs were beyond debate. On top of that, I was a distinguished citizen of the community. Without any reservation, I dropped my request. "I want to borrow the money to buy my winter supply of coal. I need five tons and the going rate is. . . ."

"Wait a minute, Reverend!" he quickly interrupted. The smile was gone. A firm, tough business look replaced the sparkle in his eye. "Reverend, we never loan money to buy coal!" The words were spoken with final authority.

I couldn't believe what I was hearing. He must have read my perplexity because he went on to explain his position.

"You must understand something about banks. The money we have to loan is not our money. Hard-working people put their savings here. They trust us to use their money to make money for them. We cannot lose their money. Therefore, we can't lend money without collateral."

"Collateral?" I asked, totally ignorant. "What's that?"

"Collateral," he said with a smile, "is when you have something of value to offset the debt. If you borrow money for a house or a car and can't make the payments, we simply take the car or house and sell it. We pay ourselves back, and any surplus is yours. That's called your equity. But if you borrow money to buy coal, the coal cannot be collateral because you will burn it in the furnace. Then if you don't pay your bill, our customers will lose their savings. Their money will literally go up in smoke! My advice to you, Reverend, is run your personal and church business so that you never need to borrow money for coal."

The banker must have sensed my panic. "I will tell you what I will do," he said with a look of mercy. "If I loaned you $75, could you pay it back in five monthly payments of $15 each? There will be interest added on top of that, of course."

"Oh, yes!" I said with a sigh of relief. "I can make those payments. There's no problem there at all."

"Good. Then we have a deal," the banker said with a smile as he shuffled some papers in front of me to sign.

As I got ready to leave, check in hand, the banker stood to shake my hand. His eyes met mine. "Reverend," he said seriously, "remember, never again borrow money for coal."

I walked out of that bank with a $75 check and one of the most important economic lessons of my life. Never again would I borrow money for something that could not be held as collateral or that would not produce a product or service that would grow and appreciate in value. It is safe to say that most, if not all, of our $5 trillion federal debt is for "coal money" and it has all been burned up! Bullets, obsolete equipment, salaries of federal employees, social security, payments on the interest on the national debt—all of this is coal money.

Every year our government borrows money to pay the interest on the national debt. It is like burning that coal in my furnace. Borrowing money to pay the interest on the debt is simply fueling our debt because we are not paying off the principal. Rather, we are adding to it. Perhaps the only difference between my borrowing money for the coal and the government's borrowing for the interest on the debt is that my monthly payment was only $15. The federal government pays $21 billion a month in interest only!

Have you ever stopped to think about what could be done with $21 billion a month? $260 billion a year? What if our nation did not have a debt? Is such a situation possible?

To find out, in 1985, we commissioned the Hudson Institute, a nonprofit public policy research organization, to study the costs, benefits, and plausibility of a fiscal strategy that would eliminate the federal debt. The results were unexpected. The implications were more serious than either we or the institute had anticipated. Although some of this information is today dated, what is both interesting and frightening is to compare the 1985 predictions with what has actually happened since that time.

A paper prepared by Dr. Arnold H. Packer under the direction of Jim Wheeler, director of economic studies of the Hudson Institute, stated that it was both wise and possible to first eliminate the federal deficit and then run sufficient budget surpluses to reduce and eliminate the debt.

According to the paper, "The benefits of reducing or eliminating the debt are great. The dangers of doing nothing are monumental."

In preparing his 1985 study, Dr. Packer assumed three scenarios: (1) the debacle, (2) muddling through, and (3) debt elimination. In each case a twenty-year projection was made, until 2005.

The worst and most fearful of the three scenarios painted by the Hudson Institute was the *debacle scenario*. The government deficits would remain at a constant $45 billion per year, *exclusive of interest on the national debt*. The total deficit would grow each year by the amount of increase in interest on the national debt. Such a scenario had the effect of adding $45 billion plus the interest on the national debt to the principal of the debt each year.

According to the report, our country's financial situation would be completely unstable under this scenario. Financial projections would be pointless because the situation could not continue until 2005. Interest on a debt of $43.7 trillion in 2005 would equal 34 percent of the gross domestic product. This amount would be more than the entire income of the federal government! This clearly presented an impossible situation!

The second scenario, called the *muddling through scenario,* assumed just that. America would barely be able to muddle through the financial mess in which it would find itself because there would be too little action too late.

Under this scenario, budget deficits would be kept in the $200 to $300 billion range, which is a diminishing percentage of the increasing gross domestic product. To achieve even this modest action, however, would require painful fiscal discipline. This plan also idealistically assumed that there would be no recessions or significant interest rate increases.

It was projected under this scenario that in 2005, the debt would be $5.9 trillion with an interest cost of $540 billion. To pay the interest, the federal government would have to take in $310 billion more than it spent exclusive of interest—and it would still have a $230 billion deficit, causing the debt to continue to grow.

The *debt-elimination scenario* was the most promising forecast, but we Americans have not yet taken the belt-tightening steps of increasing revenues or decreasing spending that were required to make this plan work. Under this plan, the $45 billion program deficit would have been eliminated by 1986, and we would have had a balanced budget—eliminating the deficit—by 1991. As a result, the entire debt would have been paid off by 2005! The revenue increases required to achieve a balanced budget were not projected to be great: only 5 percent for individuals and 15 percent for corporations.

SITUATION IN YEAR 2005 (as forecast in 1985)*

Scenario	Debt $Trillion	Deficit $Billion	Debt/GDP %	Interest/GDP % in 2005	% in 2008
1. Debacle	43.7	9,545	257	56	96
2. Muddling Through	5.9	230	33	3	0
3. Eliminate Debt	0	0	0	0	0

*Assuming a 50 basis point increase in real (and nominal) interest rates annually.

Although it might be difficult to focus on these numbers, please take a minute to realize that the muddling through scenario forecast that in the year 2005, we would have a debt of $5.9 trillion, a deficit of $230 billion, and a debt as a percentage of GDP of 33 percent. This scenario also forecast interest on the debt as a percentage of GDP at 3 percent. In some respects we are worse off in 1995 than the muddling through scenario forecast for 2005. Our debt is $5 trillion; our deficit is $200 billion; but our debt as a percentage of GDP is more than 70 percent.

This is a wake-up call, America! The time is short. We are now ten years closer to the debt bomb explosion. We are rapidly hurtling toward the debacle scenario.

According to the Hudson Institute report, deficits will continue to grow due to the increasing interest payments. Eventually, bondholders who finance the debt will lose confidence in the dollar and in America's capacity to meet its obligations. When confidence is lost, investors will rush to sell their bonds and notes at a discount. America will be faced with a financial and economic crisis. Banks will fail and credit will be abruptly restricted. This crisis will not be limited to the United States but will lead to severe worldwide recession.

However, some catastrophic financial event will probably occur first to adjust the severe debt load with which we are saddling ourselves and our children. In 1929, financial excesses were corrected in the form of a stock market collapse. In the first part of the twentieth century, the Weimar Republic of Germany had to issue million-mark notes because inflation caused its currency to collapse. We do not know what form America's next financial adjustment brought on by the huge federal debt will take. It could be a currency collapse, hyperinflation, hyper-interest rates, or some unforeseen financial event.

In the early 1980s, the Japanese yen stood at 280 yen to the dollar. By the summer of 1995, the U.S. dollar had collapsed to 71 yen to the dollar. The dollar has suffered similar devaluation against the German mark, the Swiss franc, and the British pound, although not as severe. In some respects, we have already begun to see the effects of our deficits on the U.S. dollar.

The startling fact is that the debacle tragedy depends not on a spending spree in Washington but on the federal government's continuing to run a deficit at the level that the Congressional Budget Office projected for the rest of the century. Avoiding that scenario will require a concentrated effort on the part of the American people.

We are currently muddling through because we have done too little too late. We are muddling through with budget deficits in the $200 billion range. We are muddling through with growing interest payments on the debt, which eat away at our government's capacity to perform.

At some point, we need to begin to repay our debt. If we start to balance our budget now and pay down our national debt, the nation's economic well-being will be assured. The nation's investment productivity, exports, economic output, and housing stock will be higher. Small businesses and state and local governments will have less difficulty borrowing if the federal debt is wiped out. We propose that a substantial tax reduction will also be in order.

In 1965, Singapore was billions of dollars in debt. Since 1980, however, the nation of Singapore has run a surplus. Singapore passes this surplus on to its citizens in the form of tax rebates and tax cuts. Wouldn't it be wonderful if the U.S. government could do that for us? "Of the people, by the people, and for the people" would take on a whole new meaning.

What would a debt-free economy mean to you and me? What would it mean to your children and my children? A debt-free economy would affect every area of our lives, but let's look closely at the areas of housing and health care.

To begin with, the lumber industry in the forests of Washington would go back to full employment. Glass factories in Ohio, carpet manufacturers in the Deep South, and aluminum and steel factories in the East would all find orders pouring in. Factories for small appliances for kitchens and bathrooms would be superproductive. Companies that make boxes for shipping anything from light bulbs to plumbing fixtures would have "Help Wanted" signs hanging out front. The boom in our productivity would be fantastic! In addition, our children and grandchildren could dream of owning their own homes and paying them off in their lifetimes.

The money that is spent on nonproductive interest expense servicing the national debt could be used to fund more research into cancer, AIDS, muscular dystrophy, heart disease, diabetes, Alzheimer's disease, and a host of other ailments. Low-interest loans could be made to private sector companies and individuals to find treatments and cures. How many Louis Pasteurs and Jonas Salks are there with the minds, energy, and belief that they can find a cure for these life-threatening illnesses, but they do not have the research funds available to them?

If America will decide to eliminate its national debt, it will have the financial power to provide homes for all its people, find cures for life-threatening illnesses, and build the economic foundation for the continuation of a strong and productive future. No longer will our country be laden with the emotional and financial burden of debt. Rather, it will be a country that knows the liberating power of being debt free!

4 WHY HAS NOTHING BEEN DONE?

We arrived at the warehouse of Fleetwood Enterprises where we were to meet John Crean, founder and chief executive officer of America's leading manufacturer of motor homes, travel trailers, and manufactured housing. We knew he had built his company on a no-debt policy. Curious to learn more, we arranged to meet him for lunch.

John's wife, Donna, greeted us and took us down a hallway to a room where we could find her husband. We expected to see an office with a large desk. Instead, the room was a garage. Covered with sawdust, John stopped his work on a new, experimental recreational vehicle. Over a sandwich at a nearby coffee shop, he shared his story with us.

"I started in 1950 making venetian blinds for trailers. But at the time I couldn't get any credit. I had very little credit before I started the company, and what I did have was bad because I had been late on payments. So I was forced to operate on a cash basis. I bought parts for cash and I sold only for cash. I extended no credit. My sales policy was simply to sell a better quality product at a lower price. Well, I was into the business less than a year when my major competitor filed for bankruptcy. It turned out that when I started dealing on a cash basis, he ended up with all the bad credit accounts, all the deadbeats."

Shortly afterward, John began to manufacture travel trailers, and he was extended credit from many of his suppliers. "But I didn't like it," he said. "I kept careful records so as not to miss a payment." As business volume increased, so did his credit, and so did the credit he extended to his customers.

But then the recession in 1954 hit. Suddenly, he couldn't collect his receivables, which meant he didn't have cash for his payables. "I had $300,000 due to me in receivables, but I owed the same in payables," John recalled. "Since I couldn't pay my bills, there was a total shutdown in deliveries. When you are in debt, you depend on your customers to pay their bills so that you can pay yours. If you have too many unpaid receivables, you can't extend more credit and you can't sell your product. Then you're in trouble. It was a very discomforting situation."

Determined to work things out, John took out a $10,000 loan from the bank to pay his bills. But before his checks cleared, the bank nervously recalled its money. "I had prided myself in never having a check bounce," said John. "Now they all bounced. I decided then and there never to go in debt again, not even for one quarter. It was really a simple decision. Since then I have always bought and sold for cash."

Nine months later John was operating again on a no-debt policy. "Any economist will tell you that you can't do that in our economy and grow. All I can tell you is that it worked. In 1973, when the oil crisis hit America, the recreational vehicle industry was severely affected. Sales dropped off 75 percent. But because Fleetwood was a debt-free corporation, we survived while others didn't. When the crisis ended, there was a pent-up demand for RV's. We came out that year with the same profitability as every other year."

Today Fleetwood Enterprises is the leading manufacturer of motor homes, travel trailers, and manufactured houses with sales in 1994 of more than $3 billion.

John's no-debt policy is not limited to his business. He and his wife have never had a mortgage and have always paid cash for their homes. "When you can't borrow money, and you see a goody you want, you know you can't have it unless you earn it.

That gives you tremendous motivation to work. In 1951 my wife and I lived on a tight budget, but we always had a little left over. One day I saw this beautiful Jaguar XJ 120. Suddenly, I wanted every extra bit of work I could get just to make an extra buck to buy that car. I had it in less than eighteen months."

John Crean feels that a no-debt policy would greatly benefit the United States, also. As he found with his business, he believes paying off the national debt begins with making a decision.

"I would like to see the leadership emerge that would make paying off the national debt as much a priority as winning World War II was. If everyone would produce more, tighten their belts, we could pay it off. It might hurt a bit, but if it were a national priority, it would be a pretty short-term thing. To get it done, it might take some pain and some long, hard work. But I'm willing to do it. I'll be the first to jump in!"

There can be little doubt that the rising federal debt is one of our nation's greatest problems. Then why has nothing been done about it? Why don't we hear more about it? We hear about the deficits and the need for balanced budgets, but rarely do we hear about the deeper, underlying problem of the structural debt. Why don't our highest elected officials in Congress and the executive branch of the government decide to tackle this problem? Where are the voices of concerned citizens rallying together to speak out against this tyranny?

- **Is it possible that little action has been taken because we are not aware?**
- **Or because we simply do not care?**
- **Or because we don't dare?**

Is it possible that we are not aware of the enormity of our nation's debt? Do we really care about the ensuing consequences if nothing is done about it? Even if we are aware and care, do we dare tackle a problem that seems so imposing?

Federal Deficit
(1926-1994)

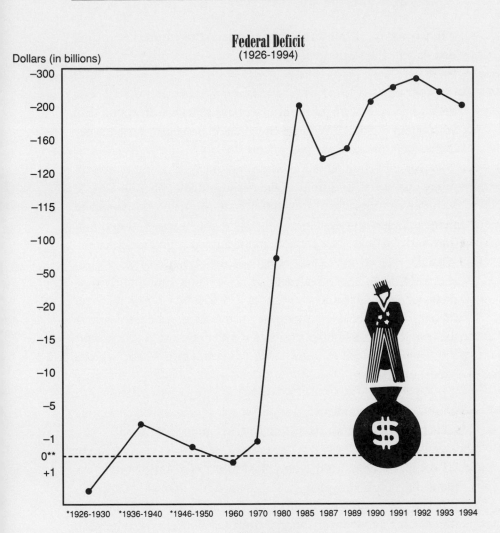

Dollars (in billions)

Fiscal Years

* YEARLY AVERAGE
** 0 INDICATES A BALANCED BUDGET

Source: Financial Management Service, U.S. Dept. of the Treasury

Are we aware of the difference between the country's budget deficit and the structural debt?

The news is filled with stories about the budget deficit. The deficit has been a major point of debate in recent elections. But what about the debt? Why are the print and electronic media virtually silent on the underlying debt?

Annual deficits of $200 billion are staggering, but these represent just annual additions to the national debt, which in 1995 is twenty-five times the size of the deficit. We need to understand that the underlying structural debt is the major cause of continuing yearly deficits. Budget deficits of any size increase the debt. And the interest on the debt remains a major cause of the budget shortfalls. With a national debt of $5 trillion, the interest payments equal $260 billion a year. In 1995, we paid $494,673 per minute simply to pay the interest on the debt! And this is more than twice the $217,000 per minute we were paying only ten short years ago. We need to know what the problem is before we can expect to discover the solution.

Are we, the American public, aware of the severity of our structural debt? Can we relate to the figure $5 trillion?

Jim Wheeler, a top economist for the Hudson Institute, explained that as he traveled around the country in the 1980s to lecture on the budget deficit and the national debt, he had tremendous interest and concern from his audience until he gave the hard facts. As soon as he wrote on the blackboard or overhead screen the figure $1,836,000,000,000 (by the way, this is not a typographical error—every zero belongs here) for the national debt in 1985, his listeners got what he called the "eglo" syndrome; that is, their eyes glazed over.

The 1995 $5 trillion debt has an unreal quality about it to all of us. We cannot comprehend this staggering amount, especially when the average American family income is only $35,939 per year. It might help to realize that $5 trillion amounts to a $43,500 debt for every one of the 115 million taxpayers in America.

Are we aware of our country's hidden debts? Are we being told the whole truth about our nation's financial picture?

Apparently not. With an ingenious stroke of the pen, our government has hidden much of our nation's true debt with an attractive accounting device. For example, unfunded social security payments, which amount to trillions of dollars, are not included in statements released to Congress and the public as part of our accumulated debt.

Government agencies and private economists project that the social security trust fund will be bankrupt between 2010 and 2015. Many quasi-government agencies are not included on the books of the federal government, but if the agencies failed, U.S. taxpayers would have to bail them out. For example, the Pension Benefits Guarantee Corporation, which insures corporate pension plans, is underfunded $71 billion. This off-budget arm of the government would be liable in the event of a financial collapse of a corporate pension through mismanagement, fraud, or other unforeseen event.

Likewise, when Mexico faced its 1995 currency crisis, the U.S. dipped into its heretofore unpublicized (and in many circles, unheard of) Exchange Stabilization Fund to borrow $20 billion of taxpayers' money to lend to Mexico. Of course, this will show up on next year's budget as a $20 billion bill to U.S. taxpayers.

High-risk loans and subsidies to special interest groups are also not included in the outstanding debt. This is called off-budget lending, which means such figures do not appear on the budget sheets as amounts that contribute to the budget deficit. In 1974, Congress created the Federal Finance Bank, which in the last twenty years has made trillions of dollars of loans to subsidize everything from energy costs for certain segments of the country to small business loans and much more.

Rather than show up in the yearly budget deficits, this eye-popping multitrillion-dollar debt is entered into the Treasury Department's books and is sold to the public in the form of Treasury securities. Although it is not paid for through taxes, this debt is unknowingly financed by people who purchase Treasury bills and bonds. The problem is that this takes money out of our economy that could otherwise be used to repay the national debt or enable our economy to expand.

Estimates of our federal government's total debt, including these hidden debts, range from $5 trillion to $17 trillion, depending on how conservative or liberal the interpretation might be. The National Taxpayers Union, for instance, says that the total federal debt is actually $17 trillion, which, assuming there are 115 million taxpayers, amounts to $147,826 of debt per taxpayer. If the Federal Finance Bank's debt and other hidden debts were included in our national debt, at least we would be aware of the problem. But now it is buried beneath a stack of accounting papers, hidden from our eyes, yet costing each one of us.

Are we aware of how we pay for the debt in our everyday lives through inflation?

The average American family pays $10,000 in federal government taxes each year, but these taxes currently finance less than 58 percent of our government's spending needs. Therefore, the government must raise money from other sources, which include sales taxes, customs duties, import taxes, corporate taxes, and a hidden tax called inflation. Inflation is one way we all pay for the debt. The National Taxpayers Union has drafted the statement of account on page 53 showing the actual liability of each United States taxpayer.

The government has seemed to prefer inflation, a subtle form of taxation. By printing money, the government is able to make up the shortfall in tax revenues needed to pay its bills. But the result is the devaluation of every dollar in proportion to the amount of

STATEMENT OF ACCOUNT

DEBT OR LIABILITY ITEM	FEDERAL OBLIGATIONS	YOUR SHARE
Liabilities		
Public Debt	$4,900,000,000,000	$42,609
Pension and Entitlement		
Programs (Estimate)	5,868,000,000,000	51, 026
Agency Securities		
Outstanding	18,000,000,000	156
Deposit Fund Accounts	21,000,000,000	183
Accounts Payable	124,000,000,000	1,078
Commitments		
Undelivered Orders	424,000,000,000	3,687
Long-Term Contracts	21,000,000,000	183
Contingencies		
Loan and Credit		
Guarantees; Insurance		
Commitments	5,355,000,000,000	46,565
Unadjudicated Claims		
& Other Contingencies	120,000,000,000	1,043
TOTAL	$16,851,000,000,000	$146,530

* Based on 115 million real taxpayers.

Source: Dept. of U.S. Treasury ("Statement of Liabilities and Other Financial Commitments of the U.S. Government") and National Taxpayers Union Foundation staff calculations and estimates of actual liabilities from government data.

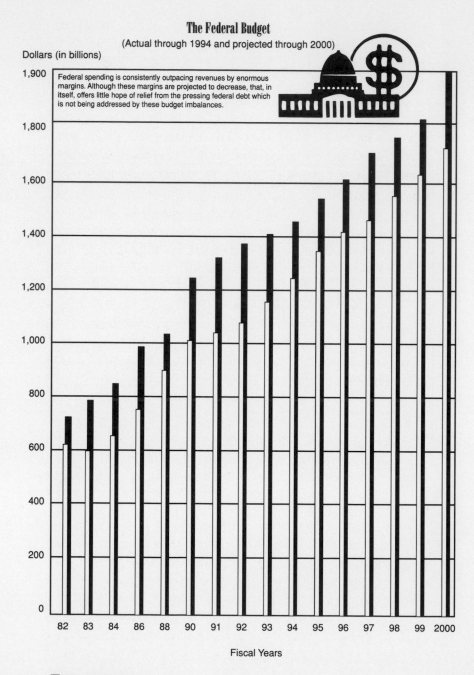

The Federal Budget

(Actual through 1994 and projected through 2000)

Dollars (in billions)

Federal spending is consistently outpacing revenues by enormous margins. Although these margins are projected to decrease, that, in itself, offers little hope of relief from the pressing federal debt which is not being addressed by these budget imbalances.

Fiscal Years

■ Federal Spending

□ Federal Revenues

Source: Financial Management Service, U.S. Dept. of the Treasury, and National Taxpayers Union Foundation.

money printed by the Treasury Department. When the government prints too much money, our dollars buy less. As the Nobel Prize-winning economist Milton Friedman said, "Who do you suppose pays for the deficit? There is no Dutch uncle. Not even an Uncle Sam to pay it. We all pay it, one way or another."[1]

It is much easier for members of the House or the president to turn to inflation as a means of raising funds rather than to declare outright that the government should raise taxes. Would you vote for someone who said, "I am going to raise your taxes by 50 percent"? But that is exactly what has happened. In the last twenty years the purchasing power of the dollar has eroded.

Although inflation is currently under control, many economists feel that it could come roaring back at any time. Some estimates are that if the deficit is not reduced, inflation could shoot up to an annual rate of 16 percent. (We must not forget that inflation was about 14 percent between 1976 and 1980 before the deficit quadrupled.) Are you aware that at an annual rate of 16 percent inflation, your 1995 dollar bill will be worth less than 11 cents in the year 2010? Everyday costs would be at unthinkable levels. Some projected costs appear in the following list:

	1995	*2010*
New home	$120,000.00	$1,112,000.00
New car	15,000.00	139,000.00
Cart of groceries	120.00	1,112.00
Gallon of gas	1.20	11.12
Pack of cigarettes	1.80	16.68
Loaf of bread	1.60	14.83

Inflation is the most insidious tax of all, for it hits not only the upper and middle classes, but also the poorest of the poor.

Although it is difficult to imagine inflation rates above 2 or 3 percent because we have enjoyed modest inflation since 1985, the storm clouds are already on the horizon in the form of a tightening of the labor markets and an upward pressure on wages. Many union contracts are up for renegotiation shortly, and union representatives are sure to remind their employers—and rightly so—of the sacrifices the union members have made over the past ten years to help American business compete.

For the past few years the producers of finished goods have not passed on to consumers the price increases of their raw materials. But eventually they will be forced to do so. The cost of raw commodities has been rising 10 to 15 percent per year as measured by the Commodities Research Bureau Index. For example, the price of wood pulp, which is used to make newsprint, has risen more than 54 percent in 1994 and 1995, but the cost of newspapers has risen only 4 percent. Primary nonferrous metals, used to make machine tools, have jumped 48 percent, but the tools themselves have jumped only 2 percent. Rubber prices have increased 90 percent, but tire prices have barely moved.

The strong Japanese yen and German mark have pushed up the prices of imported Japanese and German cars to the point that Ford, General Motors, and Chrysler have considered raising their prices. The quality and reliability of U.S. cars now equal and exceed those of many imports. Therefore, the demand for U.S. cars could add pressure to the inflation indexes.

Are we aware of the dangers of a growing federal debt as it relates to inflation and devaluation of our national currency?

Debt can throw a country into deep recession or depression or send it into an upward spiral of inflation. Rather than choose depression, our government will probably choose to print money and cripple us with inflation if nothing is done about the debt. It is even possible for our country to experience inflation and depression at the same time, accompanied by high interest rates and a devaluation of the dollar.

Devaluation of the dollar is a form of hidden inflation. Although it is true that a weak dollar makes U.S. goods and services cheaper abroad, a weak dollar permits complacency and a lack of competitive urgency. When the currency is strong, corporations must cut costs and improve efficiency. Devaluing the world's premier currency can only eventually lead to inflation, and not just in America, but in other countries as well. Oil, natural gas, and most of the world's energy markets are priced in U.S. dollars. If the dollar is devalued, it will take more dollars to buy the same barrel of oil. And that is inflationary. Never in history has a country with a weak currency prospered.

If we were to have a falling dollar and rising inflation, the Federal Reserve would probably fight inflation by raising interest rates. If it did not, the market would raise rates itself as investors demanded an increased interest premium over the rates of inflation. This increase of interest rates would increase the interest on the debt, and that would add an increasing burden to our nation's financial system.

Other countries with large debts have suffered greatly because of their inability to pay off their debts. Imagine that you are walking through a supermarket doing your weekly shopping. You wheel your cart down the aisles, carefully choosing items with the most value per dollar. You are extremely price conscious. You are on a budget and have decided to bring only the money allocated for groceries with you.

You choose a half-gallon of milk priced at $1.53. You select a carton of eggs marked 79 cents. A pound of extra-lean ground beef costs $1.99. After filling your cart, you push it to the front checkstand where you are suddenly confronted by the assistant manager hovering over your basket of goods. He begins to mark up the prices. Your milk is marked up to $1.91. Your eggs are upped to 99 cents. Your beef now costs $2.49. All of your items are marked up 25 percent! The assistant manager says, "You know why we are doing this, don't you? The government has just devalued the dollar by 25 percent."

Does this sound unthinkable? Impossible? Do you believe it could never happen? It did. This experience happened to us when we lived in Israel! And it was not the first time it happened in that country. Nor is this scenario confined to Israel alone. Mexico,

Argentina, and other countries have resorted to this method of dealing with inflation that is out of control.

Are we, the American public, aware that we have the ability to do something to solve the problem of our national debt?

So often when we hear of economic problems and government decisions, we close our ears and eyes. Our vision is confined to our small, private worlds. We tend to take the attitude that we can do nothing about it. But let us never forget that we live in a democratic society that depends on our involvement. The solutions to our problems are not in the government's hands, but in our hands.

There is a delightful story of a young boy and his friends who decided to try to trick the wise old man who lived in town. They caught a bird, and one boy held the bird tightly in his hand. He said to his friends, "I will ask the old man whether the bird is dead or alive. If he says the bird is dead, I will open my hand and let the bird fly away. But if he says the bird is alive, I will crush the bird until it is dead." And so the boys went to see the wise old man. "Is the bird dead or alive?" the boy asked. The wise old man looked down at the boy and thought a minute, then finally said, "The answer to that, my friend, is in your hands."

The answer to our country's debt problem is in our hands. But we must first be aware of what the problem is. We need to understand the severity of a debt of $5 trillion. We must be informed about the hidden debts our government does not readily disclose to us. And we must become educated about how we pay for this debt through taxes and inflation in our everyday lives.

The fact that we are not aware is not the only reason why nothing has been done about the rising federal debt. Is it possible that many who are aware simply do not care? The reasons why we do not care provide an interesting insight into our society's lifestyles and values.

Do we care if we repay our debt?

I will never forget a unique visit I once had with a dear friend, the late Congressman Clyde Doyle. Clyde was one of the most distinguished representatives, having served in the United States Congress for more than twenty-five years. He was held in the utmost respect by Democrats and Republicans alike. I remember asking his advice about debt. Our church was still very young, and we had devised a long-term plan to go in debt to acquire land, buildings, and equipment to perform our services as a church. I calculated that the church would grow enough so that we could repay our debt over a twenty-year period. I felt we had to. I am convinced that it was this attitude of planning to pay off our debt that has enabled us to be a church free of long-term debt today. I mentioned to Clyde, "We are planning to pay off our debt in twenty years. We feel this would be financially responsible. Do you agree?"

"Of course," he said.

"Okay," I ventured. "Then let me ask you how many years the federal government plans to take to repay its debt?"

I will never forget the look on his face and his answer. "Why, we will never pay off the debt, Bob." As he saw my stunned and confused expression, he went on to explain, "You see, the federal government has no life span. As individuals, we all have a life span, and we have to think in terms of paying off our debts in our life spans. Otherwise our children will inherit a terrible liability, or we will face bankruptcy as old persons when we are incapable of earning more money. So as individuals, we have to think in terms of repaying the debt in twenty to thirty years. But our government expects to stay in business forever. So we never have to pay off the debt. All we do is pay the interest on the debt and keep refinancing it. We simply roll the debt over."

Is it possible that nothing has been done about the debt because we do not care if we ever repay it? We are glad to report that at least in Congress this attitude seems to be changing. No longer are senators and representatives suggesting that we only refinance the debt. As we prepared this book we contacted every senator and representative and found that all who responded shared our concern that the debt is a problem that must be dealt with in our life spans, not passed on to future generations.

Do we care enough to take the long look?

Is it possible that we do not care because we have no sense of history? We live in "the disposable age." We are the "throw-away generation." We live in "the instant culture." We buy disposable items. We bring in sod for an instant lawn. We import full-grown olive trees for a big show. Expediency is a plight that erodes the quality of leadership. We want it now and have forgotten the power of patience.

We need to learn the lessons of history. Quality takes time. All the money in the world cannot produce instant roses. Nature takes time for the rose plant to grow and the bud to form. Don't try to chemically or artificially produce a premature blossoming of a bud!

Too often companies have sacrificed actions that would result in stable, long-term growth on the altar of needing to report short-term, quarterly profits to the financial community. Such an attitude hurts the company, its employees, and its stockholders in the long run. Our country must also begin to think in terms of long-term financial responsibility, not just in terms of how much we can spend before the next election. When we talk about paying off the national debt in twenty to thirty years, the benefit to you and me may seem to be too far away. The truth is, the stimulation from the expectation is as exciting as the reality of that goal! The anticipation of going to a party is as satisfying as the party itself. I get terribly excited knowing that one day the palm trees I have planted will be one hundred feet tall. As possibility thinkers, we must anticipate what our country will be like when it is debt free twenty to thirty years from now. Then we will find the energy and excitement to actualize it.

We need to practice the "ABCs of possibility thinking": attitude, belief, and commitment. Then by the time of our country's 250th anniversary in 2026, the United States can be the financial powerhouse of the world! Just think what tremendous excitement and anticipation that will create. It is far easier to get excited about our country's strong financial future than its coming doom. It is like comparing plastic to marble or Formica laminated plastic to solid wood. The laminated plastic dulls and chips, but the wood can be sanded down and refinished to last hundreds of years.

Integrity and quality take time. America needs to take the long look to secure its financial future.

Do we care enough to give up our selfish interests for the sake of our children's future?

Debt is the subtlest form of immorality if it serves only our own selfish indulgences and willfully passes the obligation on to others. When we take something from others without their permission, that is stealing. If we ask our government to provide a product or a service for our own purposes, no matter how legitimate, knowing that the government will never be able to repay it in our lifetimes and that the bill will be passed to our grandchildren with interest and that our children will pay our debt through taxes and inflation, are we not taking from their income in advance? Is that not stealing? When we run up a huge debt and have no plan to repay it, the voters and the elected officials form a silent conspiracy to steal from the next generation.

Do we care enough to stop our elected officials from running up a debt that will pay for our pet projects?

How much of our debt has been incurred by elected officials whose primary purpose was their own reelection? If we citizens do not hold ourselves responsible to repay our debt, we open the door for opportunistic politicians to get reelected on the promise of paying for our projects and needs. Unless we care about the debt, we cannot expect our elected officials to care either. Perhaps someday we can elect officials who ask for our votes, even if they cannot promise us what we want because they will not ask our unborn grandchildren to pay for our indulgences.

Democracy can survive only when men and women of honor run for office on honorable promises. And democracy can survive only when we citizens, with an equal sense of honor, refuse to make selfish and unreasonable demands upon our elected officials.

The responsibility falls on both the candidates and the public. President John F. Kennedy said it so well: "Ask not what your country can do for you; ask what you can do for your country."[2]

We have entered a critical time in history when we must stop asking our senators and representatives for personal financial favors. Rather, we must ask them to tell us what we can do to pull our way out of this financial trap and into a powerful future for peace, freedom, and justice worldwide. The time is coming when a senator, representative, or president will be elected when he or she promises to reduce the national debt and never increase it beyond our ability to repay it over a predetermined number of years.

Many people in America do care. One man told us, "If it means that I have to take a cut in my social security check, I'm willing." Many young people are already planning to achieve financial security so that they will never need to make demands upon their government. They plan to become part of the solution, not part of the problem.

If we are governed by greed and care only for ourselves instead of having a sense of shared community responsibility, we must question whether democracy can survive generation after generation. If our democracy survives only by people being elected to office based on our selfish demands, then the debt will continue to increase. Unless our hearts shift from "let the country help us" to "let us help our country," there will be no lasting freedom.

Do we care how our government spends the money we have entrusted to it?

Some of our elected officials don't care about the debt, and that attitude shows in their legislation. Not only do they spend money for projects that will aid them in their reelection, but many also do not give careful consideration to the financial aspects of more legitimate projects. Fiscal irresponsibility in the spending of our hard-earned tax dollars blatantly denies their concern about the debt.

Everyone has heard of the $436 hammer and $50,000 toilet seats as examples of waste in government spending. These are only the tip of the iceberg. The National Taxpayers Union reports that despite the debt about to race past the $5 trillion mark, the federal government continues to provide large amounts of money for questionable projects, many of which should be paid with private funding:

- $7 million to study "innovative methods for building wooden bridges."
- $20 million to convert the Fort Worth, Texas, stockyards into a tourist attraction.
- $7 million to help build an eighteen-story Rock and Roll Hall of Fame in Cleveland, Ohio.
- $350,000 to renovate the U.S. House of Representatives beauty salon.

We need to draw attention to such wasteful government spending practices and pork barrel politics, but we also need to recognize that successful steps are being taken to correct abuses such as these.

When President Clinton and Vice President Gore took office, they did so with a promise to "reinvent government" so that it would work for and assist the American people. On September 7, 1993, while posing with two loaded forklifts holding thousands of pounds of government regulations, they announced the formation of the National Performance Review. At the root of this effort is really problem-solving possibility thinking in action!

It is simply using common sense and listening to the ideas of the people who are doing the work.

A city worker in Phoenix, Arizona, had the "if it's going to be, it's up to me" attitude and suggested to his city manager that they use chain saws instead of hand saws for tree trimming. The city manager could have responded, "We cannot do that because chain saws are too noisy and so we need approvals and a feasibility and environmental impact study." Instead, he implemented the idea immediately. The result was happy workers who were four times more efficient.

In New York City, twenty-five thousand social workers who had complained about their rigid schedules implemented a flextime work schedule. Morale went through the roof!

The federal government has now adopted electronic transfer of funds from one government agency to another, saving millions of dollars in paper costs, postage, and record keeping.

In addition, the Pentagon and other federal agencies now allow managers to buy items off the shelf rather than requiring them to go through complicated procurement procedures.

On March 24, 1994, Congress reinvented the retirement options of federal workers by offering to buy out near-retirement-age workers through cash bonuses of up to $25,000 for early retirement. The private sector has been doing this for years.

Do we care enough to recognize that the problem is not going to go away by itself?

Hard as it is to believe, many people do not feel the debt is a problem. They feel that the productivity of future generations will be so strong that tax revenues resulting from the increased productivity will provide enough money to reduce the debt.

They claim that in the United States federal debt as a

percentage of the GDP is in line with those of other industrialized countries such as Japan and Germany. But both Japan and
Germany have savings rates that are nearly four times that of
the United States. Their currencies are among the strongest in
the world.

We need to care about our economic future. If we don't care,
who will? We need to care enough to take the long look, to face
the fact that if nothing is done about it, the debt will eventually
cripple our country's economic freedom. We need to care more
about our children's future than about our own selfish interests.
And we need to care enough to ensure that every dollar spent in
government today is being used wisely and efficiently.

If our future generations could speak, what would they
say? Would they care? In a small corner of Virginia, a group of
sixth graders studying government financing care about their
future. Every week, the members of the class pool their al-
lowances to mail $35 to Washington with a note that reads,
"Help save America for us!"

To solve the problem of our national debt, we must first become aware of the magnitude of the situation. That awareness
must make us care enough to make the sacrificial changes that are
needed to secure our economic independence. But even if we are
aware and care, nothing will ever be done if we do not *dare* to take
a stand! Change always involves risk, and unless we dare to face
the risks, we remain on a determined road to financial disaster.

Do we dare to stand up for what is right?

When we asked senators, economists, corporate leaders, and
average citizens, "Why don't we pay off the national debt? Why
don't we become a debt-free nation? There isn't a downside risk,
is there?" the reactions were predictable. We were answered by
raised eyebrows, shocked stares, a few excited reactions, and
many negative comments.

Many elected officials don't dare to even dream of paying

off the debt because it might mean budget cuts in their own back yards. They often run on the platform of promising what they will do when they are elected. Never are these promises, "I will raise taxes and cut some of your favorite programs so that America can solve its great problem of the national debt." Instead, they promise to spend money on projects requested by powerful, well-organized lobby groups that helped them get elected. This costs the unorganized majority of citizens billions of tax dollars. But we are equally guilty when we vote from self-interested positions.

Some politicians do not dare speak out against their party's platform, even if they disagree with it, for fear that they may advance no further or may severely limit their careers within the party. If a senator or representative knows within his or her heart that the party's spending policies or tax policies are wrong, he or she will rarely speak up and openly criticize the party.

Therefore, let us applaud elected officials who have the fortitude to do what they know is right, regardless of what it may do to their political careers. If we can recognize the courage of the individuals who speak out for a platform that limits government spending, gives a lower ceiling to our nation's debt, and demands a balanced budget, then we will take the first step up the mountain of financial freedom.

Do we dare to disagree with the experts who say it can't be done?

Most of us would not dare tackle the debt problem because people who are smarter than we are in the fields of economics and politics tell us it can't be done. They muster facts and figures that are researched and documented to justify their economic theories of why the debt cannot be eliminated.

The most destructive force in an institution or a society is a negative-thinking expert. (An expert is somebody who has more experience or is more knowledgeable in a specific area than the average person.) A negative-thinking expert has had experience and "knows" it won't work. But the truth is, new revelations and discoveries constantly change the scene. A positive-thinking expert is the best person we can find. But a negative-thinking expert is the worst because nobody dares challenge that individual. Creativity, however, often comes not from the authorities who are entrenched in a field of study but from an outside observer.

Consider the janitor who was cleaning the front lobby of an old landmark hotel in downtown San Diego. He overheard two well-dressed, professional-looking men talking in the lobby. "We'll just have to cut through the floor above," one of the men said. "And cut through the floor below," the other added. The janitor edged closer to hear better. The two professionals continued to discuss exactly where the holes would be made.

Finally, the janitor interrupted, "Pardon me. But it is my job to keep this place clean. What are you talking about?" They introduced themselves as an architect and an engineer, and they were designing a new elevator for the hotel so that it could keep pace with the competition of newer and more modern hotels.

The janitor protested, "But you can't cut a hole in the floors from top to bottom, not without closing down the entire hotel!"

"Of course, we can," they said. "We've done it before and we'll do it again."

Again the janitor spoke up: "But this hotel is made of plaster walls. If you knock these walls apart, dust is going to go through the hallways and into the rooms, and there's no way I can keep it clean. You'll have to close down the whole operation."

The experts smiled and tried to ignore him. But the janitor was persistent. He looked them straight in the eye and said, "Why don't you just build the elevator on the outside? That way it won't make any mess at all, and people will have a nice view of the ocean as they take the ride up!"

From the voice of a janitor came the idea of the first glass elevator on the outside of a hotel, which has since become a trademark of the finest hotels in the world!

Like all other professions, economics is too important to

leave to the economists. We will never pay off the debt if we believe we can't do it. And if an economist or politician believes we can't do it, he or she will have facts, figures, and reasons to "prove" why we can't. But attitude is more important than facts.

In a wonderful book, *Conversations with an Economist,* Arjo Klamer, professor of economics at Wellesley College, interviewed prominent economists including James Tobin, Karl Brunner, and David Gordon.[3] Professor Klamer found that economists differed widely concerning their theories, and despite volumes of publications and numerous debates, they did not change their minds. The reason, according to Klamer, is that economists develop theories to justify their own political positions.

This is not a criticism of their profession, but an observation of human nature. Facts can be gathered to support almost any economic viewpoint. Even Nobel Prize-winning economists differ on the solution to our national debt crisis. Each supports his argument with equal amounts of "undisputed facts." If the economists disagree, how can anyone else dare to believe there is a solution?

Nobel Prize-winning economist Friedrich A. von Hayek stated that "economists can observe and describe general patterns that emerge in the marketplace, but cannot make precise predictions about the course of the economy." Professor von Hayek said, "Not even a computer can keep track of the daily information that is dispersed among hundreds and thousands of people about their real intention to buy, sell, and invest. They signal them through prices. They often won't say what they intend and don't even know themselves until the moment they find out the price is right"![4]

This is when we must remember that our attitude toward a problem is much more important than any of the facts surrounding it. Consider the amazing feats people have achieved simply because they believed something was possible despite the odds and facts against them. Where a positive attitude pervades, creative solutions abound even in the face of experts who say it can't be done.

Do we dare face the facts?

A wise member of the Crystal Cathedral board of directors, John Joseph, once said, "I am a success because I learned economics from my father."

"What was your father's profession?" I asked.

"He was a lawyer," John answered. When I looked puzzled, he continued, "My dad once told me, 'John, you can't succeed unless you understand basic economics. I'll give it to you in one simple sentence: When your outgo exceeds your income, it's the upstart of your downfall!' "

Today the outgo of the government exceeds its income. Our country's economic condition is comparable to a luxury cruise ship. The orchestra is playing and the party is in full swing. The sound of laughter fills the ballroom where many couples are dancing. Some passengers have retired early to their staterooms. Unknown to all of them is that far beneath the deck of the ship, a hole has been punctured in the hull. Water is slowly leaking in. If the problem is discovered in time, the damage can be limited to the lower levels of the vessel. But if too much time elapses, the results can be devastating. To ignore the danger by listening to the music will lead to certain disaster.

We must dare to face the facts. America has a hole in its budgetary boat. Our outgo exceeds our income. This is the upstart of our downfall!

Do we dare to share the responsibility for the debt?

We must be careful when we criticize our senators and representatives who may vote to increase the debt. We are the ones who put them in office! We must shoulder the responsibility too. We must share in the liability. There can be no rescue until we share in the common goal and take common responsibility for solving this problem. No president can do it alone. No political party can do it alone. They are all powerless without the shared support of an unselfish public.

Do we dare to face the fear of failure? Do we dare to succeed?

Nothing restrains people more than the fear of failure. The major cause of failure is the fear of failure. We are so afraid we will fail that we don't try. When we don't try, our failure is guaranteed instantly and absolutely. Fear of success also keeps some people paralyzed. Whether it is fear of failure or fear of success, we must dare to face our fears to achieve our goals.

America must face the fear of failure as we seek to solve the impossible. Fifty years ago it was impossible to put a man on the moon, transplant a heart, or make a deaf person hear. The idea that we should actually try to pay off the national debt might strike fear of failure in the hearts of our president, elected officials, and top economists.

Do we dare to run the risk of failure? Do we dare to stand up for what is right? Do we dare to disagree with the experts who say it can't be done? Do we dare to share the responsibility for our economic condition? We have no choice but to take this challenge because our national debt is about to engulf us.

The answer to the federal debt is in our attitude. If we are aware, if we are willing to care, and if we have the courage to dare, then a solution is possible. We *can* find the answer!

5 PROBLEM OR SYMPTOM?

The truth is that for years we Americans did nothing about the national debt because we were not aware of its dangers and its effect on our lives. We did nothing about the national debt because we did not dare to believe that a problem that big could be solved.

But we are now ready to take action. We are ready to believe that the most seemingly hopeless problem can be solved. Even a problem as big as the national debt can be answered. Americans tackle such problems each day with success. We can eliminate the national debt and provide a strong financial future for the next generations.

In the 1980s, the South Bronx in New York City was the epitome of urban blight. It was an ugly battleground, filled with squalor and decay. If you had traveled through it on a graffiti-covered elevated train in 1985, you would have seen mile after mile of burned-out buildings and boarded-up high-rises. I'll never forget the horrible scenes I witnessed when visiting the South Bronx in those days. Rows upon rows of windows were smashed out. Rooftops were littered with dirty needles. When I went to a public school, a fully armed police officer unlocked the school door and escorted me and my companions into the building. What was more difficult to see than the physical devastation was the ruin of people's lives: the killings on the streets, the apartment buildings taken over by drug addicts, the hopelessness and fear of the people who lived there. Could such a situation ever be saved?

In 1974, the Mid-Bronx Desperadoes, a community group that has been instrumental in the turnaround of the Bronx, believed that its borough could be saved, but few others shared that belief. But the Mid-Bronx Desperadoes (renamed MBD) did not give up and encouraged others to help.[1]

One of those was a man named Billy Procida who in the late 1980s began to develop South Bronx real estate. He acquired abandoned buildings because he could not afford Manhattan real estate. Today Melrose Court, one of the projects of the Procida Organization, is a 4.5-acre development filled with working-class people in an area that had been devastated by arsonists. It includes homes with pastel façades, awnings, balconies, courtyards, patios, lampposts, and private parking spaces. The residents are excited about things the rest of us take for granted. For instance, Sara Morales, a thirty-seven-year-old single mother of two boys, says that last summer "there wasn't one time here when I heard gunfire during the night." In the South Bronx, that's a significant statement.

In addition to decent housing, retail investment is taking place in the South Bronx. Billy Procida has opened an eight-store minimall on 130th Street and has three more under construction. Rite-Aid, Pathmark, Bradlee's, CVS, Conway, and Walgreen's are all planning stores in the area.

On the drawing board for the South Bronx are a sports complex, a renovated waterfront area that may include an amphitheater, an arts center, a police academy, and a $335 million supreme court complex. The seemingly hopeless South Bronx has found hope because a small group of people followed the ABCs of mountain-moving, problem-solving, success-generating possibility thinking: They had a positive attitude, they believed that change was possible, they had a commitment to make it happen, and they made the decision to act.

If a complete change in the living conditions in parts of the South Bronx can take place because a few citizens believe they can make a difference, Americans can provide a climate for a sound financial future for our children and grandchildren by believing we can eliminate the national debt and acting on that belief. But we should also ask ourselves whether the debt could be a symptom of an even bigger problem.

The real problem of the people of the South Bronx was not living conditions characterized by drug addiction and violence, but an oppression of their spirit brought on by their circumstances. The problems you would have seen on your train ride through the area were the *results* of despair and hopelessness as well as the *cause*.

In the same way, the frightening growth of the national debt is a result of the real problems America is facing: cynicism and negativism, a lack of respect for authority, and an "us versus them" relationship with our government. Just as there were forces that tore down the spirit of the people of the South Bronx, there are forces that tear at the spirit of Americans. Paying off the national debt will be the *result* of a spirit of pulling together as well as a *cause* of an increasing spirit of unity.

Just as the environment of the South Bronx added to the despair and hopelessness the people living there felt, so the huge national debt adds to the cynicism and negativism, the lack of respect for the government, and the "us versus them" attitude concerning the government. The South Bronx became filled with squalor and decay because the residents felt helpless and despondent. And they felt helpless and despondent because they lived in the squalor and decay of the South Bronx. It was a vicious circle. The cycle had to be broken by a group of people made powerful by possibility thinking. How can we break the cycle of negativism and cynicism in government bureaucracy, which leads to wasteful government practices, which, in turn, lead to a huge national debt, which leads to more negativism and cynicism? The only way we know is through the actions of a group of people made powerful by possibility thinking.

Our Constitution begins with these words: "We the People of the United States, in Order to form a more perfect Union. . . ."

America is "the people," not the government, not a bureau-cracy. America is not "them," it is "us." I remember when we Americans felt responsibility for our government—local, state, and national—and when we felt that our voices would be heard, whether in a town meeting, at the ballot box, or through our elected officials. However, since the early part of this century, the government bureaucracy has taken away our self-reliance—and therefore our self-esteem—and increased our dependence on the government. That has driven a wedge between the government and the people. No longer is it "we the people." Now it is "they the government" versus "we the governed." Two the areas that have contributed to the separation of Americans from our government are government regulations gone haywire and our welfare system.

In his book *The Death of Common Sense,*[2] Philip K. Howard tells many stories of government regulations gone haywire which, in many cases, drives a wedge between the government and the people it is supposed to serve. He says, for instance,

A colleague of mine and his wife worked hard for several years to renovate the bathrooms and kitchen of their Brook-lyn brownstone. All plans were duly filed. Inspectors came periodically to see the work. They finally finished, got sign-offs from the inspectors, and went to get the certificate of occupancy. It was refused on the grounds that they had been living in the home. Of course, they had been living there; it is, after all, their home. But, they were told, the law prohibits "habitation" in a dwelling under renovation. No inspector, in all their visits, had ever told them of the rule. The rule itself suffered the typical defects of specificity. The language can't distinguish between a gutted home, which probably would not be appropriate to live in, and one being spruced up by the family living there. But that didn't matter to the bureaucrat at the desk. My colleague had broken the rule. It took him and his wife months to get the problem straightened out.

One of the themes of Howard's book is that laws have multiplied so fast, trying to cover every circumstance and leaving nothing to the judgment of the citizens, that they dehumanize us and sometimes make the government look ridiculous.

Bricks can fall on people, but never have bricks been considered poisonous. In 1991, the OSHA regional office in Chicago, after visiting a construction site, sent a citation to the brick maker for failing to supply an MSDS form with each pallet of bricks. If a brick is sawed, OSHA reasoned, it can release small amounts of the mineral silica. The sawing of bricks, however, does not release large amounts, and bricklayers don't spend much time sawing bricks. Bricks, after all, are not used like lumber.

Brick makers thought the government had gone crazy. . . . [But they] dutifully began sending out the MSDS form, which describes, for the benefit of workers, how to identify a brick (a "hard ceramic body . . . with no odor") and giving its boiling point (above 3500 degrees Fahrenheit). The problem, at least as seen by the brick manufacturers, was not just the paperwork, but the necessary implication that the material is, in fact, hazardous.

A specific area in which the government affects a large number of people is welfare. Welfare was originally conceived as a way of helping people in need. Decades later, it is now a source of mutual distrust between government and the people. Once a shining example of everything good about our American democracy, welfare has evolved into a government subsidy that many equate with a constitutional right. Philip Howard also summarizes what is wrong with the welfare system:

It is difficult to imagine a system that more perfectly combines the evils of inhumanity and ineffectiveness. All you have to do is visit a welfare office to believe that it was designed by a demon. It is a world where the recipient is barely known to the clerk. The "face-to-face" meetings required every six months are a form of torture: A forgotten Social Security card or other required piece of documentation leads to termination of benefits. Waiting for the interrogation under fluorescent lights is itself part of the torture. One documentary showed several elderly people sitting in the waiting area all day, the main movement being the hands of the clock. The end of the day came around, and it showed them being asked to leave. You keep asking yourself, What did they need? Were they hungry?

Our welfare system's human face has been replaced by a bogged-down mechanism of due process operating so as to establish uniformity and procedures without conscience. In the process billions of dollars are being wasted or misdirected.

One particularly controversial welfare program is Supplemental Security Income (SSI). The SSI was created in 1974 by Congress to provide what were classified as life's essentials to low-income adults too ill, old, or disabled to work. But as a recent report in the *Baltimore Sun* pointed out, the SSI's 6.3 million recipients include alcoholics and drug addicts who support their life-threatening habits with government cash. The SSI's annual cost of $25 billion represents double the expenditure of 1990, and it is expected to increase another 50 percent by the end of the century.[3]

Donna Shalala, Secretary of Health and Human Services, has pointed out problems with another controversial welfare program: "Aid to Families with Dependent Children is a $22 billion-per-year system that too often penalizes work, stigmatizes recipients, and many times locks families into a cycle of dependency."[4] When President Clinton polled one hundred children, many of whom had babies out of wedlock, he reported that 80 percent said if Aid to Families with Dependent Children was not given to people after they had had their first child, the number of out-of-wedlock births would be reduced. This fact was reported in *Reader's Digest* under the headline "Are We Encouraging Illegitimacy?" The various levels of government in America need to begin working again for the *people,* not for the *government.*

America needs leadership—a leadership that can restore the confidence of the people in the government, leadership that believes it can discover solutions to impossible problems, leadership that not only provides details of *how* to pay off the national debt, but also instills in us the *motivation* to pay off the national debt. The motivation for solving this and *all* of life's impossible problems starts with a belief and confidence in ourselves, in our communities, in our country, and in our God.

Yourself

"Why worry about paying off the national debt?" you might ask yourself. "What can I possibly do to help? What difference could I make?" This is negative thinking that leads to failure. It is a sign of a lack of self-confidence.

The beggar sat across the street from an artist's studio. From his window the portrait painter sketched the face of the defeated, despairing soul—with one important change. Into the dull eyes he put the flashing glint of an inspired dreamer. He stretched the skin on the man's face to give him a look of iron will and fierce determination. When the painting was finished, he called the poor man in to see it. The beggar did not recognize himself. "Who is it?" he asked as the artist smiled quietly. Then suspecting that he saw something of himself in the portrait, he hesitantly questioned, "Is it me? *Can* it be me?" "That's how I see you," replied the artist. Straightening his shoulders, the beggar responded, "If that's the man you see—that's the man I'll be."

To solve impossible problems, you first need a belief and confidence in yourself. They tell us that some ants are born with wings and use them, know the glory and rapture of flight, then tear the wings off, deliberately choosing to live out their lives as crawling insects. Don't make the same mistake by selling yourself short.

When you become a self-confident winner, you will be marked by four qualities:

1. *Imagination:* The self-confident person imagines being the person he wants to become. He ignores the way he is now.

2. *Commitment:* So strong is the desire to achieve a dream that the self-confident person totally commits himself to his goal. It is an unconditional, nonnegotiable commitment. The power of the totally committed person is incalculable.

3. *Affirmation:* First imagination. Then commitment. Then the self-confident person affirms that he is going to succeed by verbalizing his positive thinking. This exercises and vitalizes his self-confidence. At the same time, this causes others around that person to believe in his eventual success. Now a wonderful thing happens. As other people begin to believe, they will want to help, which adds fresh propellant to the rocketing self-confidence!

4. *Never-ending Persistence:* Never, never, never give up! Patience and persistence are the crowning qualities of a self-confident champion. Defeat and failure are heretical concepts that cannot and will not be contemplated.

The initials of these four qualities spell I C-A-N! That's self-confidence. It's those who have a belief and confidence in themselves who will be a powerful positive influence on our country. One such person is Heather Whitestone who had as her platform in her quest for the Miss America crown the belief that "Anything is possible." Heather had to overcome the obstacle of her deafness. But she imagined herself as Miss America. She then made a commitment to do what it took to achieve her goal. Her affirmation was given substance when she won the title of Miss Alabama. She never gave up, and she won the hearts of millions in September 1994 as she danced flawlessly in Atlantic City to music she could not hear. People such as Heather Whitestone who have a belief and confidence in themselves will be powerful, positive influences on our country.

Charles Ballard, a colleague of Robert L. Woodson, president and founder of the National Center for Neighborhood Enterprise in Washington, is another person who has tackled an impossible problem with confidence in himself.[5] After being released from prison in the early 1980s, Ballard adopted the son he had fathered with a woman before his arrest. From there, he started an outreach in Cleveland, Ohio, called Teen Fathers. Ballard went to maternity wards in Cleveland, researching the names of fathers of babies born out of wedlock. He then confronted the men to ask why they were not taking care of their children. Most of the young men confessed to Ballard that they did not know *how* to be fathers. Ballard therefore took it upon himself to teach the men the responsibilities of fatherhood. Over a period of ten years, Ballard eventually contacted two thousand men in this manner, and saw two hundred of them ultimately marry the mothers of their children. Because he cared and acted on his selfless idea, Charles Ballard was able to restore the foundation to hundreds of families. "Charles has demonstrated that you can change the value choices people make," Woodson said. "You can call people to themselves."

One person with a self-confident belief in himself or herself will inspire others. This, in turn, will change the attitudes of those people to ones of responsibility and self-confidence.

Your Community

If one person can make a difference, it only stands to reason that many working together can make an even more significant impact. We do not live in isolation. We have a need to belong. The foundation of our society is our families and communities. Each of us needs a sense of belonging because there is strength—both moral and physical—in numbers. But just as we need to restore a belief and confidence in ourselves, we need to restore a belief and confidence in our community.

It seems as if we have lost some of the sense of community from which we can derive such strength and stability. Increased mobility, the segregation of the generations so that young people do not learn from those with more experience, and a loss of both history and a sense of belonging have all contributed to our not having confidence in and commitment to our communities.

Unfortunately, it frequently takes a tragedy to let faith in our community flourish. When a bomb exploded at the Alfred P. Murrah Federal Building in Oklahoma City, the community pulled together. Good Samaritans offered strong hands and tender spirits to help a city mourn and then get back on its feet. Danny Cavett, for instance, spent hour after hour consoling parents and friends in crowded hospital corridors, even though he was in the midst of one of the most debilitating stages of chemotherapy for his advanced lymphoma.[6]

Two years earlier, hundreds of homes and farms were washed away by the waters of the Mississippi River in the great midwestern flood. Through a Farmers Helping Farmers hotline, people who experienced disaster were given oats, hay, corn, straw, labor, transportation, toys, money, food, clothes, and even livestock to help them get back on their feet. The larger community pulled together.[7]

The South Bronx could not have been successfully reborn until the people who lived there had restored to them a sense of community, a pride in themselves and where they live. Sara Morales said, "There was a time when you would see drug sales on the street, in front of everyone, with kids playing next to them. That has changed considerably with middle-income people moving in. At one time very few people cared. I come from the projects and a lot of people didn't work, didn't care about the development. They were always just hanging around. But here

[Melrose Court], there are all working people; they have a vested interest in the community."

If we do not feel we have a vested interest in our community, we won't care what happens to it. If we do not feel we have a vested interest in our country, we won't care whether we pay off the debt or not.

Your Country

It has become fashionable to demythologize our heroes and pry into the weaknesses of our leaders. It may be true that Benjamin Franklin was a womanizer, that Ulysses S. Grant drank too much intoxicants, and that our government acted shamefully in its treatment of Japanese Americans during World War II. But in spite of the weaknesses of our leaders and the errors we have made in the past, America is still the greatest country on earth. Our ideals, our goals, our optimism, and our energy make us great.

Most of us were born in America and did not make a decision to become citizens of this country. But the hundreds of thousands of people who would like to become Americans know that America—in spite of all its weaknesses—is still a symbol of hope.

An associate of ours recently attended a naturalization ceremony where people from England, Thailand, Nigeria, the Philippines, Bolivia, Mexico, Vietnam, Jordan, and Morocco were sworn in as new and proud American citizens. In conducting the swearing-in ceremony, United States District Judge Robert Echols spoke of the obligations inherent in being an American citizen. It is a charge that needs to be heard not only by naturalized citizens but also by all of us as well who are Americans by birth:

It is a great privilege and honor to welcome you as citizens of the United States on behalf of your fellow countrymen. Today is your own personal Declaration of Independence. You have renounced your allegiance to your country of origin and pledged your allegiance to the United States. Much of the strength of this country has come from the diversity of its people. They have made this country part of what it is today, a shining example of self-government. The real secret to the fact that this country has succeeded and that we have remained a free people is that we have a written Constitution that restrains the exercise of power and preserves the freedoms of individuals. But our Constitution requires continuing vigilance, and in that respect you have a duty to discharge your responsibility as a new citizen. If we do our duty as good citizens and preserve our inheritance, the freedom that you and I enjoy today will be available in the future for our children and our heirs, Americans will still be a free people, and there will be opportunities like this for others. But it takes your effort, your work, and your participation in the democratic process. I challenge you and I encourage you to use your new citizenship. Don't put it on a shelf or hang it on a wall and forget about it.

Your God

One of my favorite parts of the Bible is the eleventh chapter of Hebrews (vv. 33-34, 37-38) because it tells of the wonderful ways that God worked in the lives of various Old Testament men and women. It tells of these people who "conquered kingdoms, administered justice, and gained what was promised; who shut the mouths of lions, quenched the fury of the flames, and escaped the edge of the sword; whose weakness was turned to strength; and who became powerful in battle and routed foreign armies." It does not say everything went easily: "They were stoned; they were sawed in two; they were put to death by the sword. They went about in sheepskins and goatskins, destitute, persecuted and mistreated—the world was not worthy of them." But the men and women described here all had faith in God: "And without faith it is impossible to please God, because anyone who comes to him must believe that he exists and that he rewards those who earnestly seek him."

Having confidence and faith in an all-powerful God and knowing that He loves you is the fundamental basis for a belief in yourself, your community, and your country.

The destructive cycle of lack of confidence in our government, which results in spending too much of someone else's money, which generates a further lack of confidence, can be broken. Not only can we eliminate the national debt, but we can regain our faith in ourselves, in our community, in our country, and in our God. That is mountain-moving, possibility-thinking faith.

6 POSSIBILITY THINKERS— LEAD THE WAY

America is faced with a historic window of opportunity. It is now that we must take up this great challenge to balance the budget, eliminate the mounting yearly deficits, and make a plan to retire the national debt.

To some people this undertaking may seem to be an impossibility. But through the power of possibility thinking, impossibilities can be moved into the realm of the possible.

What precisely is possibility thinking? Possibility thinking is assuming that the ideal can become real. Possibility thinking is sifting carefully through all the alternatives and options, both real and fanciful, in the process of determining the grand objective that should be pursued.

The late Walter Burke was chairman of the board of Mc-Donnell Douglas Corporation in Long Beach, California, when he received a telephone call from President Kennedy. As Walter Burke described it to me, "The president said to me, 'Mr. Burke, I want to put a man on the moon. We both know that's impossible. Now let's figure out a way to make it possible. I'm calling you because we need to have a rocket with enough booster power to push a capsule away from the gravitational pull of the earth. I want you to tackle that part of the total project.'"

It was not much later that Walter Burke called me to ask if he could have a large photograph of the possibility thinker's creed. The same poster had been distributed to many locker rooms in professional athletic circles. We promptly sent the following poster to Mr. Burke, which he kept on the wall behind his desk.

WHEN FACED WITH A MOUNTAIN
I WILL NOT QUIT!
I WILL KEEP ON STRIVING
UNTIL I CLIMB OVER,
FIND A PASS THROUGH,
TUNNEL UNDERNEATH—
OR SIMPLY STAY
AND TURN THE MOUNTAIN INTO A GOLD MINE,
WITH GOD'S HELP!

Possibility thinkers listen to every positive idea. They never reject an idea because there is something wrong with it, because it might release some new tensions, or because it contains an inherent fault or negative factor, actual or implied, within the proposal. Possibility thinkers are smart enough to know there is something wrong with every good idea. Possibility thinkers clearly understand that all great ideas have their own flaws and imperfections. However, possibility thinkers believe that if there is some value or good in the proposal—no matter how preposterous and off the wall it may sound—then the proposal should be taken seriously. It is not a mark of intelligence to scorn, scoff at, or snub some way-out idea if, in fact, it does hold some positive potential. History proves that great progress has been made by great dreamers whose ideas at the outset appeared unrealistic, if not ludicrous. Possibility thinkers explore with an imaginative and open mind all of the possibilities in a proposal. Possibility thinkers make an all-out commitment to discover hitherto unknown avenues by which an impossibility could, in time, become a new breakthrough. Strangely enough, this mental attitude alone has the power to release incredible forces that will move an impossible idea into the realm of the possible.

Pay off the entire federal debt? This gives us a fantastic

example and opportunity for applied possibility thinking. The almost universal instinctive, intuitive, impulsive reaction is, "But if we can't even balance the budget, how do you expect to pay off the debt?"

It has been observed that when a positive idea comes into the mind, we can almost always expect the positive idea to be immediately followed by a negative thought that can threaten to abort the positive idea at its conception. But every positive idea deserves a fair trial. Just because some splendid dream appears fanciful and unrealistic, if not impossible, doesn't give anybody the right to rudely hiss the idea off center stage or rule it out of court. The greatest ideas are always impossible when first conceived.

If they were well within the realm of possibility and general acceptance, they would not be ideas under discussion—they would be projects already begun. The greatest ideas are ones so embryonic that they are unborn and still waiting to be taken seriously.

There is a delightful story of the old fisherman who sat at the end of the pier with his line in the water. At his side was a bucket where he put his catch of the day. Next to the bucket was a ten-inch ruler, stained and splintered. Next to the ruler was a can of worms. A passerby paused and watched the fisherman's pole bend and saw him enthusiastically land his first fish. He carefully dislodged the hook from the fish's mouth. Holding the squirming fish in one hand, he picked up the ruler with the other to measure the length of his catch. It measured just short of his ten-inch ruler. He seemed pleased and threw the fish into the bucket. The fisherman then hooked another fish, and the pole bent until the tip almost touched the water! As he landed the big one, it was quickly obvious that it was far longer than the ten-inch ruler. He threw this fish back. The passerby was puzzled, but said nothing. As he watched the old man, he observed that the little fish were put into the bucket to be taken home, but the fish larger than ten inches were thrown back. Curiosity got the better of him, and finally, he said to the fisherman, "I'm very curious. Why do you keep the little ones and throw the big ones back?"

"Well," the old fellow answered, "my frying pan is only ten inches wide."

We can laugh at this story, but in reality, we are that fisherman. Every person is that fisherman. The truth is, we throw away the biggest ideas that come into our minds. We have our plans, perceptions, and prejudices, and if an idea comes along that exceeds or doesn't fit into our plans, we intuitively, instinctively, impulsively—but not necessarily intelligently—discard it out of hand.

The hardest job in the world is to think bigger than we have been thinking before. Thus, the ideas that are bigger than we are able to understand or embrace are offhandedly and irresponsibly discarded.

Intelligent and critical possibility thinkers have learned that ideas are never to be thrown away simply because they are too big for our minds to grasp. We may reserve judgment. We may be cautious before we make a wholehearted commitment. We may quietly hesitate before we plunge ahead. But we discipline ourselves against the natural, normal, negative inclination to simply laugh the idea away and throw the big fish back into the water.

What is true for an individual or for an institution must be true for our country, too. We will all rise or fall, succeed or fail, move forward or backward depending on our willingness to master skills of good management. Management is the control of resources to maximize productivity. Success comes as we establish solid objectives and then manage our resources to achieve the determined goals that have been sensibly established. Individuals, institutions, and nations fail when they fail to manage. Some fail by mismanaging time. Others mismanage money. Still others mismanage people. But ultimately, most fail when they mismanage the ideas that flow into their minds.

Possibility thinking is the philosophy that offers universal principles for the effective management of ideas. Ultimately, no person, company, organization, or nation suffers from a shortage of money, talent, or time. The problem is always an idea problem. Money flows to dynamic ideas. Talent is attracted to the corporation or the country that has excitement-producing ideas.

In the book *Tough Times Never Last, But Tough People Do!* I listed ten commandments of possibility thinking. These commandments can help us fulfill the dream that the American people could form a national consensus to achieve the objective of becoming a debt-free nation.

This is an idea. We hope it will prove to be an idea whose time has come. But how will this idea be received in the minds of people? How do we manage the thought? How do we respond and react to the proposal? Let us keep in mind the ten commandments for possibility thinking.

Commandment Number One
NEVER REJECT A POSSIBILITY BECAUSE YOU SEE SOMETHING WRONG WITH IT!

There is something wrong with every good idea. No proposal is perfect. There are flaws in every system. It is no mark of intelligence to find something wrong with a great idea. The question is, Is there something good in it? Possibility thinkers assume they can spot the positive and the negative elements in every idea and then proceed to divide the negative from the positive. The negative elements must be isolated and eliminated, or at least insulated or sublimated. Meanwhile, the positive elements in the proposal are extracted, welcomed, nurtured, developed, and exploited with adventure and ultimate success.

Commandment Number Two
NEVER REJECT A POSSIBILITY BECAUSE YOU WON'T GET THE CREDIT!

We would plead with our fellow citizens that the proposal for achieving national financial freedom through the power of being debt free not become a political issue. A tragedy in a free society is the inclination of a cause to become a politicized issue. If Republicans are for it, then Democrats have to be against it. If Democrats advocate it, Republicans had better fight it.

When the bombs fell on Pearl Harbor, there was only one unanimous reaction: We must win the battle and save the country without concern about who gets the credit. The Republicans didn't stop to think, "Well, if we win the war, the Democratic president will get the credit." Great things will happen when a company or a community or a country pulls together to win a battle without any concern about who is going to be honored.

God can do tremendous things through the person who doesn't care who gets the credit.

Commandment Number Three

NEVER REJECT AN IDEA BECAUSE IT IS IMPOSSIBLE!

Every great idea is impossible because what makes an idea great is that it is something that isn't being done . . . yet. And it isn't being done because it probably hasn't struck anyone as being a viable venture. I'm convinced that every time a great idea comes from God it is always impossible. The contribution that religion makes to society is the reminder that greatness comes when we walk in the arena of faith. And faith is making a decision before we can see our way through the whole pilgrimage.

Someone said to me recently, "I will be glad to go along with the idea as soon as I can understand it." He elaborated, "I'm willing to become a believer once I get the answers to my questions."

I replied, "But faith is what you need when you can't get answers to the questions!"

Possibility thinkers don't reject an idea because it is impossible, because they can't get answers to their questions, or because they can't see how they are going to accomplish it. They welcome glorious impossibilities as exciting invitations to come up with a new invention, a new organization, or a new technique that could spell triumph anyway.

Commandment Number Four
NEVER REJECT A POSSIBILITY BECAUSE YOUR MIND IS ALREADY MADE UP!

Possibility thinkers recognize that ego, greed, and stubbornness are the three major causes of failure. They are the unholy trinity that block progress. Possibility thinkers do not want their own way; they want to do the right thing. "I'm not ego involved; I'm success oriented," I tell my friends and associates. After all, possibility thinking is pragmatic. I know that if I get my own way—if I'm wrong—I'm going to fail later. Then I can suffer a real ego blowout at high speed in heavy traffic!

So, possibility thinkers have the capacity to change their thinking drastically and sometimes swiftly. People who never change their minds are either perfect or stubborn. I don't know of an intelligent person who would claim to be perfect or who would want to be labeled stubborn. Therefore we need never be embarrassed about changing our minds. Rather, it can be a mark of emotional maturity.

Commandment Number Five
NEVER REJECT AN IDEA BECAUSE IT IS ILLEGAL!

Under no circumstances do we permit or advocate or approve of an illegal act. But it is true that much progress is thwarted by regulations, ordinances, and procedures, as well as by county, state, and federal laws. The beautiful thing about a democracy is that we have the power to change laws. And the positive legislators are the persons who are constantly looking for progress-restricting obstacles that exist in society. Then, through legislation, they seek to remove these growth-restricting obstacles. We simply change the laws to allow positive possibilities the opportunity to come alive and bring greater opportunity for all.

Commandment Number Six

NEVER REJECT AN IDEA BECAUSE YOU DON'T HAVE THE MONEY, THE MANPOWER, THE MUSCLE, OR THE MONTHS TO ACHIEVE IT!

The power of a dream outpaces the power of the obstructions. The weight of a positive idea tips the scale when balanced against the weight of the obstacles. In other words, a positive idea has the power to attract the kind of support that can compensate for lack of money, manpower, talent, or time. If a positive possibility is treated with respect and is carefully nurtured, it will succeed against overwhelming odds. Exciting possibilities have a magnetism that attracts the kind of support that can move them from fantasy to reality. Ideas attract money. Ideas attract talent. Ideas solve time problems, too. The important thing is *the idea*. Welcome it. Respect it. Trust it. Believe in it.

Commandment Number Seven

NEVER REJECT AN IDEA BECAUSE IT WILL CREATE CONFLICT!

Every new idea will stir some opposition. Every new proposal can offend someone. Every positive possibility has a price tag on it and not everyone will agree on the price. Every time we set a new goal we will incur some opposition. Every new commitment will produce a new set of conflicts. New tensions arise with every new move forward. Therefore, if we reject an idea because it will create conflict, we will never get anywhere.

Commandment Number Eight

NEVER REJECT AN IDEA BECAUSE IT IS NOT YOUR WAY OF DOING THINGS!

Ultimately, your way isn't important. The right way is the only thing that matters. Learn to accommodate. Prepare to compromise. Plan to adjust. A different style, a new policy, and a change in tradition are all opportunities to grow. Readjust your budget. Compromise your taste. Accommodate your lifestyle. You may have to decide that it's more important to succeed than it is to snobbishly adhere to your private preferences.

Commandment Number Nine

NEVER REJECT AN IDEA BECAUSE IT MIGHT FAIL!

Great success comes to the individual or the institution that has the freedom to fail. The *fear* of failure is the number one reason for failure itself just as the possibility of success is the number one explanation for most human achievement. What would you attempt to do today if you knew you could not fail? What goals would you set for yourself if you knew you could succeed? What promises would you make if you knew you could keep them? What dreams would you embrace wholeheartedly and completely if you knew they could come true? This is possibility thinking. It releases incredible energies, enthusiasms, and powers. Ideas that have great possibilities for failure are turned into astonishing accomplishments through the power of possibility thinking!

Commandment Number Ten

NEVER REJECT AN IDEA BECAUSE IT IS SURE TO SUCCEED!

Does this sound crazy? Ridiculous? Not really. We have seen countless people reject positive ideas because they were afraid of success. "If I succeed, will people expect more from me?" "If I succeed, will I only set higher standards for myself that I'll have to live up to?" "If I succeed, will I be able to handle the success?"

Many companies are deliberately kept small and restrained from expansion by corporate chiefs who fear success. They assume, often correctly, that if the company succeeds, they will have to delegate power and authority to others. And to many founding individuals that is a threatening prospect. In the political realm, we all see reactionary politicians voting against great ideas that could possibly succeed and in the process accrue to the advantage of their political opponent.

The ten commandments of possibility thinking help us to manage ideas so effectively that we can be assured of success. Each one has told us what *not* to do. Now let's restate them in positive terms. Possibility thinkers are slow to vote no and naturally inclined to vote yes to positive ideas. The yes vote may be qualified: yes, if; yes, when; yes, but; yes, after. But it is always yes.

The natural reaction of a possibility thinker is to vote yes to a positive idea.

Commandment Number One

Say yes to an idea
IF IT WILL HELP PEOPLE WHO ARE HURTING
NOW OR IN THE FUTURE!

Possibility thinkers recognize that we are all stewards. We are entrusted with a life and are obligated to contribute to the welfare of the human family. Anytime someone comes up with a big, bold, beautiful idea, we do not ask, "Is it possible?" Rather we ask, "Who needs it? Would it help people who are hurting?" The secret of success is to find a need and fill it, find a hurt and heal it, find a problem and solve, it, find a chasm and bridge it. If an idea would help people who are hurting, we have no right to vote against it. Our mental attitude must be yes. Perhaps yes, if. Maybe yes, when. Sometimes yes, but. Occasionally, yes, after. But never a total, obstinate, arbitrary, no!

Commandment Number Two

Say yes to an idea
IF IT CHALLENGES AND MOTIVATES
SELF-DISCIPLINE!

Every person and every institution understands the normal inclination for waste. Expendable resources can too easily be drained away through lack of self-control. Possibility thinking is interested in maximizing productivity. All of us must welcome ideas that, if embraced, would impose the pressures to work harder, save more, and increase the power base to give added strength to the institution, the organization, or the cause that perpetuates the nobler human values.

Commandment Number Three

SAY YES TO AN IDEA
IF IT HOLDS THE PROSPECT OF CONTRIBUTING
TO PEACE, PROSPERITY, AND PRIDE IN THE
HUMAN FAMILY!

In a world marred by poverty, wars, and humiliation in the human family, let there be no offhanded, impulsive rejection of sincere proposals that, however implausible and unrealistic they may seem, do hold some promise of moving the human family closer to prosperity that can eliminate poverty, peace that can eliminate war, and pride that can eliminate human shame.

Commandment Number Four

SAY YES TO AN IDEA
IF IT WILL ENDOW THE GREAT DREAMS OF
GREAT DREAMERS!

History teaches that there are dreamers, there are dreamers, and then there are dreamers! There are the dreamers who have a dream but never pull it off. There are the dreamers who make their dreams come true only to have their dreams die out when they die. Then there are the dreamers who make their dreams come true and inspire their successors to perpetuate their dreams beyond their own lifetimes.

Any idea that will prolong the life span of a great dream of a great dreamer deserves to be taken seriously. There were those great dreamers who dreamed of colleges and watched their dreams come true, only to see those dreams die out for want of a perpetual endowment fund that could capitalize the dream through stormy seasons. The history of private colleges in the United States is littered with shipwrecked dreams of colleges that were founded but were unable to survive the depressions, the wars, and other economic tough times. On the other hand, there are also colleges founded with the financial foundation that provided them an unbroken income, enabling them to survive the catastrophic economic earthquakes that history inevitably produces.

If an idea contributes to the endowment of a great dream of a great dreamer, listen to it carefully and take it seriously.

Commandment Number Five

SAY YES TO AN IDEA
IF IT MAKES GOOD FINANCIAL SENSE!

I remember the first time I met W. Clement Stone. At the time he was reputed to be one of the wealthiest men in the United States. "What does it feel like to be super rich?" I asked him.

"It gives me the feeling of power," he answered.

"And what is that feeling of power?" I asked. I'll never forget his answer.

He looked at me and said, "It is a wonderful feeling, if you want to do a lot of good for a lot of people!" And he flashed his wonderful smile.

Great wealth gives you the power to do a lot of good for a lot of people! Any idea that holds the possibility of producing financial advantages for persons or institutions controlled by the nobler human values deserves to be taken seriously.

With its ideals of freedom, peace, and prosperity, America should strive to multiply its wealth. The goal of the United States of America should be to become a richer, wealthier nation so that future generations will be empowered to do greater good for the whole world. The poor cannot solve the poverty problem. The hungry cannot solve the famine problem. The enslaved cannot solve the problems of the oppressed. It makes sense for Americans to maximize the wealth that we have today and aim at being not only a debt-free nation but also a nation that will, like a great university, have its own endowment funds. A great president of a great college or university should set as prime objectives not only the establishment of the highest academic credentials but also the building up of an endowment fund to make sure that research and development can be carried out in future generations. That president should strive to build an endowment so that worthwhile students who lack the money to attend the university could be given an opportunity for a free education.

We should call upon the presidents of the United States of America in the coming decades to understand their role to be somewhat like that of the head of a great university. They should establish endowment funds. They should start them and watch them grow. They should build endowment funds in which the capital cannot be touched but the annual earnings can be distributed. I have a dream of a day when the national radio and television networks will converge upon the nation's capital for the announcement of the winners of the scholarships given by the federal government to worthy students. Even as the president of the United States has handed out medals of honor to veterans of wars, and even as the king of Norway has the joy of handing out Nobel Prizes to international achievers, so future presidents of the United States would have the joy of handing out prize scholarship awards from the endowment funds that have yet to be established.

Commandment Number Six

SAY YES TO AN IDEA
IF IT WILL BRING BEAUTY INTO THE WORLD!

Beauty is practical, too. Ideas that contribute to color and to cleanliness upgrade the quality of human living and deserve to be taken seriously because human beings are inclined to become more beautiful persons when they live in a more beautiful environment. Environmental ugliness contributes forcefully and forthrightly to moral decline and decadent behavior.

What will happen in American society if the streets are filled with potholes and never repaired, if the paint peels and is never repainted, if windows crack and are not replaced, and if weeds grow through the cracks in the sidewalks and are never removed? We can expect those conditions to exist and to spread like a malignancy throughout the land in the decades to come if our country becomes financially bound by debt. We are one nation, after all. A debt-free America would be a wealthy America. And that would mean the power to ensure the perpetuity of beauty in our cities, in our streets, in our countrysides. We see beautiful parks. We see rolling hills. We see clean streets and clean cities. But it will be in direct proportion to the financial health of our land.

Commandment Number Seven

SAY YES TO AN IDEA IF IT CONTRIBUTES TO A SENSE OF A CARING COMMUNITY!

If an idea has within itself the power or possibility of bringing divergent peoples together into a sense of brotherhood and sisterhood, it has enough value to be looked at honestly.

Many ideas are malicious in their intent. Some individuals and institutions thrive on being divisive. This, after all, is a natural, age-old, reactionary technique of insecure people who elevate themselves by demeaning their real or fanciful competitors.

The truth is that all human beings are living on the same

planet, drinking the same water, and breathing the same air. Earth is a space vehicle traveling at an incredible speed of sixty-seven thousand miles per hour around the sun. And if planet Earth blows up, all nations will blow up together.

There is a beautiful teaching in the Bible that all people are created by God and accountable to Him. That makes us accountable to one another. The world is too dangerous a place today for any nation to be isolationist in its mentality. If one nation suffers, all of us will eventually feel the pain. If water penetrates a boat by entering the most insignificant room of the vessel, it will be only a matter of time before the captain in his luxurious quarters will be affected, too.

We must recognize the truth in the phrase that no man is an island. No nation can stand alone. We must constantly keep before us a vision of a world that is a united collection of human beings. And the universality of the human family's needs must transcend our individual selfish goals. If an idea will contribute to the possibility of happiness and health for all nations, then of course, it must be taken seriously, however grandiose it may appear. We will not say no to any idea that holds within itself the prospect of a world of brotherhood and sisterhood of human beings. We may qualify our response and say yes if, yes but, yes after, or yes when, but we will not say no. We have a dream of an America that is so financially powerful, a country with all its debts paid, a mature institution well endowed with cash surpluses, that it will have the power and clout to produce peace and prosperity for our whole world!

Commandment Number Eight

SAY YES TO AN IDEA IF IT WILL CONTRIBUTE TO THE COLLECTIVE SELF-ESTEEM OF A PERSON OR A NATION!

Self-esteem and possibility thinking are philosophical Siamese twins. The "I am" always determines the "I can." The individual or institution that has a strong self-image will dream noble dreams. The individual or institution that suffers from an inferiority complex will never dare to dream what it can do, what it can be, or what it can accomplish. More than anything else an individual's self-image will contribute to the quality of the visions the mind creates.

All the wealth and all the power, without genuine, healthy pride, are nothing. For nearly one hundred years now a new "science" called psychiatry has tried to arrive at an understanding of the ultimate motivation that makes a human being a person. Dr. Viktor Frankl, lecturing at Claremont Theological Seminary in Claremont, California, said that to Sigmund Freud the ultimate human motivation was the will to pleasure. Freud thought the single, strongest need within the human being was the need for pleasure drives to be fulfilled. Alfred Adler, said Frankl, thought the ultimate human motivation was not the will to pleasure, but the will to power. Frankl himself, however, thought the ultimate human motivation was the will to meaning. He said that more than anything else, people need to see that there is some meaning, some value, some purpose, to what is going on.

I thought about that lecture for many years. It directed me down avenues of study in books and in conferences. Years later in a three-hour private dialogue with the esteemed Dr. Frankl, I shared my position: "Dr. Frankl, I submit that deeper than the will to pleasure, deeper than the will to power, deeper than the will to meaning is the *will to dignity*."

Even meaning loses meaning unless and until it feeds my need for self-esteem and human dignity. We now know from behavioral sciences that the lack of self-esteem is the single most important cause of almost every negative human behavior imaginable. Any idea, therefore, that contributes to a personal or collective sense of self-esteem ought to seriously attract our vote and our support.

The goal of a debt-free America holds the prospect of building a nation that will enjoy a patriotic self-esteem at the highest level of any nation in the history of the human race. Psychologists have long known that people with a strong sense of self-esteem tend to be open, generous, and nondefensive. Therefore, they are easy and wonderful to live with. That's the kind of America that the world would welcome! On the other hand, insecure people and insecure nations, suffering from inferiority complexes or a lack of noble pride, are defensive, selfish, and basically dangerous.

Commandment Number Nine

SAY YES TO AN IDEA IF IT IS A POSITIVE SOLUTION TO A NEGATIVE CONDITION!

Possibility thinkers are aware of the fact that there is a positive and a negative solution to every problem.

The challenge of morality is to accept the restraints of law that would protect us from the temptation to select the negative solutions to human problems. For instance, the Ten Commandments in the Old Testament given by God to Moses were not designed to keep human beings from enjoying life. They were given to protect us from the negative solutions to human pressures and problems. Reckless antisocial behavior will ultimately rob us of the joy of living. For instance, people who kill can expect to be killed. Men who commit adultery can expect to have a fight with a husband of a philandering wife. People who lie can expect to lose the confidence and trust of fellow human beings. Moral restraints protect us from the inclination to accept negative solutions to problems. To get out of a problem by lying is the negative approach. We welcome, then, solutions to problems that are within the restraints of moral law and that would protect us from taking the cheap and easy way out of a predicament.

The vast majority of religious people have always opposed abortion. Why? Because they view abortion as a negative solution to a problem. The positive solution would be to allow a unique creature, a one-of-a-kind individual, to come into human existence and have his or her chance to contribute to society. Ideas that restrict our moral freedoms are not to be viewed as violations of our liberty but are to be seen primarily as screens that can protect us from the temptation to accept negative solutions.

The elimination of our federal debt is a moral issue. To continue to increase the debt for our personal self-indulgences today and pass on the expense of servicing that liability to unborn generations is a form of taxation without representation. It is theft!

Commandment Number Ten

SAY YES TO AN IDEA IF IT CHALLENGES US TO THINK BIGGER AND HAVE MORE FAITH!

Any idea that would help the human family and at the same time would appear to be impossible is to be welcomed as a challenge to our belief system. In 1967, the World Psychiatric Congress was held in Madrid, Spain. The closing session dealt with the subject "Human Values of Psychotherapy." The first lecturer dealt with the human value of faith. The second lecturer dealt with the human value of hope. The third lecturer dealt with the human value of love. More than four thousand delegates at the convention, including me, heard the challenge to welcome opportunities that would build faith, inspire hope, or generate love. These qualities mark emotionally and mentally healthy persons.

The same can apply to a nation. How can we build faith? Any great idea that appears to be impossible holds the fabulous potential of becoming a faith-building experience. Individuals and institutions are only as strong as their inner confidence and belief systems. Ultimately, this inner spirit of dynamic faith cannot be inherited, nor can it be institutionalized effectively in a Declaration of Independence, a Bill of Rights, or a national Constitution. Ultimately, it must be discovered by each new generation. Each new generation must face its own mountain and move it! Each new generation must confront its own wars and win them! Each new generation must tackle its own impossible challenge and overcome it! This continuous process of discovery, rediscovery, and renewal of belief and faith is made possible as new ideas come to challenge us to move some glorious impossibility into the realm of the possible.

Possibility thinkers, let's unite! Let's proclaim America's Declaration of Financial Independence by tackling the great idea of creating a debt-free America for the peace, the prosperity, and the pride of all human beings on planet Earth.

7 THE POWER OF BEING DEBT FREE

We Americans have a history of producing innovative solutions to unsolvable problems, of creating new ideas for new tomorrows. In the 1940s, scientists were certain that an airplane could not travel faster than the speed of sound. But a group of United States Air Force pilots believed it was possible, and in 1947, Captain Charles Yeager broke the sound barrier. Since then, airplanes have traveled in excess of five times the speed of sound.

In a Los Angeles ear clinic, deaf children and adults are being made to hear for the first time in their lives. Through an ingenious electronic implant in the inner ear, microscopic hair follicles are stimulated to transfer the vibrations of sound into nerve impulses, successfully restoring the sensation of sound to hundreds of hearing-impaired people.

In the Midwest, the lithotripter, a kidney stone crusher, was developed to treat patients with shock waves in order to dissolve kidney stones without the usual painful surgery and prolonged recovery time.

In all fields of life, human beings have solved unsolvable problems or created new and innovative methods of dealing with their problems. The imagination of the human being constantly amazes us with the wonderful products and services being created.

If we can break the sound barrier, make people who are deaf hear, and develop machines to heal our hurts, isn't it possible that we can creatively solve the problem of the federal debt? Or is this a bit crazy? Is it too idealistic? Who will really make the world a better place, the realist or the idealist? The cynic or the dreamer? No dreamer is ever crazy because the dreamer becomes the uplifting force that gives people and institutions a vision. Without dreams and visions, we will die!

The Man of La Mancha is a musical play based on the Spanish classic *Don Quixote*. The dreamer Don Quixote sees windmills as evil knights, his decrepit horse as a noble steed, and an ugly cleaning lady in an inn, who is also an abused prostitute, as a beautiful and high-bred maiden. The beautiful part of the story is that those who listen to him become more like Don Quixote's dreams. He gives them self-esteem.

When confronted by the cold, calculating cynics for being a wild dreamer, Don Quixote responds, "Who's crazy? Am I crazy because I see the world as it could become? Or is the world crazy because it sees itself as it is?"

The dream of a debt-free society through possibility thinking is the hope our future generations have for a fiscally stable society. Unless as a nation we are motivated to believe that our economic freedom is possible, then we will give in to the crippling forces of our rising federal debt.

The solution does not lie in intricate details of economic theory. The key is not found by finely tuning government policies. The answer centers on motivating all Americans. The solution is within each of us.

In researching the national debt, we had a delightful interview with Arthur Laffer, one of our country's leading economists. As we sat down to breakfast, he immediately offered us a copy of the book *Foundations of Supply-Side Economics,* which he wrote with Victor Canto and Douglas Joines. We opened it to one of the middle pages, and it appeared to be in a foreign language. We couldn't understand any of it.

We attempted polite smiles, showing that we appreciated his gift, and hoping to convince him that we were dying to go home and read it. But Dr. Laffer anticipated our thoughts. "Have you ever tried teaching a lot of students?" he asked. "Especially teaching them the stuff in that book? They sit there thinking, 'Oh, I should never have come to this class.' What do you do to keep their attention? You have to provide incentives, motivation. In fact, economics is the study of motivation."

His words shocked us. He made us realize that it is time for our nation to make a major shift in its economic thinking. *We must change from mathematical economics to motivational economics.* Possibility thinking must play a major role in developing an attitude that leads to finding solutions to our national debt crisis.

There will be people who will read this and think, *How simple. How shallow. I must have a more intricate plan, one full of numbers and projections in order to convince me that we should take the first step toward eliminating the national debt.*

But we were encouraged by Dr. Laffer who said, "There's an old motto: 'Just because it's simple doesn't mean it's wrong.' I would rather be approximately correct than precisely wrong. And even the top economists can be precisely wrong. The spirit of what you are saying—far more than the exact recipe—strikes me as being right."

Dr. Laffer went on to say, "I was the chief economist for two years with George Schultz. And any time I had a debate with David Stockman or an economist in front of the president, we would get into talking about tiny, detailed numbers. But they have nothing to do with the truth. Because of the immensity of the federal budget, no human being can handle a discussion of those tiny numbers. They will kill any effort to look at the real problem. The simple answer is the right answer. We need to get back to basic principles that even a congressman can understand. Then you will be able to answer the problem!"

We spoke with other economists, and they also gave us their encouraging support. Martin Feldstein, former chairman of the president's Council of Economic Advisors and economics professor at Harvard University; Gary Shilling, president of Shilling and

2. The Supply of Labor 109

In general, V may rise more or less than R when the wage rate rise. We assume, however, that the tax rates are low enough and workers get a high enough share of the benefits from government spending so that

$$V_w > R_w \tag{25}$$

In that case, individual n chooses to work if the wage rate exceeds w^*, for then $V > R$; and he chooses not to work if the wage rate falls short of w^*, for then $V < R$. Define w^* to be zero if $\lim_{w \to 0} (V - R) > 0$ and to be infinite if $\lim_{w \to \infty} (V - R) < 0$. It then follows that

$$w^* = W(\tau_1, \ldots, \tau_m; \gamma_1, \ldots, \gamma_m; k_1, \ldots, k_m; n) \tag{26}$$

is a well-defined function if the τ_is are not too large and if the k_is are not too small.

Equation (22) implies that

$$W_{\tau_i} = \frac{(R_{\tau_i} - V_{\tau_i})}{(V_w - R_w)}, \qquad i = 1, \ldots, m \tag{27}$$

$$W_{\gamma_i} = \frac{(R_{\gamma_i} - k_i V_{\gamma_i k_i})}{(V_w - R_w)}, \qquad i = 1, \ldots, m \tag{28}$$

$$W_{k_i} = \frac{(R_{k_i} - \gamma_i V_{\gamma_i k_i})}{(V_w - R_w)}, \qquad i = 1, \ldots, m \tag{29}$$

and

$$W_n = \frac{-V_n}{(V_w - R_w)} \tag{30}$$

It is straightforward to use Eqs. (20), (21), (2) and (8)–(13) to show that

$$V_{\tau_i} = \frac{U_c\{-w^2 U_c \sum \gamma_i k_i \tau_i + (1 - \gamma_i k_i)[(1 - \tau)^2 w^2 U_{cc} + 2(1 - \tau)w U_{ch} + U_{hh}]\}}{D}$$

$$< 0, \qquad i = 1, \ldots, m \tag{31}$$

$$V_{\gamma_i k_i} = -\frac{\tau_i w h U_c[(1 - \tau)^2 w^2 U_{cc} + 2(1 - \tau)w U_{ch} + U_{hh}]}{D}$$

$$> 0, \qquad i = 1, \ldots, m \tag{32}$$

$$V_n = -f'(n) < 0 \tag{33}$$

$$R_{\tau_i} = U_c[w H_{\tau_i} \sum (1 - k_i)\gamma_i \tau_i + w H(1 - k_i)\gamma_i] \gtreqless 0, \qquad i = 1, \ldots, m \tag{34}$$

$$R_{\gamma_i} = U_c[k_i w H_{\gamma_i k_i} \sum (1 - k_i)\gamma_i \tau_i + (1 - k_i)\tau_i w H] \gtreqless 0, \qquad i = 1, \ldots, m \tag{35}$$

and

$$R_{k_i} = U_c[w \gamma_i H_{\gamma_i k_i} \sum (1 - k_i)\gamma_i \tau_i - \gamma_i k_i w H] < 0, \qquad i = , \ldots, m \tag{36}$$

Company, an economics consulting firm; John Templeton, founder of the Templeton Fund and one of the leading investment analysts in the world; and the late J. Peter Grace, former chief executive officer of W. R. Grace Company, all agreed with the spirit of our desire to motivate the American public to get involved in our economic process. Most of them felt that we had a greater chance to bring the importance of this issue to the American people than they did as "experts." Their responses reaffirmed the universal principle that economics is too important to leave to the economists.

When we published the first edition of this book, we sent a survey to every United States senator and member of the House of Representatives, asking their opinion on the budget deficit and the reasons for the underlying debt our nation has accumulated. The response then was impressive and informative. It encouraged us to survey our senators and representatives for this project. In the spring of 1995, we again sent a letter to each, asking them whether they agreed or disagreed with the following statements:

> The federal debt never needs to be repaid. We simply refinance it, generation after generation, and continue to pay interest on that debt as part of the federal budget.

> A plan should evolve and a decision be made to repay the entire federal debt with the goal of becoming a nation that does not have to spend part of its budget to pay the interest on debts.

We received a great response, with nearly a unanimous vote that disagreed with the first statement and agreed with the second. The elected officials shared our concern that we must plan now to deal with the debt in our lifetimes. Many senators and representatives not only answered the brief questionnaire but also responded with lengthy letters and reports on their own efforts to creatively eliminate the budget deficit and reduce the federal debt. They were reacting to the many letters they had received from voters in their districts and states. They were eager to share their views with us and support us in the movement to balance the budget and pay off the debt. Here are a few of their comments:

> As a nation we should come to the awareness that two rules must govern. Rule #1: We are broke. Our nation's obligations, including the federal debt and trust fund obligations, exceed our assets. Rule #2: All decisions must be based on Rule #1. Only then, when the public is fully aware, can we find the fiscal sanity to preserve this great nation and the freedom and liberty that uniquely resides within our borders.
> Congressman Todd Tiahrt (R., Kansas)

> It is my strong belief that we must remain focused on reducing the deficit rather than increasing the debt by enacting tax cuts we cannot afford. It is my concern that by passing tax cuts before making real cuts in spending, the same mistakes made in the 1980s will be repeated. As you probably recall, in the 1980s Congress enacted a series of tax cuts but did not make the corresponding budget cuts that it promised. As a result, our federal debt exploded from one to four trillion dollars. I am firmly committed to the belief that the most effective way the government can help people at all income levels is to reduce our federal deficit.
> Congressman Michael Doyle (D., Pennsylvania)

> I strongly support plans to repay the entire national debt. For the last forty years, Congress has failed to confront the difficult choices necessary to bring the budget into balance. If, for instance, there were twenty quality programs competing for scarce dollars, we would fund all of them, even if there were revenues for only fifteen. We have mortgaged our children's future. We owe it to our children and our grandchildren to

make the difficult choices so that they will inherit a federal government that lives within its means.

Congressman Greg Ganske (R., Iowa)

If the Congress does not get the deficit under control, studies show that future generations will face average lifetime tax rates of an incredible 82 percent! Unless action is taken today, the debt will continue to spiral out of control, leading to political wars between different generations of Americans.

Congressman John J. Duncan, Jr. (R., Tennessee)

For the future of our children and grandchildren, we must cut spending to first balance the budget and then begin to pay off our national debt. I believe it is our moral obligation to do this.

Congressman Tom Latham (R., Iowa)

The federal deficit and accompanying huge federal debt severely weaken our economy by requiring the federal government to pull capital out of private markets to make federal interest payments, threatening our capacity to invest here at home and to compete internationally.

Senator Paul D. Wellstone (D., Minnesota)

I wholeheartedly share the goal of balancing our federal budget and then eliminating the national debt. As you know, interest payments on that mountain of debt now cost taxpayers $203 billion a year, about 14 percent of the total annual budget of the United States government. In my view, that is $203 billion that could be spent much better by working families.

Although the balanced budget amendment to the Constitution has yet to win approval, Congress has a greater prospect this year than at any time in the past four decades of setting America on the path to a balanced budget.

Senator Phil Gramm (R., Texas)

As someone who has worked for decades to control excessive government spending, I believe that passing the Balanced Budget Amendment to the Constitution represents the very best way to eliminate the federal deficit and begin dealing with our nation's tremendous government debt.

Senator Strom Thurmond (R., South Carolina)

I believe we must move immediately to reduce our national debt. The national debt, which has more than quadrupled since 1981, now approaches $5 trillion. We are now the largest debtor nation in the world.

The debt is an enormous drain on federal resources. . . . [It] is more than we spend on all domestic discretionary programs combined. And we get absolutely nothing in return for this spending, nothing for education, job training, housing, health care and research, or environmental protection.

It will take a lot of effort and commitment to resolve this problem. We must begin by reducing our huge federal budget deficit. The Budget Reconciliation Act of 1993, recommended by President Clinton—the largest deficit reduction measure in history, nearly $500 billion—was a good first step.

Senator Paul Simon (D., Illinois)

If Congress does not act to balance the budget, current estimates show a child born today will owe 82 cents of tax for every dollar earned and will pay $187,150 over his or her lifetime just in interest on the national debt. It is unconscionable for Congress to continue to put off the hard spending choices, leaving future generations to pay the price.

The U.S. government is paying $550 million a day in interest on the debt, which is now the second largest item in the federal budget. Spiraling interest payments are eating up dollars which we could use to reduce the debt, pay for priority programs, or return to the taxpayer in the form of lower taxes.

Senator Dan Coats (R., Indiana)

Under a no-debt constitutional amendment, members of Congress would not be obligated to say yes to demands that exceed actual needs and available means such as some so-called uncontrollables which are just as controllable as Congress votes to make them. For the coming decade, the price of freedom is the long road back from self-deception and debt to the ways of prudence and productivity.

Representative Andrew Jacobs, Jr. (D., Indiana)

Representative Mark Neumann of Wisconsin responded with a detailed plan not only to balance the budget but also to repay the debt completely:

For all the government spending, let us ask ourselves, "Is it okay to spend our children's money to pay for this program?" We came to balance the budget. . . . In twenty years, let us look back and be proud as we explain to our grand-children what we did. America's future—*our children's future*—depends on us having the courage to do what is right for our great nation—today.

Representative Mark Neumann (R., Wisconsin)

Although the senators and representatives differed in their views on how the deficits and debt should be financed, they all agreed that somehow it should be done. With additional pressure from the public, our elected officials can put aside their differences and devise a plan to eliminate federal deficits and repay our national debt. There is no substitute for a determined public, Congress, and administration who will muster the political will to resolve this problem. All Americans must put aside self-interest for our national interest and our children's secure future.

With all the agreement as to the need for a balanced budget, why do we not have one? Until recently, senators and representatives have addressed this issue only in vague terms and have refused to get down to the tough choices, the specific issues, and the specific means. We applaud the efforts that have recently been made by Congress to deal with the difficult choices that must be made to reduce deficits and pay off the debt. There are more difficult choices ahead. Senators and representatives must not lose their resolve. And they should not assume that the American public will object to cutbacks. The backbone of the American public is stronger and straighter than they might believe.

Time magazine interviewed citizens in Fargo, North Dakota, the heartland of America, who are sure to be hurt financially by federal budget cuts. Its findings were amazing. "Surprise of surprises: the people of Fargo don't seem to mind very much," *Time* reported in its May 22, 1995, issue. Citizens such as Larry Akers, a construction foreman, said, "It's going to hurt. But we are borrowing from our grandchildren. And it's got to stop somewhere." Marlene Brown, a mother, said, "People here will figure out a way to get by. We're good at looking after our needs." "People here think a lot about surviving. They survive the winters. They will survive the cuts," added Julie Eyestone.

The solution to our economic challenge, the way to stop the theft of our children's financial future, is to be found in two words: *attitude* and *commitment*. As a nation, we need a positive attitude that arises from a firm belief that we can succeed, and we need a strong commitment to accomplish the goal, no matter what the cost. That commitment should be the result of a careful decision. If we have an open, creative, positive attitude as we seek ways to pay off the debt and if we make a solid commitment to pay it off before we know how to solve all of the problems, then we will have taken the most important step.

Attitude

Consider the difference an attitude makes within a financially troubled company. Two corporate giants—the Manville Corporation and Chrysler Corporation—both faced financial problems that would make even the most optimistic financial consultant cringe. One company chose bankruptcy; the other has risen to reclaim its rightful place among the leading corporations of America. What made the difference? It wasn't the rescue loans. It wasn't the quality of the product. It wasn't the cooperation of the unions. All of those factors were important to Chrysler, but the real difference was a positive attitude.

In August 1982, the directors of the Manville Corporation sat around their boardroom table discussing their corporate problems and bleak future. The billion-dollar forest products and construction company was faced with 16,500 lawsuits as a result of its role in producing asbestos-related products. Although the corporation was financially sound and had a low debt-to-equity ratio, it filed for bankruptcy because of the potential loss from the lawsuits. The directors had decided their problems were unsolvable. Why should they drag out the inevitable? Why not just declare bankruptcy? Throw in the towel. Let's quit!

The *Wall Street Journal* reported that the move was "highly unusual and unexpected."[1] The stockholders' equity plummeted from a high of $26.50 per share to nothing. The corporate leaders had lost control, and the company and all the investors had lost their money and faith.

In another part of America several years earlier, the directors of the Chrysler Corporation met to discuss their financial problems. The country was in a deep recession. Auto sales had fallen off dramatically. The company was billions of dollars in debt. In 1980, it lost $1.7 billion, the largest operating loss in United States corporate history. The future looked bleak. If any company should give up, it should have been Chrysler. But after hours of deliberation, a decision was made: We will not quit! There will be a way. We don't know what it is, but we will find it. We are willing to make changes. We are willing to listen.

Over the next six months, the unions agreed to unprecedented "givebacks." Twenty thousand white-collar jobs were eliminated as overhead was cut. The federal government made loan guarantees of $1.2 billion (on which it has earned an estimated $800 million in interest and fees). The engineers designed new and better products. The number of different parts needed fell from fifty-three thousand in 1981 to less than forty thousand in 1984. Chrysler's directors had a positive attitude that arose from a firm belief that they would succeed in their goal of putting their corporation back on its feet as a leading automaker in America.

By August 1982—the same month Manville declared bankruptcy—Chrysler had paid off all of its government-backed debts. It reemployed and offered job security to thousands of union members. It designed a new and exciting line of products, including minivans and the reborn convertible! Chrysler stock soared from $2 to $36 a share. Its investors made money and gained renewed confidence in the company. Its challenging slogan became known nationwide: If you can find a better built car, buy it! Chrysler's corporate chief, Lee Iacocca, was acclaimed by several polls as one of the most respected corporate leaders in America.

What was the difference between Chrysler's success and Manville's bankruptcy? Attitude! There were many important factors along Chrysler's comeback road, but the most important element, the impulse that pushed the company to the top, was the decision not to quit but to win and succeed. The directors realized they didn't have a money problem; they just had an idea problem.

The effect of the attitude factor goes beyond the financial boardrooms of America. It can also make the difference in a country's survival as a sound financial entity.

In the late 1970s, the country of Turkey was the world's most experienced down-and-outer. Now it has become a shining example to which international bankers point when they say there is hope for countries that are unbelievably burdened by debt. The head of the International Monetary Fund, Jacques de Larosière, pointed out that Turkey took a bold step to make the necessary changes to pay off its national and foreign debt. The Organization of Economic Development has said that Turkey's successes are far-reaching and courageous. The World Bank has called Turkey's restructuring program one of the most significant undertaken by a developing country in recent history.

At the peak of its debt crisis, Turkey owed billions of dollars. Inflation was more than 107 percent yearly. Exports were virtually flat. Interest rates were rising. But Turkey made a decision, a decision to pay off its foreign loans and indebtedness. The country's leaders asked for support from the people of Turkey. The people decided they should vote for their grandchildren, not for themselves. Both peasants and businesspeople made sacrifices. It wasn't easy, but the people had a new attitude. A poor farmer resigned to earning less said, "Of course, Turkey owes money. Every one of us knows that." The Turks hardly complained. Rather, they stood behind their government's new policies in hopes that it would make a difference.

It did. Annual inflation dropped from 107 percent to 37 percent; exports rose to 11 percent of GDP; the debt fell to $16 billion. And during a world recession, Turkey's economy grew at a pace of more than 4 percent. In the fall of 1984, the Turkish government took another bold step by preparing to sell hundreds of state-owned companies to private investors. As many as 263 enterprises, including the Turkish airlines, Turkish Petroleum Company, and the National Post, Telegraph, and Telephone Administration, were offered for sale at the new Istanbul Securities Exchange. The *Wall Street Journal* called the move Turkey's "most daring gamble yet to spur a free market economy."[2] Turkey has come a long way, and the attitude of its citizens has made a difference!

More recently Chile, once regarded as a high risk, third world country with a poor corporate and government bond rating, huge deficits, an unstable currency, and an unfunded social security system, has made a dramatic turnaround.

The people of Chile made tough choices. They challenged their assumption that only the government could provide for an individual's retirement. While guaranteeing the elderly's social security payments, Chile offered its younger workers the option of investing their social security withholdings in privately managed mutual funds and other investment vehicles. A prerequisite was that these monies would still be deducted from the workers' paychecks, although the government would not administer the social security plan. Through hard work, prudent financial management, and a positive attitude, Chile has a balanced budget and no deficit. It also has successfully privatized most of the nation's pensions, and it has fully funded its social security payments.

Commitment

A positive attitude that arises from a firm belief that one can succeed is essential. But action is also necessary. There needs to be a strong commitment to accomplish a goal, no matter what the cost.

The famous scientist René DuBos once said in effect that the human being has a natural and overwhelming inclination to adjust downward. It was one of the reasons why he could be tempted to be a cynic and pessimist.

Adjustment is always a downward movement. Upward movement is never an adjustment; it is always a commitment. Chrysler made a commitment. Turkey made a commitment. Any great company or country that has faced financial disaster and pulled out of it did so because of a commitment.

Not to make a commitment is to commit to do nothing. Without a commitment, the natural adjustment downward will begin to take control. It is time for the American people to stop accepting the downward pressures that could lead to financial ruin. We need to make a commitment to move forward and upward again to become a stronger, more financially secure country.

I personally experienced this commitment-making process and the outcome when our church was in the process of building our new sanctuary, the Crystal Cathedral. Architect Philip Johnson delivered a six-inch plastic model of what is today an all-glass church 414 feet long and 126 feet high. I took one look at it and said, "Wow! That has to be built! How much will it cost?"

Philip Johnson answered, "About $7 million."

I quickly calculated in my mind what that would cost if it were mortgaged at the then current interest rate. To borrow $7 million at 9 percent interest, our annual interest payment would be approximately $630,000 the first year! And our total church income was only $2 million. I could not envision how we could have a capital funds drive that would bring in an additional $630,000 a year. We simply did not have that kind of financial base.

The project was financially impossible. But I could not accept the word *impossible*. I also could not think of borrowing that much money and increasing our indebtedness. It was a totally impossible dream from a financial perspective, unless I could make a radical, revolutionary, 180-degree turn in my thinking, namely, to pay cash and dedicate the building debt free. But that brought out a contradiction: If we couldn't make a $630,000 annual payment, how could we possibly raise $7 million?

Desperate, I decided to play the possibility thinking game. I started to write down ten ways to do what I knew was impossible. When you do this, you will be surprised how your attitude will change from "it's impossible" to "it might be possible." I wrote down ways we could pay cash for the building:

1. Find 1 person who could donate $7,000,000. (That was good for a laugh, which at least relaxed me to keep going.)
2. Find 7 people who could donate $1,000,000 each.
3. Find 14 people who could donate $500,000 each.
4. Find 28 people who could donate $250,000 each.
5. Find 70 people who could donate $100,000 each.
6. Find 100 people who could donate $70,000 each.
7. Find 140 people who could donate $50,000 each.

8. Find 280 people who could donate $25,000 each.
9. Sell all 10,866 windows in the Cathedral for $500 each. (That would raise more than $5 million.)

That was as far as I got. I was already enthusiastic. I believed that the project was possible when only minutes before I believed it was a total impossibility. Creativity happens when you are released from anxieties and tensions. As I relaxed and had fun dreaming up ways to pay for the cathedral, I was able to break out of my negative-thinking predicament.

I knew I had to get one $1 million kickoff gift to lead the enthusiasm for this project. But I didn't know anyone that rich. I remembered reading about a local businessman who had given a $1 million gift to the YMCA. I didn't know him, but I contacted him. When I arrived at his home and showed him the model of the Crystal Cathedral, he whistled with excitement.

"What will you need to get it going?" he asked.

"A leadoff gift of $1 million. That would show everyone that this is something big that is going to happen. Then people will take it seriously. I'd like you to give that $1 million."

Suddenly, he lost his enthusiasm. "Well," he stammered, "I would like to, but I can't."

"Okay," I said. "I'd like to close our visit with prayer." And with that I prayed, "Thank You, God, that John wants to give $1 million. But he says he can't. Please make it possible for him to give it."

I left his house never expecting to see him again. The next morning I received a phone call from him. "Reverend," he said, "it is not a question of *if*. It is a question of *how* and *when*."

I almost fainted with ecstasy. He continued, "That building has to be built. I'll give you a million dollars, but I cannot tell you how or when I'll give it."

Within sixty days he delivered fifty-five thousand shares of his company's stock valued at more than $18 a share. Suddenly, the $7 million building looked feasible. But then we decided to build a complete basement, which immediately increased the cost by 50 percent. So we launched a donation campaign to "sell" 10,866 windows at $500 each. The response was fantastic. It looked as if we could pay cash for the building after all.

Then the unexpected happened. Double-digit inflation hit the marketplace. In just twelve months our project was no longer costing $10 million but $13 million. One year later, when we were twenty-four months into planning the program, the cost had increased by another $3 million. We were up to $16 million. Suddenly, before we knew it, the cathedral was going to cost $20 million!

What could we do? I knew what I would do. I took a break. I was on vacation when the church board met to consider an unexpected commercial loan offer for $10 million. It would allow us to proceed without the enormous strain of fundraising. I returned home to find that the board had accepted the loan.

I was not enthusiastic. How could we pay the interest on $10 million? And the loan was to be tied to the prime rate! Neither I nor a single member of that church board could foresee that by the time the cathedral was completed, the prime rate would be 20 percent!

All I knew was that once we accepted the loan, the pressure would be off my back to try to solicit major gifts from people I hadn't even met yet. Getting a loan has a way of making a person feel as if the job is done! In fact, it is only a big show. You've only deferred the payment.

I was still consumed by my grandest dream: pay for the building and dedicate it debt free. Then when the dedication ceremony was over, I wouldn't be left with the horrendous job of balancing the budget year after year. I made a personal decision not to finish the building unless it could be totally underwritten by cash gifts or cash pledges.

It meant crisscrossing the country building new friendships, selling the cathedral idea, and soliciting funds to get it built. I kept remembering the saying, "Whatever the mind can conceive, the human being can achieve."

On September 18, 1980, the Crystal Cathedral opened its doors. It was an international press event noted and photographed in major media publications around the world. But the only thing that impressed me was that God had answered our prayers.

The cost topped $20 million. We had collected just under $17 million. Almost $4 million had been pledged to be given over the next thirty-six months. That was covered by a 9 percent fixed-rate mortgage by our local bank. We announced that the building was dedicated debt free, and in fact, all of the pledges were made good in the next three years.

I felt free! Feelings of "isn't it great not to have a debt" flooded over me. I thought, *Isn't it wonderful not to have to take money out of the offering plate to pay the interest on the mortgage? All the money can go to programs that meet human needs here and now.*

There is nothing like the power of being debt free. It is time for our country to experience that feeling. It is time for our elected officials to know the feeling of not owing $5 trillion and not having to raise more than $260 billion for an interest payment. It is time to stop stealing from our children. If America were debt free, all of our money could go to programs to meet human needs here and now.

A Movement

Our country can experience this power. It all starts with an attitude. Then it takes a commitment. With a total commitment made by the entire American public to do their part to pay off the federal debt, it is possible to do it. When people unite to solve a problem, anything is possible. When movements mount, mountains move!

We are calling for a movement of the American people to come up with creative, innovative, possibility-thinking, problem-solving solutions. Top economists and corporate leaders, secretaries and salespeople, educators and businesspeople—if everyone in America will join this movement, we will come up with an avalanche of creative ideas to solve the problem of the federal debt.

The solution is in our attitude. There is no hopeless situation until we become hopeless people. Great ideas to solve our national debt will come from ordinary people, for great people are ordinary people with an extraordinary amount of determination.

Already an underground movement to reduce the national debt is appearing throughout the United States across a wide spectrum of people, from the very wealthy to retired individuals who live on nothing more than social security pensions.

Since 1961, a little-known fund deep in the caverns of the U.S. Treasury has accepted the small change of deeply moved Americans dedicated to repaying the national debt. The Public Debt Reduction Fund in the Bureau of Government Financial Operations in the U.S. Treasury was established after Texas multi-millionaire Sarah Vaughn Clayton willed $20 million to the federal government. Her hope was that her millions might help government control the deficit spending.

Although it did not stop the spending, it did begin a small movement of other like-minded believers to donate to the fund. What was a big wave of support from Sarah Vaughn Clayton is now little ripples of donations by concerned citizens such as the retired military man who wrote that the army gave him an extra $200 when he was discharged and he wanted to give it back.

Two examples are the elderly man who sends a "Happy Birthday America" card every year with a check equal to his age, and the Hollywood producer who pledged to the Treasury at least one-fourth of the ticket sales from his movie. From one dollar to hundreds, the Public Debt Reduction Fund inspires persons to give to the government with Sarah Vaughn Clayton's leadership in mind.

But the movement does not stop there. In Washington, D.C., the National Taxpayers Union monitors government spending and lobbies to control government waste. It has successfully pressured Congress into saving millions of dollars.

A grassroots movement all across America is starting to grow. An aware, aroused, impassioned constituency can make a difference. Members of the public are not powerless. We have voices. We can vote. And our representatives in Congress are listening. There will be change if the American people demand it! Already much of the congressional debate centers on the budget deficit issue. There is pressure on representatives, senators, and all elected officials to do something to balance our budget. Let's see how to accomplish this impossible task.

8 TEN WAYS TO ACCOMPLISH THE IMPOSSIBLE—PART ONE

A debt-free America is a big, bold, beautiful dream! The fulfillment of this dream will require the unrestrained commitment of courageous Americans wholeheartedly dedicated to producing creative solutions and willing to pay the price to carry them out. We believe Americans understand the severity of our country's debt crisis and are willing to make the necessary commitment to do something about it.

During the months of research for this book, we asked economists, corporate leaders, senators, representatives, former presidents, relatives, waiters, secretaries, flight attendants, ministers, and anyone else who would give us the time what they thought of our dream of a debt-free America. Almost everyone agreed that, yes, it would be a wonderful idea, but almost everyone qualified that *yes*.

- Yes, if we do so without surrendering our position in the international marketplace.
- Yes, but not at the sacrifice of medical and social programs that insure the well-being of the underprivileged.
- Yes, but not at the expense of the collapse of our highways and infrastructures.

- Yes, but not at the price of eliminating research that can lead to incredible medical advances.
- Yes, when the nation can provide financial security out of its surplus rather than from its deficits financed by government notes and bonds.
- Yes, but how? How do you accomplish the impossible?

We have often proposed that an impossible situation moves close to the realm of possibility once we begin to play the possibility thinking game, which is an exercise in creative thinking, a variation of brainstorming. In the final analysis, all problems are the same, whether intensely personal and apparently small, or whether they are urgent national problems of massive proportions. Essentially, the problems are the same: challenges to creative thinking. That's all they are. Problems are pressures to be more productive and inventive in our thinking. As we have said, "No person has a money problem, only an idea problem!"

I have seen small problems as well as enormous problems solved by playing the possibility thinking game. The technique is amazingly simple. Take a sheet of paper, write down the numbers one to ten, then force yourself to come up with ten solutions to what you have accepted in your mind as an unsolvable problem. Inevitably, in the process you will come up with enough possibilities to give you, at the very least, a sense of hope.

Be mentally open to any wonderful, wild, eyebrow-raising, even preposterous solution to your problem that may come into your mind. You can expect to break out laughing more than once, for some of the wackiest ideas will quite understandably develop from what has now become your truly liberated imagination. The point is that creativity happens in an environment of relaxation. The tranquil mind is receptive to genuinely creative ideas that form the seeds for real breakthroughs. Humor naturally relaxes a person, which sets the stage for creativity. Hence, what oftentimes starts as a lark continues to become a spark.

People who know my ministry remember that just "as a lark" I was joking about putting glass elevators in our church steeple. That was not taken seriously by anyone at first, but out of it emerged the concept of the Tower of Hope, which stands today with an elevator and offices. Once "as a lark" the thought was jokingly suggested that we make the entire church out of glass. And out of that "lark" emerged the "spark" that turned into the Crystal Cathedral. It is important that we come up with creative solutions to what appear to be unsolvable situations.

So let's play the possibility thinking game and apply it to the problem of wiping out the federal debt. We shall offer ten possibilities that can contribute to paying off the debt. You will probably come up with ten better ideas, but let these suggestions stimulate you to believe that *paying off the debt is possible.* At least the possibility will emerge as potentially viable enough so that the goal should be taken seriously. In view of the immense far-reaching value that could be secured by achieving a debt-free status, the burden would fall upon the scoffer to come up with a better idea. If we play this game, by the time we finish these possibilities, the real issue will not be if eliminating the national debt is possible, but why we should not take it seriously and exercise leadership to go for it.

Possibility One: Eliminate Government Waste

As Americans dedicated to paying off the national debt, let's first tackle perhaps the most obvious area, even if it is not the most critical one: government waste. Each year the government wastes billions of dollars, which contributes to growing deficits and larger debts. Therefore, the first possibility we propose to pay off our national debt is cutting back government waste.

Some people will immediately reply, "The government has been wasting money for centuries, ever since George Washington threw a silver dollar across the Potomac. You'll never get government to quit wasting money. You'll always have waste in the government; there is nothing you can do about it!"

Stop right there! That is a negative attitude! That type of thinking defeats you before you even get out of the starting gate. Remember, change starts with your attitude. Simply because it has been difficult to stop wasteful government spending in the past does not mean it cannot be done now. It is not a hopeless situation until we become hopeless people.

We applaud the efforts made in 1995 to cut government waste by the newly elected Republican majority in the House. We also applaud similar efforts by President Clinton and Vice President Gore begun two years earlier with their plan to reinvent government. Such efforts are encouraging and, we hope, have a chance of making a significant impact.

In the first edition of this book we shared an extraordinary interview with the now late J. Peter Grace. We stated that no one knew more about government waste than he. Peter Grace had led, at the request of President Reagan, the Private Sector Survey on Cost Control, a commission that studied detailed ways in which the government could save money. It produced 2,478 cost-cutting and revenue-enhancing recommendations that could save, it said, $1.9 trillion per year by the year 2000.

After hearing that we were planning to write a book, Grace agreed to meet with us. We sat in a wonderful little restaurant in Newport Beach, California, where he listened intently as we shared with him our concern over the debt we are incurring for our children and our dream of a debt-free America. The interview was so powerful and so timeless that we still believe his wisdom on the national debt captures the enormity of the problem and the perspective of the businessperson, even though the examples he gave are now more than ten years old.

Mr. Grace wholeheartedly supported our goal and pointed out that rampant waste in government was a major problem that needed to be resolved immediately. Grace explained that the major aim of the president's Private Sector Survey on Cost Control was to force the government to run our nation as efficiently as American private enterprise would run its own businesses. "If America can do this," he said ten years ago, "we will drastically reduce the deficit and debt."

Grace showed us the tremendous value of saving just $1. "Let's say I argue with a congressman about $1, but he won't take it out of the budget. I will ask him, 'Where will you get that dollar?' He will say, 'I'll borrow it.' What's the interest? Eleven percent. If that dollar stays in the budget the next year, he has to borrow last year's interest and this year's interest, as well as the original $2—$1 for each year. The compounding calculation is that one wasteful dollar left in the budget today will amount to a cumulative $71 in the national debt by the year 2000. Seventy-one dollars! Therefore, $100 billion in reduced government spending in the first year will equal a cumulative $4.1 trillion savings in the national debt by the year 2000."

Grace continued, "We found $424.4 billion in waste and inefficiencies that could be saved over the next three years. That's about $140 billion a year. Multiply that by $71 and you've got $10 trillion! That's what we're talking about. If Congress will get with it and stop spouting off about things it knows are not true, then we'll save $10 trillion for ourselves and our grandchildren.

"There are 535 people in Congress, and I have said that two-thirds of them are clowns. The reason I say that is because they are clowning around with a terrible problem that faces not only us but our children and grandchildren who are going to have to pick up the tab for this terrible spending over the next fifty years. . . . Instead of improving the quality of life in this country and making our nation stronger, we will be trapped in a terrible financial problem."

According to Grace, the government not only wasted $140 billion a year, it also lacked critical information to collect the money owed to it.

"The government is owed $850 billion," he said to us, "but

that money has never been aged. The government doesn't know whether it is due, overdue, or when it is due at all. Eight hundred fifty billion dollars is three times the total taxes owed by all the taxpayers in America for three years! In addition to not knowing when the debt is owed, our government's computers are so obsolete that they are not interfaced with one another nor can they furnish the information needed. At least 50 percent of everything that one needs to run the government is not available to those who are making the decisions!"

The commission found that more than six thousand dead persons were still receiving checks regularly from the government. "Between the years 1980 and 1982," Grace said, "there was $14.6 billion paid out in false payments by the Social Security Administration, including payments to dead people. The families who received some of this $14.6 billion apparently forgot that the people had died!"

Grace explained that fraud was a major problem in government, especially in the area of social programs. "There's at least $20 billion a year in fraud," he said. "When we worked with the Office of Management and Budget we asked, 'How many social programs are there?' They said, 'About 120 to 130.' But we found a book in Washington called *Fat City: How to Get Yours*. We came back to the office and said, 'Look at this book! There are more social programs than 120 or 130.' We later found out that there are 963 different social programs, and you can get in 17 of them at the same time if you try hard enough.

"There are all kinds of fraud. The General Accounting Office just said it had discovered more than $1 billion in food stamp fraud. We don't need 963 social programs. We need only 10 or 20. There's a lot of fraud all through the government, and a lot of people in the bureaucracy are making their way of life by doling out money in both state and federal governments with the federal government picking up the tab."

Poor people were not getting the money allocated to them, according to Grace. His commission found that only thirty cents of each dollar allocated to help the poor reached them. The rest was lost or used in the administration of the programs. "Where did the money go?" Grace asked. "It's siphoned off to the bureaucracy. The needy people don't need that kind of help!"

In his book *Burning Money,* Grace told of another case of fraud that the commission uncovered:

> There was a contractor for the National Institute of Education who managed to do quite well at taxpayer expense. How? Let us count the ways: First, he held onto $71,000 he was supposed to pay to people attending a conference; then, he neglected to return another $25,000 in unused cash advances. Next, he used an undetermined amount of Institute money to support his other businesses. Afterward, he loaned over $100,000 of government money to friends and associates. Next, he overstated salaries by $23,000. Finally, this sterling citizen accepted, without comment, overpayments of $20,000 resulting from the Institute's inept accounting procedures.[1]

Inefficiency and poor management have led to some amusing but true stories reported in the media concerning the government's expenditure of our tax dollars. Mr. Grace asked us if we had heard the one about the $436 hammer that was identical to a $7 hammer in a local hardware store. In the same book, he gave the Defense Department's explanation.[2] Added to the basic $7 cost of the hammer were the following amounts:

- $41 to pay general overhead costs for the engineering involved in mapping out the hammer problem. This included twelve minutes in secretarial time preparing the hammer purchase order, twenty-six minutes of management time spent on the hammer purchase, and two hours and thirty-six minutes the engineers spent on determining the hammer's specifications.

- $93 for the eighteen minutes it took for "mechanical sub-assembly" of the hammer, four hours for engineers to map out the hammer assembly process, ninety minutes spent by managers overseeing the hammer manufacturing process, sixty minutes for a project engineer to ensure the hammer was properly assembled, fifty-four minutes spent by quality control engineers examining the hammer to ensure it did not have any defects, and seven hours and forty-eight minutes devoted to other support activities involved in assembling the hammer.
- $102 spent toward "manufacturing overhead."
- $37 for the sixty minutes the "spares repair department" spent gearing up for either repairing or finding parts should the hammer ever break.
- $2 for "material handling overhead," representing the payroll costs for the people to wrap the hammer and send it out.
- $1 for wrapping paper and box.

This brought the subtotal of costs for the hammer to $283. This figure was increased by $90, representing the defense contractor's general administrative costs, and another $56 was added for a finder's fee for locating the specific hammer that fit the navy's needs. Another $7 was added as the "capital cost of money" for the hammer purchase.

A navy spokesman explained that large defense contractors are permitted to charge off general costs against all contracted items, and that in the case of relatively inexpensive items, these costs may appear disproportionately large. We have to agree; $436 for a $7 hammer does appear to be a "disproportionately large" price to pay.

Along with the $436 hammer, the military paid $511 for a 60-cent light bulb and $100 for an aircraft simulator part that actually cost only 5 cents at a hardware store. For the simulator part, that's a 200,000 percent markup!

But military officials were not the only generous people in the government or the only ones who lacked control over their department. The commission found that inefficiency seemed to be a trademark of the United States government.

The Veterans Administration's hospital construction staff of eight hundred employees did the same work that in the private sector a work force of only fifty people did. Bureaucracy in the VA caused a project to take seven years to complete compared to the private sector's two years. And it would cost four times as much.

Subsidized mortgage loans made by the government in 1982 often went to people who didn't need help to buy their homes. Most who received help had incomes of $20,000 to $40,000 a year, and 53 percent were affluent families.

Some of these items may seem trivial, but Grace explained that they were indicative of a philosophy that leads to overspending by billions of dollars year in and year out.

Civil service and military personnel also received their share of government dollars through excessively generous pension plans. According to Grace in a letter to the president, the civil service and military retirement systems provided three to six times, respectively, the benefits of the best pension plans in the private sector. The government's employees also retired at an earlier age with the added luxury of having their pension funds indexed for inflation, something virtually unheard of in the business world. Is it any wonder that most government employees spoke disparagingly of the findings of the Grace Commission?

Representatives and senators also enjoy the benefits of government service. According to the National Taxpayers Union, thirty-six members of Congress could receive more than $1 million each from federal pension benefits during their lifetime if they leave office after their current terms expire. Members of Congress who elect to participate in the retirement system contribute 8 percent of their salary and become eligible for benefits after five years of service. According to the taxpayer group, the federal plan far exceeds the benefits of a typical private company.

Another benefit for the elected elite is that they are allowed to eat in the posh restaurants found at NASA, the Department of Labor, the State Department, the Pentagon, and other agencies. A lunch at one of these government-subsidized restaurants usually costs only about 40 percent of what the same lunch would have cost at an unsubsidized Washington restaurant.

In cash management, budgeting improvement, and accounting measures, the government could save more than $30 billion in three years, according to Grace's calculations of ten years ago. He said improvements could be made in the areas of revamping the government's system of "first in, first out" payment of bills. When the government received a bill, it paid it immediately, although the bill might not have been due for six to eight months in the future. By using electronic fund transfers instead of direct mail in paying bills and in sending salary checks to government employees, the government could save hundreds of millions of dollars. The Postal Service, for instance, issued 22.4 million checks annually through the Treasury Department at a cost of $1.01 per check. Commercial banks would have provided the same service for 10 cents per check. If taxes collected from import duties and from the alcohol and tobacco industries were paid electronically instead of by mail, hundreds of millions of dollars could be saved.

If the government had managed by the following principles, it could have saved $30 billion in three years:

- Pay bills when they are due and not earlier unless there is sufficient beneficial reason to do so.
- Deposit checks immediately after receiving them.
- Keep as little money as possible in accounts that do not earn interest and as much as possible in interest-bearing accounts.

Grace's list of inefficiencies, waste, and mismanagement in government seemed endless. In almost every kind of agency, Grace said, some waste seemed apparent.

In the Department of Labor, there was virtually no control over long-distance telephone usage. One regional office did restrict long-distance use and was able to save $1 million per year, but other offices had not followed suit. In the private sector, one telephone for every employee was considered to be an unusually high telephone-to-employee ratio. But in the Department of Labor, the ratio was nine to seven, more telephones than employees. And 90 percent of those were more expensive multiline phones, whereas 30 percent or less was usually considered adequate in private industry.

If you had written a letter to the director of the Health and Human Services Department, your letter would have been physically handled by fifty-five to sixty people. More than forty-five days would have passed before you received an answer. Compare that to an average of five days if you wrote a major corporation in the private sector.

If you wanted to patent or trademark something, your letter would have been one of twenty thousand arriving daily at the United States Office of Patents and Trademarks. Your letter would have been filed by hand before taking its place in a backlog of applications that were two years behind in being acted upon.

The government as a whole should be entitled to major corporate discounts for travel because its work force is larger than that of any private corporation in America. However, more than $2.4 billion, or 50 percent of the government's travel allowance, was used to pay for travel tickets at full-fare rates. If all arrangements could be made through centralized or regional agencies that made an all-out effort to secure low-cost fares, the government could save $984 million in three years.

Government waste was illustrated in our preparations for this book when we ordered copies of the U.S. Government's Federal Budget, the *Economic Report of the President to Congress,* and other financial statistics—a total of forty pounds of paper. We were shocked when the Government Printing Office official taking the order and credit card number said that Federal Express overnight priority shipping cost for the forty pounds would be $8.00—less than it normally charges for an overnight letter. The normal cost for a forty-pound overnight delivery is $78. It is unlikely that Federal Express gives the government that big a discount. Even so, if the government receives a discount, the charge to us should have been the normal $78, and any money saved should be returned to taxpayers. This may sound trivial, but how many shipments every day go out of government offices to private citizens at government expense?

Many public power utilities throughout America receive subsidies from the government so that recipients are charged less than one-half what those persons receiving power from privately run public utility plants are charged. Taxpayers in other states pick up the difference.

The maintenance and construction of dams and waterways for commercial traffic cost $850 million in 1981. Only $24 million was collected from those who used the waterways. The rest was paid by public tax dollars.

The stories of government waste can go on and on. There can be little doubt that government waste, mismanagement, and inefficiency greatly contribute to our rising national debt.

According to the Grace Commission, one-third of all taxes were being consumed by waste and inefficiency in the federal government. Another one-third escaped collection as the underground economy grew in direct proportion to tax increases. That placed pressure on law-abiding taxpayers. Two-thirds of income taxes were wasted or not collected, and 100 percent of what was collected was absorbed *by interest on the federal debt* and by federal government contributions to transfer payments. All individual income tax revenues were gone before one nickel was spent on services taxpayers expected from their government.

The Grace Commission projected that unless something were done to stop government waste, the national debt would reach $13 trillion by the year 2000. "What can possibly be done?" you might ask. There are many answers.

Although groups and task forces are beginning to combat government waste, there is still no substitute in our electoral system for direct pressure on the House and Senate to be accountable to a concerned and aware public. You can write your elected officials. Share this book with ten people, and ask them to get involved by writing their representative and senators. Let it be known to these elected officials that you will vote for those who do the most to secure our economic future.

Eliminating government waste is just one of the positive possibilities for paying off the federal debt, but it is the first step we must take to meet this challenge. It is also the most important step because it will not cost taxpayers anything.

Our government can learn a lot from an old parable.

A wife came to her husband and said, "I would like to buy a new bed cover."

The husband answered, "What will you do with the old bed cover?"

The wife replied, "I will cut it up and make new pillow covers."

"What will you do with the old pillow covers?" he asked.

"I will use them for dust cloths," the wife answered.

"What will you do with the old dust cloths?" he questioned.

She answered, "I will tie them together and make a new mop."

He asked again, "What will you do with the old mop?"

"Oh," she said, "I will chop it up, mix it with ashes, and use it to stuff the holes in the outside of the house."

The husband was silent. Finally, he spoke. "All right. You can buy a new bed cover."

9 TEN WAYS TO ACCOMPLISH THE IMPOSSIBLE—PART TWO

Ten years ago, we called for the following suggestions that then seemed like a hopeful dream. But today these possibilities are much closer to reality. Had these ideas taken root and been implemented ten years ago, we would not be in the financial difficulty we find ourselves today. Over the past ten years, the federal debt has nearly tripled. The lack of fiscal discipline and responsible budgeting has driven up the deficits. Today we have no choice but to buckle down and take back control of the government from the politicians.

Americans are finally ready to put their votes where their hearts are. The presidential election of 1992 showed that the voters wanted a change. Again, the elections in the fall of 1994 showed an overwhelming consensus for more change. The voters are seeking a change that will lead us out of a dark hole and into the light of positive leadership.

The tools we suggested ten years ago are still waiting to be used by elected officials. Unfortunately, we still need them because even with the changes in the executive and legislative branches of government, there is no guarantee that the federal government will not fall back into wasteful spending sprees and mismanagement of our—the taxpayers'—money.

Currently, the way Congress is set up resembles a situation in which 535 people have joint access to a major credit card—all with the same account number. Everyone can spend as much as he or she wants, but when the bill comes, each person will owe exactly 1/535th of the bill, regardless of how much he or she personally spent. Unlike your personal credit cards, there is no credit limit. There is no one telling Congress its purchase is denied because it is over its limit! Where is the incentive to limit spending?

Imagine standing at a retail counter, having selected all of your purchases. The clerk runs your credit card through for verification, and it is denied. Then you say to the clerk, "I'm going to take these things anyway," and walk toward the exit. How far do you think you would get? But Congress does just that. In spite of the Gramm-Rudman Act requiring Congress to limit its spending, it raises its spending limit and the ceilings on the debt, and then reaches into the pockets of taxpayers or—worse yet—borrows the money and lets it compound for our children and grandchildren to repay with interest. This is done year after year with no plan to pay the money back!

Because the congressional credit card and checkbook are joint accounts, it is not hard to imagine what happens. Everyone tries to get more at everyone else's expense. After all, the bill is going to be divided among 535 representatives and their constituents.

We need to set limits on how much Congress can spend—immediately! Every other business and personal household has limitations on the amount of money it can spend. Now is the time to propose a legal limit to federal spending.

Possibility Two: Set Up a Legal Spending Limit through the Balanced Budget Amendment to the Constitution

A constitutional amendment requiring the federal government to balance the budget on a yearly basis would impose limits on the amount of money Congress could spend. Congress would not be allowed to raise the debt ceiling and borrow money to fund pet projects and please special interest groups. However, a balanced budget amendment could have a provision for it to be waived in times of national emergencies, such as war or natural disaster.

The Constitution provides the following procedures for adding an amendment: "The Congress, whenever two-thirds of both Houses shall deem it necessary, shall propose Amendments to this Constitution, or, on the Application of the Legislatures of two-thirds of the several States, shall call a Convention for proposing Amendments, which, in either case, shall be valid ... when ratified by the Legislatures of three-fourths of the several States."

In other words, there are two ways to amend the Constitution. First, Congress may propose amendments. This is how all twenty-seven existing amendments to the Constitution have started. The second way is for the states to call for a constitutional convention to propose and discuss amendments. When two-thirds of the states request a convention, it must be held. Once proposed—either by Congress or by a constitutional convention—an amendment must be ratified by three-fourths of the states to become a part of the Constitution.

In 1981, a constitutional amendment to balance the budget and limit federal taxes was drafted. While it was approved in the United States Senate by a wide margin, it received less than the two-thirds majority vote required for passage in the House of Representatives.

When we first supported the balanced budget amendment ten years ago, we were told, "Forget it. It won't happen!" The naysayers cited every possible reason why it would fail. The amendment would have to be ratified; Congress would never give the majority approval; such an amendment would open up the Constitution to frivolous changes. There are always problems with every great idea.

A major criticism of a constitutional convention is that extremists might want to question the Bill of Rights or make other proposals that would severely limit our freedoms or change the character of the Constitution as we know it today. To help ease the fear of a runaway constitutional convention open to any subject, a limit of one issue—the balanced budget amendment—should be imposed on the convention. A specific time frame, such as 120 days, could also be appointed for deliberation on this issue. Leadership requires recognizing problems before they become problems. We can't throw out a great idea because of problems that can be managed aggressively.

Other problems plague the balanced budget amendment. Senator Dianne Feinstein told me privately that she personally favors a balanced budget amendment and had previously supported it, but she refused to vote for it because "they wouldn't take social security off the table." The problem has been that on one side people want a balanced budget, but they want all the sacrifices to be made by the military; others want all the cuts to be in social programs such as social security. The respective parties must get together and be prepared to make sacrifices on both sides. If they don't, everything will fail. There will be no money for the military or the social programs.

Senator Byron Dorgan of North Dakota met with me in 1994 and was concerned as well, but he rejected the balanced budget amendment in light of the proposed cuts in social security. These elected officials have understandable fears that other politicians will be unsympathetic to the legitimate needs of our society, and so they will not vote for blanket deficit reductions without the assurance that the people who really need help will not be abandoned.

In spite of such problems, the constitutional amendment to balance the budget lost in 1995 by only two votes, one of which was a procedural maneuver by Senator Bob Dole. Although he supported the amendment, Senator Dole voted against it so that he could call for a new vote sometime before the 1996 elections. As the majority leader, Senator Dole is allowed to change his vote and call for a new vote. What had once seemed like an impossible idea is on the brink of becoming part of our nation's Constitution. This issue is so serious and the needs are so pressing that no elected official should get in the way of its success by insisting on the support of his or her pet project.[1]

Possibility Three: Impose an Across-the-Board Spending Freeze

Strong support is growing in Congress and still exists among the American people to freeze government spending. A spending freeze would limit any *increase* in funds to existing programs for the next three to five years. Funding for existing programs would not be cut back; it simply would not be increased.

A flaw in the budgeting process needs to be corrected. Currently, a division of the government receives an increase in its next year's budget simply by spending its entire allocated budget for the current year. Although the percentage of increase varies, the principle still motivates federal employees to spend their entire budget. If they were to be frugal, however, their budget would be reduced. An across-the-board spending freeze would take away the incentive to spend the entire budget and should be coupled with an incentive plan to reward fiscal frugality. The economics of motivation would then take over.

Supporters of such a freeze say that if spending is held at current levels as the economy continues to grow, revenues will increase, and deficits will therefore decline. When revenues catch up with the existing spending level, we will have a balanced budget. Over the past fifteen years, revenues and spending have increased almost every year. Estimates are that if spending is held in check, it will take three to five years for the rise in revenues to eliminate the yearly deficit and balance the budget.

An across-the-board spending freeze would be an effective way of eliminating the deficit now without much hardship rather than paying for the cumulative deficits later at a greater cost. A balanced budget would be achieved without cuts in current services and without increases in taxes.

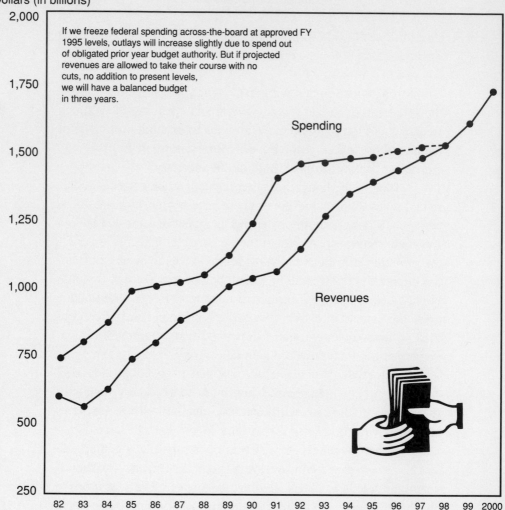

Federal Spending Freeze

Dollars (in billions)

If we freeze federal spending across-the-board at approved FY 1995 levels, outlays will increase slightly due to spend out of obligated prior year budget authority. But if projected revenues are allowed to take their course with no cuts, no addition to present levels, we will have a balanced budget in three years.

Spending

Revenues

Fiscal Years

One of the first critical actions an emergency medical team takes in treating a traumatized hemorrhaging accident victim is to stop the bleeding. Congress needs to stop the bleeding of the red ink and deficits, and then it can focus its attention on healing America of its debt disease.

Possibility Four: Permit a Line-Item Veto

Currently, the president has the option of allowing an entire bill passed by both houses of Congress to become law or of vetoing the entire bill. It's all or nothing. A line-item veto would give the president the power to veto or negate any portion of a bill while approving the balance of it. This would give the president greater ability to eliminate government spending that is wasteful or favors special interest groups.

Popular bills that are sure to be passed and approved by the president frequently contain many amendments unrelated to the main bill that ordinarily would not pass on their own if presented as independent bills. Representatives and senators have found this to be an attractive way to please special interest groups, and so it has become a much-abused practice that leads to government waste. The president and members of Congress alike, although they recognize the abuse and waste of these special attachments to major bills, are forced to approve them in order to pass the major bill itself.

For example, suppose the president supports a major bill calling for an increase in Medicare and social security payments to older people. But attached to the bill are twenty unrelated items calling for a variety of government subsidies such as low-interest loans to a major building contractor in one state or a subsidy of electric power for another state. While the president recognizes that the majority of Americans will not benefit from subsidized electricity in one state or low-interest loans in another, he is powerless to do anything about it if he wants to pass the primary bill.

A line-item veto would give the president the power to delete from the bill the lines that are unfair to the majority of Americans. The president is the only elected official voted into office by all Americans. Therefore he is not as susceptible to the pressure of powerful lobbies in individual states as are senators and representatives. Rather, the president is responsible to the majority of the people.

Congress would, of course, be able to override a line-item veto with a two-thirds majority vote just as it can now override the veto of an entire bill.

A line-item veto would give the president the power to veto anything that he felt was wasteful government spending, and thereby help save each dollar to be put into effective use. With a line-item veto we would start to see results immediately!

Possibility Five: Establish a Federal Debt Reduction Bank

We propose that the Congress of the United States establish and charter a Federal Debt Reduction Bank that has as its one objective to be the guardian of the financial future of unborn American citizens. How irresponsible would we be in our own personal debt expansion if we had no tough lending institution looking over our shoulders every time we wanted to borrow more money? If we could borrow money from a bank without the need to present a financial statement showing our assets and liabilities and our ability to handle the financial obligations, is it not likely that we would quickly borrow money irresponsibly and recklessly?

Our government has operated without any fiscal restraint for more than two hundred years. The Federal Debt Reduction Bank of the United States would monitor funds, collect funds, make payments, and manage funds arising from all sources to pay off the debt. The monies received could not be used for anything else.

At present Congress and/or the president have the power simply to expand the federal debt without having a financial review of the government's ability to pay off the increased debt.

We have a Supreme Court to ultimately pass judgment on legal cases. Does it not also merit consideration to establish a Federal Debt Reduction Bank of the United States for the purpose of passing judgment on the government's ability to repay its indebtedness? The Federal Debt Reduction Bank would actually assume the liabilities of the government and be responsible for paying off the debt. In turn it would hold title to the physical assets of the government in the name of the people. The collateral in the bank could be government lands and properties.

The Federal Debt Reduction Bank of the United States would have the responsibility of making sure that elected officials did not become reckless and irresponsible in their approval of budgets. The bank, along with its board of directors consisting of nonelected persons, would ensure that politicians could not manipulate the budget to strengthen their chances of reelection at the expense of future generations.

Since the Federal Debt Reduction Bank would agree to take over the liability of the government's $5 trillion debt, the income potential of the country would have to be carefully studied. A repayment schedule, including interest and principal payments, would need to be approved by Congress.

The Federal Debt Reduction Bank would assume liabilities of the government debt under the following provisions:

1. The Congress of the United States could not incur any new debt without the bank's approval.
2. In emergency situations Congress could discuss with the Federal Debt Reduction Bank temporary loans with predetermined obligations to repay the principal over an agreed-upon period of time, not to exceed our own generation.

The Federal Debt Reduction Bank could be the managing force to channel the funds that come from a multitude of sources. This would assure us that specific funds allocated for the repayment of the debt would not be siphoned off to meet the needs of other programs but would be used solely to help reduce our $5 trillion debt obligation.

What would this do to the morale of our country if we knew we were on a program that would gradually, dollar by dollar, reduce our federal debt and at the same time promise a bright and prosperous future for our children and grandchildren?

Possibility Six: Increase Revenues through Change in the Tax System

"When your outgo exceeds your income," John Joseph's father told him, "it's the upstart of your downfall." If we are to pay off the national debt, we must decrease outgo, increase income, or both. Therefore, possibility number six is that we should increase revenues so that the government has more money coming in.

Ten years ago, we issued a call for a radical change in the tax system and suggested that the flat tax or a variation of it might be most effective. The impact of such a change on the national debt, we predicted, would be dramatic through the increased productivity of the personal and corporate sectors. A decade ago, we felt like lone voices, repeating the wisdom of economists Milton Friedman and Arthur Laffer. Today we are no longer alone. In fact, there is a groundswell of support for a radical change in the tax system.

In 1985, a drastic change in the tax system such as the proposed flat tax seemed like a distant possibility. Today that possibility is nearing reality with proposals set forth by such congressional heavyweights as House majority leader Dick Armey, the retail sales tax proposed by presidential hopeful Richard Lugar, a Republican senator, and the USA (Unlimited Savings Allowance) tax backed by Democratic Senator Sam Nunn and Republican Senator Pete Domenici.

The bipartisan support for a major tax change is fueled by the fire of tax zealots like Sharon Cooper, a nurse who, after spending $15,000 in legal and accounting fees to settle a $1,800 case with the IRS, joined the fight to reform the system. Polls indicate public support is growing steadily for the proposed flat tax, primarily because people viewed it as a fair tax.

It's no wonder taxpayers are upset. The current tax system is burdened with regulations and constant revision and changes so that the average taxpayer spends the weeks before April 15 having lengthy meetings with accountants and attorneys, organizing tax receipts, documenting expenditures, worrying about missing a deduction, getting nauseated at the thought that he or she is working until May 3 each year just to pay the taxes.

A change in the tax system must be dramatic enough to cause a significant underlying change in people's behavior. Currently, people work diligently to avoid paying taxes. We should encourage people to work diligently—at their work.

One might think that in discussing changes to the tax system to reduce the national debt, we would be seeking ways to increase revenue by increasing taxes. However, the best way to increase revenues is to eliminate the entire existing federal income tax structure and impose a true flat tax. With a flat tax, people making $10,000 a year would pay the same percentage of their incomes as people making $100,000 a year. Various deductions that are currently available would be eliminated.

Opponents of the flat tax claim that the tax burden would shift to the poor. But according to economist Milton Friedman, every class of society would benefit. The poor and middle classes would pay less taxes due to higher personal exemptions and lower rates. And although the rich would pay more taxes, they would actually be better off because money they now spend for nonproductive tax shelters could be freed up to be used in more productive ways.

But how would a flat tax actually yield as much or more revenue as the present system?

In *Tyranny of the Status Quo,* which he wrote with his wife, Rose, Friedman explains the process,

The reason is that although the tax rates are steeply graduated on paper, the law is riddled with loopholes and special provisions so that the high rates become window dressing. The income tax does indeed "soak the rich," but that soaking does not yield much revenue to the government. It rather takes the form of inducing the rich to acquire costly tax shelters and rearrange their affairs in other ways that will minimize actual tax payments. There is a very large wedge between the cost to the taxpayer and the revenue to the government. The magnitude of that wedge was illustrated by the reduction in 1981 of the top rate on so-called unearned income from 70 to 50 percent. Despite an ensuing recession, the taxes actually paid at rates of 50 percent and above went up, not down as a result.[2]

Raising revenue by changing the tax structure to a flat tax is a viable option. But another possible way to increase revenue might be to actually lower taxes altogether. "Taxes are always a negative incentive," economist Arthur Laffer told us.

When the amount of taxes a person needs to pay is decreased, he will be encouraged to work harder and keep more. When taxes are lowered, people are motivated to earn as much as they possibly can. For instance, a person in the 40 percent tax bracket might have the opportunity to earn an additional $10,000 if he works longer hours or increases his sales. But after taxes, he keeps only $6,000. His motivation to earn that additional income is clearly less than it would be if he keeps $8,000.

If we increase motivation to work by lowering taxes, our country will see an increase in productivity. This increase in productivity will provide a broader base from which the government can collect revenues. The result is, for instance, that the government is better off with 20 percent of $200,000 ($40,000) than with 30 percent of $100,000 ($30,000).

Arthur Laffer is a strong proponent of this concept. He explained to us more fully how motivation plays an important role in productivity and how taxes and government programs affect motivation.

"When it comes to taxes," he said, "you know exactly what people will try not to do. They will try not to report taxable income. But you won't know how they will avoid reporting that taxable income. They may use tax shelters. They may participate in the underground economy in which all work is done for cash and all goods are sold for cash so that the transaction cannot be recorded. But you know they will try to avoid reporting their taxable income.

"However, if the government subsidizes a certain activity, you know exactly what people will do. They will try to do whatever gives them the subsidy. When you tax something, you get less of it. When you subsidize something, you get more of it."

Dr. Laffer went on to explain that the federal government is basically "taxing work output and employment and subsidizing nonwork, leisure, and unemployment. It should come as no shock to anyone why we are getting so little work out of those who are employed and such nonwork and leisure from those who are not employed.

"If you want people to be fully and productively employed and wealthy, you should provide them the incentives to do so. It just doesn't make sense to say, 'Raising taxes on workers and producers is going to give us more workers and producers.' "

According to Laffer, if people can gain more from being unemployed and staying on government programs or from not reporting income, then they naturally will do so. This, in turn, raises deficits through the subsidy of more social programs. In Laffer's opinion, the deficits exist largely because the tax system stifles incentives for people to work and pay fair and reasonable taxes.

"I dream of a debt-free society," concluded Dr. Laffer. "And the only way we can get there is through growth and prosperity."

As we consider increasing revenues through change in the tax system, we must keep three principles in mind. First, whether the change in taxes is to be a flat tax, a retail sales tax, or a USA tax, the rate must be low enough that people do not focus their energies on trying to avoid taxes through the use of tax shelters, unreported income, unreported cash transactions, barter trades, and other devices. Rather, taxpayers should feel good about paying their portion of taxes.

Second, taxpayers should feel good about the goods and services on which the government is spending their taxes. There must be a level of confidence that taxes are not being wasted. The best way to achieve this is through the immediate and appropriate spending cuts discussed earlier, coupled with our elected officials' demonstrating fiscal discipline through the appropriate stewardship of taxpayers' hard-earned dollars.

Third, the tax code should encourage savings, not punish savers by taxing the accumulated earnings on savings. This could be accomplished through expanded super IRAs, a USA savings account, or savings for health care and education. Incentives need to be established to encourage savings. Already, many young people wish to opt out of social security and establish their own private secured pensions so that they will not be dependent on the government when they retire. Programs to encourage savings are essential in order to diminish the effects of our current welfare state.

In talking with Dr. Beurt SerVaas, trustee and fellow of the Hudson Institute and successful corporate leader, he advised us that capital gains taxes should be reduced dramatically. Dr. SerVaas said, "The media has confused capital gains tax reduction with a rich-versus-poor issue. In fact, many Americans have large portions of their personal assets in homes, farms, or small businesses that have appreciated over many years. If capital gains tax rates (which are in many cases higher than the individual's adjusted gross federal income taxes) were low enough to induce or encourage these Americans to sell, a large well of capital would be freed up, which in turn would stimulate the economy."

Dr. SerVaas suggested, for example, that assets held for one year could be taxed at 22 percent. If an asset were held for three years, it would be taxed lower at 18 percent, five years at 15 percent, and ten years at 10 percent. This would be a particular incentive to the elderly who have built and owned a family business over many years and who would be faced with a huge tax burden if the business were sold.

We are not tax experts, and we make no claim as to what tax system is best. However, we do know that there needs to be a change made soon to encourage productivity. We propose that the experts, with the public's participation, hammer out the details and come up with the best plan—one that is fair and equitable to all sectors of society.

Imagine how much easier it would be if when April 15 approaches, you pull out a one-page simplified tax form that reports your earnings and your appropriate share of taxes. You simply sign the return, stick it in your mailbox, and use the rest of the week to be productive in your work or your home or to enjoy your favorite hobby in the constitutionally described inalienable right of the pursuit of happiness.

Possibility Seven: Take Advantage of Lower Interest Rates

Ten years ago, in the first edition of this book, we predicted that interest rates would fall dramatically. We pointed out that the real rate of return (which is the difference between what you earn on your money and what inflation eats away) historically had been two to three percentage points. In 1985, the real rate of return was 9 percent.

Using the historical norm of 2 to 3 percent for a real rate of return and the then current inflation rate of around 3 percent, we predicted that interest rates could go as low as 6 percent for a thirty-year Treasury bond. In 1995, interest on a thirty-year Treasury bond ranged from 5.86 to 8.25 percent.

All of this is a blessing in that it enables us to lower the interest rate on our $5 trillion debt. Now is the time for us to create a new debt instrument known as a Federal Debt Reduction Bond. It would have characteristics similar to Treasury bonds and notes, except that the money received from investors who buy these bonds could be used only to pay down the principal of the national debt. We believe that as the principal of the debt is reduced, interest rates could fall even farther because more money would be available. Moreover, as the debt shrinks, the servicing costs of the debt would go down proportionately. In fact, some economists believe that if we had no federal debt, our interest rates could be in the 2 to 3 percent range.

If you went to the bank to borrow money and you had no debt, the bank would be much more willing to lend you money on better terms than if you wanted to borrow money to pay the interest on your other debts.

The interest rate on the Federal Debt Reduction Bonds should be lower than that on Treasury bills, but the interest on the bonds could be exempt from federal income tax or exempt from federal estate taxes so that wealthy individuals could pass them on to their children and grandchildren. This would encourage older Americans who have a large concentration of the nation's wealth to purchase Federal Debt Reduction Bonds to accomplish two things: (1) help reduce the national debt and (2) pass on part of their estate to their heirs tax free.

10 TEN WAYS TO ACCOMPLISH THE IMPOSSIBLE— PART THREE

Our government and economic leaders can explore a myriad of traditional, mainstream problem-solving solutions to pay off the national debt. They include eliminating government waste, implementing a constitutional amendment to limit government spending, imposing an across-the-board spending freeze, using a line-item veto, establishing a Federal Debt Reduction Bank, increasing government revenues through a change in the tax system, and taking advantage of lower interest rates. But our possibility thinking game can take us beyond these obvious answers to our nation's great financial predicament.

As we let our imagination run freely, what other creative problem-solving possibilities can we dream up?

Possibility Eight: Sell or Lease Government Assets

Many government-owned properties could be sold or leased to the private sector with the income going to the Federal Debt Reduction Bank. Obviously, this sale or lease needs to be done in such a way as to avoid exploitation of the environment. Of course, there is potential for abuse or problems. But this just underscores a fundamental principle of possibility thinking: There is something wrong with every good idea. Don't reject an idea just because it has a problem with it. Every positive idea needs to be analyzed and dissected. Separate the negative part of the idea, isolate it, and eliminate it. Then release the positive element of the idea for its fullest potential.

Many government assets could be sold to raise large sums of money. Consider federal buildings and the current value of these properties. Does it make sense for the government, a nonprofit institution, to hold title to office buildings? As pastor of a church, I can say it does not pay for a nonprofit organization to hold title to apartment buildings or office buildings that have to compete with those built and operated by for-profit corporations. The simple reason is that for-profit corporations can deduct the interest on the mortgages as an expense as well as depreciate the value of the properties, all of which translates into a stronger bottom line after taxes for the corporation. Perhaps it would make better sense for the government to sell its office buildings to profit-making corporations in the private sector and then lease them back.

In addition, the government could consider leasing equipment and property it owns to the private sector. For instance, the government could protect special parcels of land by leasing them rather than selling them.

Services could also be leased. For years we have tried to get the Marine Band to perform at one of our church services, but we have been told repeatedly that the band is not allowed to play at a sectarian church service unless the president or vice president of the United States is in attendance. We would happily make a gift to the government if we could "rent" the band for certain religious functions.

There was a time when California did not allow public school buildings to be rented for church purposes. That was until the state had an urgent need for cash. Today public schools that used to stand empty on Sunday mornings are now rented to churches for their Sunday services. The citizens of the state benefit and the congregations benefit. It is a win-win situation.

Are there ships or other vessels that the government could charter to corporations and private groups for seminars at sea? Undoubtedly, many unused government properties, equipment, and services could be leased or sold to the private sector and generate billions of dollars to help pay off the national debt.

With the advent of new technologies, heretofore undreamed of and unrealized assets of the United States suddenly become potential sources of huge amounts of revenue that could be leased or sold to help pay off the national debt. Recently, the government raised billions of dollars by auctioning off a small spectrum of the FCC-controlled bandwidth for use by personal digital assistance, an upcoming technological marvel that will allow people to communicate, send faxes, receive messages, and perform computer functions by hand-held battery-operated devices. The future holds unlimited potential for the government to raise resources in the constantly evolving field of technology.

When originally doing our research, we had a discussion with former President Gerald Ford concerning the elimination of the national debt and brought up the topic of charitable gifts. "Do you realize," I asked the former president, "that in 1983, the American people contributed $65 billion to charity? Why couldn't we solicit volunteer gifts to help pay off the federal debt?"

"Well," he said, "that is a new approach. Maybe we could offer a tax deduction to people who make gifts to reduce the debt."

We were shocked. We assumed that any gifts to the federal government were currently deductible from income taxes. The fact is that they are not. In addition, we wondered how much cash was available in the hands of Americans to give charitably to the government. To find out, we asked financial expert John Templeton.

Again we were in for a shock as Templeton nonchalantly told us the amount of liquid cash available: "Not counting real estate, stocks, or long-term bonds, there is $10 trillion [in 1995] in cash or financial instruments in the hands of the American people. This is more money than the entire available supply of stocks and warrants on the New York and American stock exchanges and the

NASDAQ [National Association of Securities Dealers Automated Quotation] over-the-counter securities system."

Encouraged by this report, we came up with our next solution.

Possibility Nine: Provide Tax Incentives and Solicit Voluntary Contributions

Where did the billions of dollars in contributions to charity come from last year? How was it raised? It was contributed by people who were motivated to give money to a project or organization in which they believed. If billions of dollars were raised for charity last year, how much more could be raised by the people of this country if they knew that their gifts would help make America financially stable? Are we so jaded and so cynical that we do not believe that our fellow citizens would not share the same sense of sacrifice and devotion as our founding fathers who pledged their lives, fortunes, and honor for their freedom?

We feel confident that this may be one of the best solutions that we have yet presented, for we believe that the American people are generous and grateful for the terrific opportunities they have inherited by being citizens of the United States. We propose that $20 billion a year could be raised from caring and concerned individuals. Billions of dollars in benefits through Medicare, social security, and aid to the homeless and under-privileged were distributed in 1994. Why can't we contribute voluntarily, not just by heavy taxation, to help pay for these important programs?

What price can we put on our freedom? How much would each one of us be willing to give if we knew it would secure that same freedom for our children and grandchildren? We believe that many people would be willing to give money if they knew it was specifically earmarked for a fund that would help pay off the federal debt. The Federal Debt Reduction Bank could receive all monies in a special account that would let people know that their gifts were not being wasted by excessive government spending.

I have raised millions of dollars in cash gifts. People love to contribute large amounts of money to great causes. In the building of the Crystal Cathedral, we received seven gifts of more than $1 million. We are convinced that there are hundreds, perhaps thousands, of persons in America who would be willing to make gifts of more than $1 million each if they knew their money would be secured in a bank that guaranteed the management of our country's indebtedness.

Is it unrealistic to think that there are potential gifts to the federal government in the billion-dollar bracket? And what about the millions of small gifts that could be raised? We believe this idea has countless possibilities. For a start, here are a few ways to implement this.

A Supertelethon

Imagine a live television program from Washington, D.C., hosted by our country's most respected politicians, the president, and famous entertainers that had as its sole objective to raise a certain amount of dollars to help repay the federal debt.

Every year, Jerry Lewis raises tens of millions of dollars in only twenty-four hours during a telethon for the Muscular Dystrophy Association. What a fantastic possibility a super-telethon would be to help pay off the national debt! It could last for a week, and private corporations could sponsor it to help pay for the air time, advertising, and production costs. All fifty states would have a role to play in raising funds. The personal involvement of hundreds of thousands of Americans would stimulate incredible momentum. It would help bring the country together to achieve a common goal. A financial upswing of confidence would also stimulate creativity and productivity to expand our national net worth to a degree that is unimaginable.

Even with possible large gifts in the million- and billion-dollar range, we know that most organizations continue to be supported by the millions of people who give smaller donations. The same is true with our federal government today. It is not the rich people who support our nation with taxes but average people who give their share. We know that millions of people would want to give their smaller gifts to the government to help repay the federal debt, and the results would be overwhelming.

Patriot Class Mail

One way to help make this possible is for the postal service to create a special "patriot" stamp that would cost 2 or 3 cents more than a regular stamp. However, the extra money would mandatorily be deposited into the Federal Debt Reduction Bank. Both the sender and the recipient would know that the person purchasing these special stamps was a part of a committed group of Americans dedicated to making our country financially secure for future generations.

The Walk of Freedom

More than ten thousand people proudly donated $500 each to have a window in the Crystal Cathedral dedicated to them or the person of their choice. We created an endowment fund to maintain the beauty of the gardens and grounds of the cathedral for generations to come through what we called the Walk of Faith. These are steppingstones around the property that have inscribed on them the name and favorite Bible verse of the donor who gave $2,000. The mile-long Walk of Faith not only served as a successful fundraising campaign, but it also has become a spiritual treat for everyone who visits the cathedral.

Perhaps the government could establish a Walk of Freedom to raise funds to help pay off the debt. For a $2,000 or $500 gift, individuals would have their names, or the names of their loved ones, inscribed on plaques or steppingstones. These could adorn the Capitol gardens or the grounds around the monuments or other important sites in the city, and the millions of visitors in years to come would be inspired by them.

Incentives to give are very important in any fundraising campaign. The incentives the government could offer are endless.

Recognition on Currency and Stamps

With all due respect to George Washington, Abraham Lincoln, and some of our country's other great leaders, no law states that only their faces may appear on America's currency or that pictures on currency can't change from time to time. In consideration of major contributions of several million dollars, donors could be recognized and thanked by their fellow citizens through an act of Congress so that the donor's face would appear on a determined number of $1, $5, $10, even $100 bills. The largest bill in circulation today is a $100 bill. Wouldn't it be possible to print $200, $500, $1,000, and $10,000 bills in honor of the Americans who led us out of our national debt crisis?

Postage stamps could also be printed with the names and faces of donors who greatly contributed to our financial freedom. Private and public corporations and institutions could also be honored for their fundraising efforts.

Highways and Parks

What federal highways and parks remain unnamed? Thousands of highways that crisscross America's countryside are designated only by a number or letter. Why couldn't they bear the names of persons or institutions that made efforts to reduce the debt? Beautiful countryside parks could be named after the people who campaigned together to secure our nation's financial freedom.

Today between the Capitol Building and the Washington Monument spreads the magnificent Washington Mall. An inspiring Gallery of National Heroes could line the marvelous plaza, bearing in granite the slogans that are the foundation of our country along with the names of the people who made major gifts to win an all-out war against the nation's greatest enemy, the federal debt. Let us give living Americans in the twentieth century the opportunity to make a contribution to their country that can be recognized for years to come as a major factor in securing our freedom for future generations.

Irreversible Trusts

Charitable fundraisers have been successful when they take the long look. Colleges, universities, and nonprofit organizations do not always receive the gifts at the moment they are promised. Many gifts are given in the form of irreversible trusts.

By law, a person can give a sizable gift of property to his or her favorite charity. Then the person can continue to enjoy the capital earnings of that property or live in that property during his or her lifetime. The children can also be allowed to live in the property after the parents have died, and in some cases, even the children's children can benefit before the property is turned over to the charitable organization.

But in the meantime, the original donor can take a tax deduction of the value of the gift. For example, Mr. and Mrs. Smith live in a home valued at $500,000. They want to live in the house during their lifetimes. They also have a child and want the child to live there after they are gone. They turn the title of their house over to their favorite charity, whether it is a church, a university, or a hospital. Based on its current appraised value, the Smiths claim a sizable tax deduction that reduces their tax payments for the rest of their lives. And yet they and their child can live in the house. When the child dies, the charity can sell the house, probably at an appreciated price.

Many systems and procedures in operation today offer great incentives for people to give enormous as well as small gifts to charities. In a similar manner, an enormous amount of private capital in property and various equities could be left in wills and estates to the Federal Debt Reduction Bank of the United States with the understanding that the estate would be used to liquidate the federal debt.

Does this sound far-fetched? Was it crazy for us to think that we could raise $20 million from voluntary gifts to pay for an all-glass cathedral? Yes! But big ideas do come to pass. And when a big idea holds the prospects of laying a firm foundation that can stand for hundreds of years, we have an idea that can capture people's imagination. We sincerely believe that tens of millions of people would be willing to give whatever they can to secure freedom not only for themselves but also for their children, their children's children, and many generations.

Every time we consider a new possibility, we give birth to a new set of problems. Every time we set a new goal, we generate new tensions. Every time we make a new commitment, we can expect to produce new conflicts. Every time we make a positive decision, we can expect to be involved in a new set of frustrations.

Possibility thinking challenges us to exceed our limits. This leads us to our tenth possibility.

Possibility Ten: Encourage Superproductivity by a Supernation

Our country has vast, untapped industrial and information-based potential in existing industries and the ability to create new ones. We have no idea how large we can grow in a healthy economy with low interest rates and virtually no inflation! Our tendency is to estimate our future accomplishments by our past achievements and that too frequently limits our thinking.

Over the last two hundred years the average increase in the gross domestic product of our nation has been 2 percent per year. Many economists say this is the most we can do in the next two hundred years. But is it? History is no proof of what the future can be, nor should it be the guideline.

Let us challenge ourselves to grow at an increased GDP of 4 percent, 6 percent, or even 10 percent annually. Is it so unthinkable? Many people will object that such growth will bring back inflation and high interest rates. But will it? Many of the emerging economies of the world are growing at rates much in excess of 2 percent annually. Several times over the last decade our country has had periods of growth of 7 to 10 percent quarterly, most notably after the tax cuts of the early 1980s. And we did this without any significant increase in inflation.

As our economy expands at possibility-thinking growth rates approaching 10 percent, vast surpluses of capital would be available to pay off our national debt. Superproductivity by a supernation is the most beneficial way to pay down the debt. Everyone will benefit. It is the total fulfillment of the American dream—growth and prosperity for all!

During times of national crisis, such as World War II, our country had a phenomenal growth in GDP. In 1940, there was a 10 percent growth, followed by 25 percent in 1941, 26.7 percent in 1942, and 21.3 percent in 1944.[1] People sacrificed, saved, and cut back to achieve the goal of winning a war. Everyone worked more and spent less. It is possible to become a superproductive nation. Today our national debt constitutes no less a national crisis and deserves our full and utmost commitment. America must learn to be cutthroat in its competitive efforts in the free world market. This means productivity so great that we would be exporting cars to Japan!

We must not look at our reflections in history to set our limits for the future. One fall in the Rocky Mountains a bighorn ram approached the home of Ed Bailey while he was watching football on television. The bighorn stopped suddenly, seeing its reflection in a plate glass window. Thinking it was another ram, the bighorn bowed its head, ready to charge. He backed up and immediately saw that the other ram backed up, too. Every time he moved, his reflection moved. Finally after a three-hour duel, the ram shook its head and charged full force into the window, knocking himself unconscious.

Like the ram in the Rocky Mountains, if we focus on our reflection in history, we will be our own worst enemy. We must not look at the past to measure what we can achieve in the future.

America is a superpower with superpeople who have superpotential for superproductivity. All we need is some superpossibility thinking!

11 A DECLARATION OF FINANCIAL INDEPENDENCE

The famous philosopher Sören Kierkegaard told the story of a flock of geese that prepared to fly from the cold regions of Norway to the warmer southern climates in their annual winter migration. After their first day's journey the geese settled in a farmer's field where they found a huge harvest of gathered corn. They quickly gobbled up their food, curled their necks to tuck their heads under their wings and, with full and satisfied stomachs, slept until morning. Awakened with the dawn, the geese stretched their long necks, looked into the crisp blue sky, and obeyed their instinct as they flew off to complete their migration.

But one goose could not resist the temptation to remain one more day to indulge in the extravagance of the food around him. He stayed behind, confident that he could catch up with the flock the next day. The second day the goose awoke with an even larger appetite, for his stomach was stretching from his daily indulgences. The more he ate, the more he wanted. He was hopelessly and helplessly addicted to what seemed to be an unending supply of miraculous wealth. Days stretched into weeks as the goose kept eating his fill of the farmer's food.

One morning, a cold and biting wind awakened the goose with a start. Rain fell from thick gray clouds and quickly turned to ice at his feet. Alarmed by a revived instinct to survive, the goose stretched his neck, spread his wings, and began to waddle, then run as fast as he could. He had to leave today. Tomorrow would be too late. But why couldn't he run faster? Why did his legs move so slowly? Why were his wings so heavy? Why did his heavy body not lift to the wind?

Belatedly, the goose discovered his tragic fate. He had waited too long, indulged too recklessly, ignored the call of his inner instinct too often. Now he suffered from the inevitable consequences of his pitiful procrastination. He could not take off because he was too fat to fly!

How serious is the economic situation facing our country? Have we been overindulging? Are we resisting or ignoring our instinctive call to self-sacrifice, self-denial, and self-discipline? Could we face the same fate as the fatted goose?

What is the greatest problem facing America for the next twenty years? There will probably not be a famine in America in the proportions of the one that haunted Ethiopia. Pockets of hunger? Yes. Famine? Hardly. Not many Americans would predict a nuclear war launched by some foreign power against the United States as long as we maintain sensible defensive strength. We may fear the prospect of the thermonuclear war, but such fear is not widely verbalized lest it become a self-fulfilling prophecy.

But a growing majority of United States citizens are suddenly becoming painfully aware of an economic crisis that looms over the horizon if we keep traveling the road we are on today!

An economic holocaust is certain if we, like the fat and distracted goose, continue to procrastinate. We are creating a legacy of debt and financial bondage for our children. The following projections of what will happen if we do not reduce the government program deficit are frightening:

- Annual budget deficits of $200 billion or more will continue to add to the $5 trillion national debt.

- The debt will become truly unmanageable and form a financial crisis of unprecedented proportions.
- Interest on the debt will be unthinkable, even higher than the 18 percent of the budget that it currently consumes, especially if interest rates increase.

Continuing deficits and a growing debt will create a situation so unstable that banks will fail, interest rates will rise beyond what we have experienced, and a worldwide recession will occur. That is why the following questions will not go away:

- If the government has to borrow hundreds of billions of dollars a year simply to pay the interest on the debt, where will the money come from for banks to lend to individuals for the purchase of homes, cars, and refrigerators?
- With the small amount of lendable money left over, isn't it likely that interest rates will soar? After all, the law of supply and demand will not disappear.
- How will our children and grandchildren be able to afford a house? Where will they get the money to make astronomical monthly mortgage payments?
- How will our country handle massive unemployment when businesses foreclose and factories shut down because they are unable to meet their obligations?
- Will America, limping in financial fatigue, see its influence and benevolent power reduced drastically? Will its power to help oppressed nations overcome their poverty, famine, and disease be virtually eliminated?
- Will an economically crippled United States lose its power to maintain world peace? Will there be aggressive nations that wait like devouring beasts to leap on the wounded, weaker prey in the world?

A Declaration of Financial Independence

The power of being debt free is the power of financial independence. It is the power to promote peace, prosperity, and human pride worldwide. Of all people in history, Americans enjoy more freedom than any other citizens of any other country have ever known. How did we come to this freedom? It happened when people of vision, courage, and integrity signed the Declaration of Independence and then formulated the Constitution with its Bill of Rights. These documents guarantee to every citizen in America the right to pursue peace, happiness, and the path of prosperity.

You can be a millionaire! You can enjoy the power of becoming a financially independent person if you make a decision to save wisely, invest smartly, and live with long-range goals. For instance, you could spend $2,000 this year on a home entertainment center or a trip to the Caribbean. Or you could invest it in an Individual Retirement Account (IRA). To invest it means you must reduce your disposable income this year and give up the home entertainment center or the trip. It means you must exercise some self-sacrifice, self-denial, and self-discipline. But if you invest $2,000 each year in an IRA account that earns 13 percent interest (the average annual return on stocks for this century), you will have $182,940 in twenty years, $351,700 in twenty-five years, $662,630 in thirty years, and $1,235,499 in thirty-five years. That $1,235,499 could earn more than $160,000 in interest annually.

The truth is, each of us has the freedom to choose to become financially independent on a personal level. We can enjoy the feeling of being debt free and of knowing that we are giving that sort of heritage to our children. With this freedom comes the feeling of having the power to choose a variety of options in our personal lives.

What is true for individuals is true for our country also. America can know the power of being debt free, but like the individual who invests in an IRA, the American people will have to make a decision to save wisely and live with long-range goals. We will have to exercise some self-sacrifice, self-denial, and self-discipline.

The other key to financial freedom is time. Anyone who sets aside $2,000 a year can become financially independent, but that person must have time to make it happen. A twenty-year-old woman or a thirty-year-old man has the thirty-five years of wage-earning time necessary to build a fortune of $1.25 million. Most fifty-year-olds do not. The key to financial freedom is to begin now and have enough years that will work for you. The longer you wait to begin, the harder it will be.

Today America's debt, huge though it may be, is still manageable in the sense that if we take action now, we can eliminate the debt and discover the joy of financial freedom. *But we must take action now*. The energy and the enthusiasm that come from anticipating the fulfillment of this dream will release forces for productivity that will generate growth in gross domestic product. Then that growth will hasten the arrival of the golden future.

Once an individual or institution catches the vision of being forever debt free, the positive motivation and compulsion to be thrifty catches on. The motivation becomes a movement. With mounting momentum, the movement attracts forces that mysteriously appear to lead the impossible dream to startling, stunning success.

When is success really achieved? At the moment of triumph? At the moment of conquest? No. Success is achieved at the moment of decision. Decisions that become commitments hold within themselves seeds of success. Decisions become confident commitments that somehow the wheel will roll; the ship will float; the pistons will fire; the atom will split; human beings will fly faster than the speed of sound; we will walk on the moon!

Today we who live in America enjoy the freedom to make decisions that are commitments. We have constitutional freedom

- to elect those who govern us,
- to choose our careers,
- to purchase our homes,
- to select the state and community where we wish to live,
- to manage our incomes,
- to launch our own businesses,
- to succeed—and to fail,
- to exercise our faith,
- to plan a family,
- to speak our minds, and
- to practice the religion of our choice.

We are the envy of nations around the world. Of all people on earth, we are most blessed because we enjoy the benefits of a historic decision that was made in 1776. Once in human history a firm decision was made to declare that we would become and forever remain an independent nation. The price paid by our founding fathers who signed the Declaration of Independence has been documented. Their sacrifice was tremendous.

In the past two hundred years an enormous price has been paid to protect, preserve, and pass on that freedom to each one of us. The price can be measured by counting the white crosses in Flanders Field in France, in the Philippines, in the Punchbowl in Hawaii, and in many foreign countries. For two hundred years our best and brightest young men and, more recently, women willingly put on the uniform and marched off to defend the inherited freedoms of our land.

Our country was founded on personal sacrifice that arose from a decision that led to a commitment. Each generation for the past two hundred years has had its own unique and timely challenge that if its members had selfishly chosen to ignore or neglect, our freedom would have been lost forever. All that is required for the grand and glorious American experiment to die suddenly is for only one generation to fail in meeting and fulfilling its historic responsibility.

Do we naively think there is no price that *we* have to pay to preserve and perpetuate our inherited freedom to future generations? The unique historic challenge that comes to our generation today is to embark on a war against poverty and oppression. An institution not committed to improving itself is bound to decline. Our challenge is to improve the living standards in America for unborn generations by supplementing the 1776 Declaration of Independence with a 1995 Declaration of Independence.

Attitude and Commitment

We *can* succeed. Our children can know a country that is financially free, but that will require an attitude and a commitment on your part and mine. A positive attitude arising from a firm belief that we can succeed is essential, but action is also necessary. A careful decision that leads to a strong commitment is necessary to accomplish our goal, no matter what the cost. This commitment will forever shape the future destiny of our nation and people. It is not too late. We are young enough as a nation to set a goal today and know we can make it.

Recently, a young couple moved from Connecticut, where they lived in a mobile home, to Nashville, Tennessee. There they found a small house, which to their delight they were able to secure with a small down payment and a long-range mortgage. It is a modest home but a beautiful one. Now they enjoy the pride of ownership! Their comment upon moving into their own home was touching. They said, "We thought we had been born too late!" They had thought they were among the newly married couples of the late twentieth century who, because of high interest rates, could no longer fulfill the American dream of owning a home of their own. Their financial future, they thought, had already been stolen from them by those who had already built up a staggering national debt.

It is not too late if we act *now*. We shall declare war on the national debt. In the process, we shall declare war on the poverty certain to fall in catastrophic proportions upon our children if nothing is done today. We shall declare that a fiscal plan will be established to guarantee that our children and grandchildren can own a home of their own in a beautiful new suburb or a comfortable apartment in the city.

But the time is rapidly running out. Listen! Can't you hear the clock ticking? Decisions must be made today, or our children will, in fact, be born too late!

Take Action Now!

What can you do now? In a nation of possibility thinkers, you can do many things. Join the growing consensus of concerned Americans committed to paying off the national debt. Either join a movement or start one. The national debt may seem like an incredible mountain to move, but remember, when movements mount, mountains move! We will mention just a few of the things you can do.

1. Get together a group of women committed to paying off the national debt. If you are already involved in a women's group, share with them your concern and the facts given in this book. Get them involved. After all, their children and grandchildren will have to suffer if nothing is done about this national problem.

A group of dedicated women can accomplish amazing victories. In the early 1960s, Brazil was threatened with a Communist revolution. The nation was ruled by morally corrupt men who allowed themselves to be manipulated by Communist subversives. Through a concerted effort on the part of thousands of concerned citizens, the Communist threat in Brazil was finally defeated.

> To the women of Brazil belongs a huge share of the credit for stopping the planned Red takeover. By the thousands, on a scale unmatched in Latin American history, housewives threw themselves into the struggle and, more than any other force, they alerted the country. "Without the women," says

one leader of the counterrevolution, "we could never have halted Brazil's plunge toward communism. While many of our men's groups had to work undercover, the women could work in the open—and how they worked!"[1]

If you are not a part of a group, then start one. If there is no leadership, then take on this responsibility. There is a critical need for dynamic leadership. American women need to have the same fervor to battle this threat to our economic freedom as Brazil's women had in battling the Communist threat to Brazil's political freedom. They said,

This nation which God has given us, immense and marvelous as it is, is in extreme danger. We have allowed men of limitless ambition, without Christian faith or scruples, to bring our people misery, destroying our economy, disturbing our social peace, to create hate and despair. They have infiltrated our nation, our government administration, our armed forces, and even our churches with servants of totalitarianism.[2]

After you read this book, share it with ten other people who can catch the vision!

2. Write your representative and senators about your concern over the rising federal debt and deficits and about your desire to see the debt paid off. Letting your elected representatives know how you feel is still one of the greatest privileges you have as an American in a democratic system. Your letter will be read and it will have an influence. Can you imagine the effect you and others would have on the senators and representatives if suddenly forty to fifty million Americans flooded their desks with mail demanding that government waste be controlled, a balanced budget be enforced, and a plan implemented to pay off the national debt?

Let your representative and senators know that you will vote in the next election based on how they handle this important national issue. After all, you want leadership in government that will provide for the future, not borrow from it. If you don't know the name and address of your representative or senators, see Appendix II for a complete list of addresses and telephone numbers of the members of the 104th Congress.

3. Encourage others to write their representatives and senators, too. Your children in grades three through six should write these officials to ask them to please save the future for them. High school and college students (a powerful voting group) could form a lobby and pressure their elected officials in Congress to pass legislation and enforce laws to lead toward a balanced budget and to pay off the national debt. Wouldn't it be wonderful if students across the country on university and college campuses gave as much enthusiasm to this purpose as they did in the past to demonstrations for peace?

4. Lend your support to national organizations committed to balancing the budget. The National Taxpayers Union, 713 Maryland Avenue NE, Washington, D.C. 20002, is a Washington-based lobby that seeks to limit government spending and waste of your tax dollars. Its phone number is 202-543-1300. Citizens Against Government Waste (formerly known as the President's Private Sector Survey on Cost Control), 1301 Connecticut Avenue NW, Suite 400, Washington, D.C. 20036, continues the study and the monitoring of government expenditures begun by the Grace Commission. Its phone number is 202-467-5300.

5. Contact the producer of a local radio talk show and suggest that he or she devote a week to the subject of the national deficit and the debt. The show can have as guests representatives, senators, economists, syndicated news columnists, and chief executive officers of local organizations to discuss their views and concerns.

6. Contact your local newspaper to ask it to have various editorials on the deficit and the debt. You could submit one to be included for publication. Feel free to draw from the material in this book as you write your editorial.

7. Many radio and television stations devote a few minutes

each evening to a commentary of interest to their viewers. Ask the station manager to air some commentaries on the national debt. Perhaps you yourself could be given time to speak out on this issue.

8. Sign the following Declaration of Financial Independence and petition to the President of the United States and the Congress of the United States. Secure as many signatures as you can and mail them to

> Americans for Financial Independence
> c/o Rutledge Hill Press
> 211 Seventh Avenue North
> Nashville, Tennessee 37219

If one hundred thousand persons each gathered one hundred signatures, or if one million persons each gathered ten signatures, there would be ten million names to give to the president of the United States and to Congress. What a terrific gesture that would be to demonstrate the concern and commitment Americans have toward achieving the goal of financial independence!

Since these petitions will be sent to the president and to Congress, it is important that they be in the correct form. Each petition should be on one side of 8½-by-11-inch paper with the wording of the petition at the top of each page. Each individual must *print* his or her name and address, including zip code, as well as sign the petition. It is also important that each person sign one of these petitions only once.

We will present these petitions to the president and the Speaker of the House.

PETITION
to the President of the United States
and
to the Congress of the United States

We the undersigned are concerned with the economic crisis

that looms because of our current federal budget deficits and increasing national debt. We therefore request that the president of the United States and both houses of Congress work together to balance the budget and take positive steps to repay the national debt.

Signature   *PRINT Name and Address*
                               (including zip code)

_____   _____

_____   _____

_____   _____

_____   _____

_____   _____

_____   _____

_____   _____

9. Contact your representatives in your state legislature and share with them your concern over the national debt crisis. In 1995, more than $100 billion in grants went directly to state and local governments from the federal government. A commitment on the part of state and local officials to the value of paying off the national debt will make it easier for federal officials to balance the budget. Ask your state representatives to keep you informed as to how federal funds allocated to your state are being used. Explain that you will support representatives who responsibly use your tax dollars.

10. In this book, we have listed ten possibility-thinking solutions to the debt crisis, but surely, there must be more. Why don't you, the reader, play the possibility thinking game and come up with three, five, or ten new solutions to repay the debt? Send them to us so that we can channel them to the appropriate congressional and senatorial authorities. Send your suggestions to

Americans for Financial Independence, c/o Rutledge Hill Press, 211 Seventh Avenue North, Nashville, Tennessee 37219.

We have a dream for a debt-free America. Won't you help us make it a reality? Let's believe it can be done. Let's work to make it happen. Let's start today!

The First Step

The spring sunshine cast its warm rays on the young family standing at the entrance to the hospital. The government official had left as quickly as possible after delivering the bill for $43,500. The parents stood stunned in silence. The young father looked at his wife. A tear rolled down her cheek. "It's not fair!" she sobbed. The proud father hugged his wife and child. "No, it's not fair. But it would be more unfair to our child if we did nothing about it. If we start today, we can pay this bill for him so that he can begin his adult life debt free!"

APPENDIX I

Assumptions

As we began work on this book, we very quickly realized that different economists and groups use different figures for the same thing. One report would have one figure for the national debt, while another report would have a different figure. The difference, of course, arises from differences of definitions and assumptions when compiling the figures. In addition, change has occurred with increasing speed in recent years. No longer do interest rates, for instance, stay fairly constant for years on end.

As much as possible, we have tried to be consistent in our use of figures throughout this book. When we quote others, however, consistency is impossible. We have used the following figures:

Federal debt	$5 trillion
Federal budget deficit	$200 billion
Interest paid on the debt	$260 billion
Population	260 million
Total taxes collected by U.S. government	$1.354 trillion

The report prepared by Arnold Packer for the Hudson Institute contained a number of forecasts, and we tried as much as possible to use those forecasts as normative for consistency's sake. Selected highlights of those forecasts are as follows:

	1984	*1990*	*1995*	*2000*	*2005*
Gross National Product					
(in current dollars, trillions)					
Muddling Through	3.683	5.822	8.261	12.196	17.465
Debt Elimination	3.683	6.030	8.767	13.096	19.078
Population (millions)	238.2	252.0	262.2	271.5	280.4
Federal Government Receipts					
(in current dollars, trillions)					
Muddling Through	.711	1.257	1.823	2.753	4.015
Debt Elimination	.711	1.343	1.986	3.006	4.406
Federal Government Expenditures					
(in current dollars, trillions)					
Muddling Through	.876	1.460	2.087	2.996	4.245
Debt Elimination	.876	1.384	1.951	2.778	3.958
Federal Government Surplus or Deficit					
(in current dollars, trillions)					
Muddling Through	−164.5	−202.8	−263.9	−242.3	−230.1
Debt Elimination	−164.5	−41.1	35.4	228.0	447.7
Interest on Federal Debt					
(in current dollars, trillions)					
Muddling Through	114.3	230.5	323.7	439.7	537.1
Debt Elimination	114.3	132.9	110.1	69.5	−24.1

APPENDIX II

104th Congress

To declare your own commitment to America's financial independence we encourage you to contact your U.S. senator and representative. A complete list of the 104th Congress follows.

ALABAMA

Senators
Senator Howell T. Heflin (D)
728 Hart Senate Office Building
Washington, D.C. 20510
Phone: 202-224-4124
FAX: 202-224-3149

Senator Richard C. Shelby (D)
509 Hart Senate Office Building
Washington, D.C. 20510
Phone: 202-224-5744
FAX: 202-224-3416

Representatives
Rep. Sonny Callahan (R)
(First District)
2418 Rayburn House Office Building
Washington, D.C. 20515
Phone: 202-225-4931
FAX: 202-225-0562

Rep. Terry Everett (R)
(Second District)
208 Cannon House Office Building
Washington, D.C. 20515
Phone: 202-225-2901
FAX: (Unlisted)

Rep. Glen Browder (D)
(Third District)
1221 Longworth House Office
   Building
Washington, D.C. 20515
Phone: 202-225-3261
FAX: 202-225-9020

Rep. Tom Bevill (D)
(Fourth District)
2302 Rayburn House Office Building
Washington, D.C. 20515
Phone: 202-225-4876
FAX: 202-225-1604

Rep. Robert "Bud" Cramer (D)
(Fifth District)
1318 Longworth House Office
   Building
Washington, D.C. 20515
Phone: 202-225-4801
FAX: 202-225-4392

Rep. Spencer Bachus (R)
(Sixth District)
216 Cannon House Office Building
Washington, D.C. 20515
Phone: 202-225-4921
FAX: 202-225-2082

Rep. Earl F. Hillard (D)
(Seventh District)
1007 Longworth House Office
    Building
Washington, D.C. 20515
Phone: 202-225-2665
FAX: 202-226-0772

ALASKA

Senators
Senator Ted Stevens (R)
522 Hart Senate Office Building
Washington, D.C. 20510
Phone: 202-224-3004
FAX: 202-224-2354

Senator Frank H. Murkowski (R)
706 Hart Senate Office Building
Washington, D.C. 20510
Phone: 202-224-6665
FAX: 202-224-5301

Representative At Large
Rep. Don Young (R)
2331 Rayburn House Office Building
Washington, D.C. 20515
Phone: 202-225-5765
FAX: 202-225-0425

ARIZONA

Senators
Senator John Kyl (R)
328 Hart Senate Office Building
Washington, D.C. 20510
Phone: 202-224-4521
FAX: 202-224-2302

Senator John S. McCain (R)
111 Russell Senate Office Building
Washington, D.C. 20510
Phone: 202-224-2235
FAX: 202-228-2862

Representatives
Rep. Matt Salmon (R)
(First District)
1607 Longworth House Office
    Building
Washington, D.C. 20515
Phone: 202-225-2635
FAX: 202-225-2607

Rep. Ed Pastor (D)
(Second District)
408 Cannon House Office Building
Washington, D.C. 20515
Phone: 202-225-4065
FAX: 202-225-1655

Rep. Bob Stump (R)
(Third District)
211 Cannon House Office Building
Washington, D.C. 20515
Phone: 202-225-4576
FAX: 202-225-6328

Rep. John Shadegg (R)
(Fourth District)
2440 Rayburn House Office Building
Washington, D.C. 20515
Phone: 202-225-3361
FAX: 202-225-1143

Rep. James Thomas Kolbe (R)
(Fifth District)
405 Cannon House Office Building
Washington, D.C. 20515
Phone: 202-225-2542
FAX: 202-225-0378

Rep. J. D. Hayworth (R)
(Sixth District)
1024 Longworth House Office
    Building
Washington, D.C. 20515
Phone: 202-225-2190
FAX: 202-225-8819

ARKANSAS

Senators
Senator Dale Bumpers (D)
229 Dirksen Senate Office Building
Washington, D.C. 20510
Phone: 202-224-4843
FAX: 202-224-6435

Senator David H. Pryor (D)
267 Russell Senate Office Building
Washington, D.C. 20510
Phone: 202-224-2353
FAX: 202-224-8261

Representatives
Rep. Blanche Lambert (D)
(First District)
1204 Longworth House Office
  Building
Washington, D.C. 20515
Phone: 202-225-4076
FAX: 202-225-4654

Rep. Ray Thornton (D)
(Second District)
1214 Longworth House Office
  Building
Washington, D.C. 20515
Phone: 202-225-2506
FAX: 202-225-9273

Rep. Tim Hutchinson (R)
(Third District)
1541 Longworth House Office
  Building
Washington, D.C. 20515
Phone: 202-225-4301
FAX: 202-225-7492

Rep. Jay Dickey (R)
(Fourth District)
1338 Longworth House Office
  Building
Washington, D.C. 20515
Phone: 202-225-3772
FAX: 202-225-1314

CALIFORNIA

Senators
Senator Barbara Boxer (D)
112 Hart Senate Office Building
Washington, D.C. 20510
Phone: 202-224-3553
FAX: 202-224-6252

Senator Dianne Feinstein (D)
331 Hart Senate Office Building
Washington, D.C. 20510
Phone: 202-224-3841
FAX: 202-224-0656

Representatives
Rep. Frank Riggs (D)
(First District)
114 Cannon House Office Building
Washington, D.C. 20515
Phone: 202-225-3311
FAX: 202-225-7710

Rep. Wally Herger (R)
(Second District)
2433 Longworth House Office
  Building
Washington, D.C. 20515
Phone: 202-225-3076
FAX: 202-225-1609

Rep. Vic Fazio (D)
(Third District)
2113 Rayburn House Office Building
Washington, D.C. 20515
Phone: 202-225-5716
FAX: 202-225-0354

Rep. John T. Doolittle (R)
(Fourth District)
1542 Longworth House Office
  Building
Washington, D.C. 20515
Phone: 202-225-2511
FAX: 202-225-5444

Rep. Robert T. Matsui (D)
(Fifth District)
2311 Rayburn House Office Building
Washington, D.C. 20515
Phone: 202-225-7163
FAX: 202-225-0566

Rep. Lynn Woolsey (D)
(Sixth District)
439 Cannon House Office Building
Washington, D.C. 20515
Phone: 202-225-5161
FAX: 202-225-5163

Rep. George Miller (D)
(Seventh District)
2205 Rayburn House Office Building
Washington, D.C. 20515
Phone: 202-225-2095
FAX: 202-225-5609

Rep. Nancy Pelosi (D)
(Eighth District)
240 Cannon House Office Building
Washington, D.C. 20515
Phone: 202-225-4965
FAX: 202-225-8259

Rep. Ronald V. Dellums (D)
(Ninth District)
2108 Rayburn House Office Building
Washington, D.C. 20515
Phone: 202-225-2661
FAX: 202-225-9817

Rep. Bill Baker (R)
(Tenth District)
1714 Longworth House Office
   Building
Washington, D.C. 20515
Phone: 202-225-1880
FAX: 202-225-2150

Rep. Richard W. Pombo (R)
(Eleventh District)
1519 Longworth House Office
   Building
Washington, D.C. 20515
Phone: 202-225-1947
FAX: 202-226-0861

Rep. Tom Lantos (D)
(Twelfth District)
2182 Rayburn House Office Building
Washington, D.C. 20515
Phone: 202-225-3531
FAX: 202-225-3127

Rep. Fortney H. "Pete" Stark (D)
(Thirteenth District)
239 Cannon House Office Building
Washington, D.C. 20515
Phone: 202-225-5065
FAX: (Unlisted)

Rep. Anna G. Eshoo (D)
(Fourteenth District)
1505 Longworth House Office
   Building
Washington, D.C. 20515
Phone: 202-225-8104
FAX: 202-225-8890

Rep. Norman Y. Mineta (D)
(Fifteenth District)
2221 Rayburn House Office Building
Washington, D.C. 20515
Phone: 202-225-2631
FAX: (Unlisted)

Rep. Zoe Lofgren (D)
(Sixteenth District)
2307 Rayburn House Office Building
Washington, D.C. 20515
Phone: 202-225-3072
FAX: 202-225-9460

Rep. Sam Farr (D)
(Seventeenth District)
1216 Longworth House Office
   Building
Washington, D.C. 20515
Phone: 202-225-2861
FAX: 202-225-2861

Rep. Gary Condit (D)
(Eighteenth District)
1123 Longworth House Office
   Building
Washington, D.C. 20515
Phone: 202-225-6131
FAX: 202-225-0819

Rep. George Radanovich (R)
(Nineteenth District)
1226 Longworth House Office
  Building
Washington, D.C. 20515
Phone: 202-225-4540
FAX: 202-225-5274

Rep. Calvin Dooley (D)
(Twentieth District)
1227 Longworth House Office
  Building
Washington, D.C. 20515
Phone: 202-225-3341
FAX: 202-225-9308

Rep. William M. Thomas (R)
(Twenty-First District)
2209 Rayburn House Office Building
Washington, D.C. 20515
Phone: 202-225-2915
FAX: 202-225-8798

Rep. Michael Huffington (R)
(Twenty-Second District)
113 Cannon House Office Building
Washington, D.C. 20515
Phone: 202-225-3601
FAX: 202-226-1015

Rep. Elton William Gallegly (R)
(Twenty-Third District)
2441 Rayburn House Office Building
Washington, D.C. 20515
Phone: 202-225-5811
FAX: 202-225-0713

Rep. Anthony C. Beilenson (D)
(Twenty-Fourth District)
2465 Rayburn House Office Building
Washington, D.C. 20515
Phone: 202-225-5911
FAX: (Unlisted)

Rep. Howard P. "Buck" McKeon (R)
(Twenty-Fifth District)
307 Cannon House Office Building
Washington, D.C. 20515
Phone: 202-225-1956
FAX: 202-226-0683

Rep. Howard L. Berman (D)
(Twenty-Sixth District)
2201 Rayburn House Office Building
Washington, D.C. 20515
Phone: 202-225-4695
FAX: 202-225-5279

Rep. Carlos J. Moorhead (R)
(Twenty-Seventh District)
2346 Rayburn House Office Building
Washington, D.C. 20515
Phone: 202-225-4176
FAX: 202-226-1279

Rep. David Timothy Dreier (R)
(Twenty-Eighth District)
411 Cannon House Office Building
Washington, D.C. 20515
Phone: 202-225-2305
FAX: 202-225-4745

Rep. Henry A. Waxmon (D)
(Twenty-Ninth District)
2408 Rayburn House Office Building
Washington, D.C. 20515
Phone: 202-225-3976
FAX: 202-225-4099

Rep. Xavier Becerra (D)
(Thirtieth District)
1710 Longworth House Office
  Building
Washington, D.C. 20515
Phone: 202-225-6235
FAX: 202-225-2202

Rep. Matthew G. Martinez (D)
(Thirty-First District)
2231 Rayburn House Office Building
Washington, D.C. 20515
Phone: 202-225-5464
FAX: 202-225-5467

Rep. Julian Carey Dixon (D)
(Thirty-Second District)
2400 Rayburn House Office Building
Washington, D.C. 20515
Phone: 202-225-7084
FAX: 202-225-4091

Rep. Lucille Roybal-Allard (D)
(Thirty-Third District)
324 Cannon House Office Building
Washington, D.C. 20515
Phone: 202-225-1766
FAX: 202-226-0350

Rep. Esteban E. Torres (D)
(Thirty-Fourth District)
1740 Longworth House Office
  Building
Washington, D.C. 20515
Phone: 202-225-5256
FAX: 202-225-9711

Rep. Maxine Waters (D)
(Thirty-Fifth District)
1207 Longworth House Office
  Building
Washington, D.C. 20515
Phone: 202-225-2201
FAX: 202-225-7854

Rep. Jane Harman (D)
(Thirty-Sixth District)
325 Cannon House Office Building
Washington, D.C. 20515
Phone: 202-225-8220
FAX: 202-226-0684

Rep. Walter R. Tucker, III (D)
(Thirty-Seventh District)
419 Cannon House Office Building
Washington, D.C. 20515
Phone: 202-225-7924
FAX: 202-225-7926

Rep. Steve Horn (R)
(Thirty-Eighth District)
1023 Longworth House Office
  Building
Washington, D.C. 20515
Phone: 202-225-6676
FAX: 202-226-1012

Rep. Ed Royce (R)
(Thirty-Ninth District)
1404 Longworth House Office
  Building
Washington, D.C. 20515
Phone: 202-225-4111
FAX: 202-226-0335

Rep. Jerry Lewis (R)
(Fortieth District)
2312 Rayburn House Office Building
Washington, D.C. 20515
Phone: 202-225-5861
FAX: 202-225-6498

Rep. Jay C. Kim (R)
(Forty-First District)
502 Cannon House Office Building
Washington, D.C. 20515
Phone: 202-225-3201
FAX: 202-226-1485

Rep. George E. Brown, Jr. (D)
(Forty-Second District)
2300 Rayburn House Office Building
Washington, D.C. 20515
Phone: 202-225-6161
FAX: 202-225-8671

Rep. Ken Calvert (R)
(Forty-Third District)
1523 Longworth House Office
  Building
Washington, D.C. 20515
Phone: 202-225-1986
FAX: (Unavailable at T.O.P.)

Rep. Sonny Bono (R)
(Forty-Fourth District)
2422 Longworth House Office
  Building
Washington, D.C. 20515
Phone: 202-225-5330
FAX: 202-226-1040

Rep. Dana Rohrabacher (R)
(Forty-Fifth District)
1027 Longworth House Office
  Building
Washington, D.C. 20515
Phone: 202-225-2415
FAX: 202-225-0145

Rep. Robert K. Dornan (R)
(Forty-Sixth District)
2402 Rayburn House Office Building
Washington, D.C. 20515
Phone: 202-225-2965
FAX: 202-225-3694

Rep. C. Christopher Cox (R)
(Forty-Seventh District)
206 Cannon House Office Building
Washington, D.C. 20515
Phone: 202-225-5611
FAX: 202-225-9177

Rep. Ronald C. Packard (R)
(Forty-Eighth District)
2162 Rayburn House Office Building
Washington, D.C. 20515
Phone: 202-225-3906
FAX: 202-225-0134

Rep. Brian Bilbray (R)
(Forty-Ninth District)
315 Cannon House Office Building
Washington, D.C. 20515
Phone: 202-225-2040
FAX: 202-225-2042

Rep. Bob Filner (D)
(Fiftieth District)
504 Cannon House Office Building
Washington, D.C. 20515
Phone: 202-225-8045
FAX: 202-225-9073

Rep. Randy "Duke" Cunningham (R)
(Fifty-First District)
117 Cannon House Office Building
Washington, D.C. 20515
Phone: 202-225-5452
FAX: 202-225-2558

Rep. Duncan Lee Hunter (R)
(Fifty-Second District)
133 Cannon House Office Building
Washington, D.C. 20515
Phone: 202-225-5672
FAX: 202-225-0235

COLORADO

Senators
Senator Ben Nighthorse Campbell (D)
380 Russell Senate Office Building
Washington, D.C. 20510
Phone: 202-224-5852
FAX: 202-224-3714

Senator Hank Brown (R)
716 Hart Senate Office Building
Washington, D.C. 20510
Phone: 202-224-5941
FAX: 202-224-6471

Representatives
Rep. Patricia S. Schroeder (D)
(First District)
2208 Rayburn House Office Building
Washington, D.C. 20515
Phone: 202-225-4431
FAX: 202-225-5842

Rep. David E. Skaggs (D)
(Second District)
1124 Longworth House Office
  Building
Washington, D.C. 20515
Phone: 202-225-2161
FAX: 202-225-9127

Rep. Scott McInnis (R)
(Third District)
512 Cannon House Office Building
Washington, D.C. 20515
Phone: 202-225-4761
FAX: 202-226-0622

Rep. Wayne Allard (R)
(Fourth District)
422 Cannon House Office Building
Washington, D.C. 20515
Phone: 202-225-4676
FAX: 202-225-8630

Rep. Joel Hefley (R)
(Fifth District)
2442 Rayburn House Office Building
Washington, D.C. 20515
Phone: 202-225-4422
FAX: 202-225-1942

Rep. Dan L. Schaefer (R)
(Sixth District)
2448 Rayburn House Office Building
Washington, D.C. 20515
Phone: 202-225-7882
FAX: 202-225-7885

CONNECTICUT

Senators
Senator Christopher J. Dodd (D)
444 Russell Senate Office Building
Washington, D.C. 20510
Phone: 202-224-2823
FAX: 202-224-5431

Senator Joseph I. Lieberman (D)
316 Hart Senate Office Building
Washington, D.C. 20510
Phone: 202-224-4041
FAX: 202-224-9750

Representatives
Rep. Barbara B. Kennelly (D)
(First District)
201 Cannon House Office Building
Washington, D.C. 20515
Phone: 202-225-2265
FAX: 202-225-1031

Rep. Samuel Gejdenson (D)
(Second District)
2416 Rayburn House Office Building
Washington, D.C. 20515
Phone: 202-225-2076
FAX: 202-225-4977

Rep. Rosa DeLauro (D)
(Third District)
327 Cannon House Office Building
Washington, D.C. 20515
Phone: 202-225-3661
FAX: 202-225-4890

Rep. Christopher Shays (R)
(Fourth District)
1034 Longworth House Office
  Building
Washington, D.C. 20515
Phone: 202-225-5541
FAX: 202-225-9629

Rep. Gary Franks (R)
(Fifth District)
435 Cannon House Office Building
Washington, D.C. 20515
Phone: 202-225-3822
FAX: 202-225-5085

Rep. Nancy Lee Johnson (R)
(Sixth District)
343 Cannon House Office Building
Washington, D.C. 20515
Phone: 202-225-4476
FAX: 202-225-4488

DELAWARE

Senators
Senator William V. Roth, Jr. (R)
104 Hart Senate Office Building
Washington, D.C. 20510
Phone: 202-224-2441
FAX: 202-224-2805

Senator Joseph R. Biden, Jr. (D)
221 Russell Senate Office Building
Washington, D.C. 20510
Phone: 202-224-5042
FAX: 202-224-0139

Representative At Large
Rep. Michael N. Castle (R)
1205 Longworth House Office
 Building
Washington, D.C. 20515
Phone: 202-225-4165
FAX: 202-225-2291

FLORIDA

Senators
Senator Robert Graham (D)
524 Hart Senate Office Building
Washington, D.C. 20510
Phone: 202-224-3041
FAX: 202-224-2237

Senator Connie Mack, III (R)
517 Hart Senate Office Building
Washington, D.C. 20510
Phone: 202-224-5274
FAX: 202-224-9365

Representatives
Rep. Joe Scarborough (D)
(First District)
2435 Rayburn House Office Building
Washington, D.C. 20515
Phone: 202-225-4136
FAX: 202-225-5785

Rep. Pete Peterson (D)
(Second District)
426 Cannon House Office Building
Washington, D.C. 20515
Phone: 202-225-5235
FAX: 202-225-1586

Rep. Corrine Brown (D)
(Third District)
1037 Longworth House Office
 Building
Washington, D.C. 20515
Phone: 202-225-0123
FAX: 202-225-2256

Rep. Tillie Fowler (R)
(Fourth District)
413 Cannon House Office Building
Washington, D.C. 20515
Phone: 202-225-2501
FAX: 202-226-9318

Rep. Karen L. Thurman (D)
(Fifth District)
130 Cannon House Office Building
Washington, D.C. 20515
Phone: 202-225-1002
FAX: 202-226-0329

Rep. Cliff Stearns (R)
(Sixth District)
332 Cannon House Office Building
Washington, D.C. 20515
Phone: 202-225-5744
FAX: 202-225-3973

Rep. John L. Mica (R)
(Seventh District)
427 Cannon House Office Building
Washington, D.C. 20515
Phone: 202-225-4035
FAX: 202-226-0821

Rep. Bill McCollum (R)
(Eighth District)
2266 Rayburn House Office Building
Washington, D.C. 20515
Phone: 202-225-2176
FAX: 202-225-0999

Rep. Michael Bilirakis (R)
(Ninth District)
2240 Rayburn House Office Building
Washington, D.C. 20515
Phone: 202-225-5755
FAX: 202-225-4085

Rep. C. W. Bill Young (R)
(Tenth District)
2407 Rayburn House Office Building
Washington, D.C. 20515
Phone: 202-225-5961
FAX: 202-225-9764

Rep. Sam M. Gibbons (D)
(Eleventh District)
2204 Rayburn House Office Building
Washington, D.C. 20515
Phone: 202-225-3376
FAX: (Unlisted)

Rep. Charles T. Canady (R)
(Twelfth District)
1107 Longworth House Office
  Building
Washington, D.C. 20515
Phone: 202-225-1252
FAX: 202-225-2279

Rep. Dan Miller (R)
(Thirteenth District)
510 Cannon House Office Building
Washington, D.C. 20515
Phone: 202-225-5015
FAX: 202-226-0828

Rep. Porter Goss (R)
(Fourteenth District)
330 Cannon House Office Building
Washington, D. C. 20515
Phone: 202-225-2536
FAX: 202-225-6820

Rep. Dave Weldon (D)
(Fifteenth District)
432 Cannon House Office Building
Washington, D.C. 20515
Phone: 202-225-3671
FAX: 202-225-9039

Rep. Mark Foley (R)
(Sixteenth District)
2351 Rayburn House Office Building
Washington, D.C. 20515
Phone: 202-225-5792
FAX: 202-225-1860

Rep. Carrie Meek (D)
(Seventeenth District)
404 Cannon House Office Building
Washington, D.C. 20515
Phone: 202-225-4506
FAX: 202-226-0777

Rep. Ileana Ros-Lehtinen(R)
(Eighteenth District)
127 Cannon House Office Building
Washington, D.C. 20515
Phone: 202-225-3931
FAX: 202-225-5620

Rep. Harry A. Johnston, II (D)
(Nineteenth District)
204 Cannon House Office Building
Washington, D.C. 20515
Phone: 202-225-3001
FAX: 202-225-8791

Rep. Peter Deutsch (D)
(Twentieth District)
425 Cannon House Office Building
Washington, D.C. 20515
Phone: 202-225-7931
FAX: 202-225-8456

Rep. Lincoln Diaz-Balart (R)
(Twenty-First District)
509 Cannon House Office Building
Washington, D.C. 20515
Phone: 202-225-4211
FAX: 202-225-8576

Rep. E. Clay Shaw, Jr. (R)
(Twenty-Second District)
2267 Rayburn House Office Building
Washington, D.C. 20515
Phone: 202-225-3026
FAX: 202-225-8398

Rep. Alcee L. Hastings (D)
(Twenty-Third District)
1039 Longworth House Office
  Building
Washington, D.C. 20515
Phone: 202-225-1313
FAX: 202-226-0690

GEORGIA

Senators
Senator Samuel A. Nunn (D)
303 Dirksen Senate Office Building
Washington, D.C. 20510
Phone: 202-224-3521
FAX: 202-224-0072

Senator Paul Coverdell (R)
200 Russell Senate Office Building
Washington, D.C. 20510
Phone: 202-224-3643
FAX: 202-224-8227

Representatives
Rep. Jack Kingston (R)
(First District)
1229 Longworth House Office
Building
Washington, D.C. 20515
Phone: 202-225-5831
FAX: 202-226-2269

Rep. Sanford Bishop (D)
(Second District)
1632 Longworth House Office
Building
Washington, D.C. 20515
Phone: 202-225-3631
FAX: 202-225-2203

Rep. Mac Collins (R)
(Third District)
1118 Longworth House Office
Building
Washington, D.C. 20515
Phone: 202-225-5901
FAX: 202-225-2515

Rep. John Linder (R)
(Fourth District)
1605 Longworth House Office
Building
Washington, D.C. 20515
Phone: 202-225-4272
FAX: 202-225-4696

Rep. John R. Lewis (D)
(Fifth District)
329 Cannon House Office Building
Washington, D.C. 20515
Phone: 202-225-3801
FAX: 202-225-0351

Rep. Newton L. Gingrich (R)
(Sixth District)
2428 Rayburn House Office Building
Washington, D.C. 20515
Phone: 202-225-4501
FAX: 202-225-4656

Rep. Robert Barr (D)
(Seventh District)
2303 Rayburn House Office Building
Washington, D.C. 20515
Phone: 202-225-2931
FAX: 202-225-0473

Rep. Saxby Chambuss (R)
(Eighth District)
2134 Rayburn House Office Building
Washington, D.C. 20515
Phone: 202-225-6531
FAX: 202-225-7719

Rep. Nathan Deal (D)
(Ninth District)
1406 Longworth House Office
Building
Washington, D.C. 20515
Phone: 202-225-5211
FAX: 202-225-8272

Rep. Charles Norwood (R)
(Tenth District)
226 Cannon House Office Building
Washington, D.C. 20515
Phone: 202-225-4101
FAX: 202-226-1466

Rep. Cynthia McKinney (D)
(Eleventh District)
124 Cannon House Office Building
Washington, D.C. 20515
Phone: 202-225-1605
FAX: 202-226-0691

HAWAII

Senators

Senator Daniel K. Inouye (D)
722 Hart Senate Office Building
Washington, D.C. 20510
Phone: 202-224-3934
FAX: 202-224-6747

Senator Daniel K. Akaka (D)
720 Hart Senate Office Building
Washington, D.C. 20510
Phone: 202-224-6361
FAX: 202-224-2126

Representatives

Rep. Neil Abercrombie (D)
(First District)
1440 Longworth House Office
  Building
Washington, D.C. 20515
Phone: 202-225-2726
FAX: 202-225-4580

Rep. Patsy T. Mink (D)
(Second District)
2135 Rayburn House Office Building
Washington, D.C. 20515
Phone: 202-225-4906
FAX: 202-225-4987

IDAHO

Senators

Senator Dirk Kempthorne (R)
367 Dirksen Senate Office Building
Washington, D.C. 20510
Phone: 202-224-6142
FAX: 202-224-5893

Senator Larry Craig (R)
313 Hart Senate Office Building
Washington, D.C. 20510
Phone: 202-224-2752
FAX: 202-224-2573

Representatives

Rep. Helen Chenoweth (R)
(First District)
1117 Longworth House Office
  Building
Washington, D.C. 20515
Phone: 202-225-6611
FAX: 202-226-1213

Rep. Michael D. Crapo (R)
(Second District)
437 Cannon House Office Building
Washington, D.C. 20515
Phone: 202-225-5531
FAX: 202-334-1953

ILLINOIS

Senators

Senator Carol Moseley-Braun (D)
320 Hart Senate Office Building
Washington, D.C. 20510
Phone: 202-224-2854
FAX: (Unlisted)

Senator Paul Simon (D)
462 Dirksen Senate Office Building
Washington, D.C. 20510
Phone: 202-224-2152
FAX: 202-224-0868

Representatives

Rep. Bobby L. Rush (D)
(First District)
1725 Longworth House Office
  Building
Washington, D.C. 20515
Phone: 202-225-4372
FAX: 202-226-0333

Rep. Melvin J. Reynolds (D)
(Second District)
514 Cannon House Office Building
Washington, D.C. 20515
Phone: 202-225-0773
FAX: 202-225-0774

Rep. William O. Lipinski (D)
(Third District)
1501 Longworth House Office
  Building
Washington, D.C. 20515
Phone: 202-225-5701
FAX: 202-225-1012

Rep. Luis V. Gatierrez (D)
(Fourth District)
1208 Longworth House Office
  Building
Washington, D.C. 20515
Phone: 202-225-8203
FAX: 202-225-7810

Rep. Michael Flanaghan (D)
(Fifth Distruct)
2111 Rayburn House Office Building
Washington, D.C. 20515
Phone: 202-225-4061
FAX: 202-225-4064

Rep. Henry John Hyde (R)
(Sixth District)
2110 Rayburn House Office Building
Washington, D.C. 20515
Phone: 202-225-4561
FAX: 202-226-1240

Rep. Cardiss Collins (D)
(Seventh District)
2308 Rayburn House Office Building
Washington, D.C. 20515
Phone: 202-225-5006
FAX: 202-225-8396

Rep. Philip Miller Crane (R)
(Eighth District)
233 Cannon House Office Building
Washington, D.C. 20515
Phone: 202-225-3711
FAX: 202-225-7830

Rep. Sidney R. Yates (D)
(Ninth District)
2109 Rayburn House Office Building
Washington, D.C. 20515
Phone: 202-225-2111
FAX: 202-225-3493

Rep. John E. Porter (R)
(Tenth District)
1026 Longworth House Office
  Building
Washington, D.C. 20515
Phone: 202-225-4835
FAX: 202-225-0157

Rep. Gerald Weller (R)
(Eleventh District)
1032 Longworth House Office
  Building
Washington, D.C. 20515
Phone: 202-225-3635
FAX: 202-225-4447

Rep. Jerry F. Costello (D)
(Twelfth District)
119 Cannon House Office Building
Washington, D.C. 20515
Phone: 202-225-5661
FAX: 202-225-0285

Rep. Harris W. Fawell (R)
(Thirteenth District)
2342 Rayburn House Office Building
Washington, D.C. 20515
Phone: 202-225-3515
FAX: 202-225-9420

Rep. John D. Hastert (R)
(Fourteenth District)
2453 Rayburn House Office Building
Washington, D.C. 20515
Phone: 202-225-2976
FAX: 202-225-0697

Rep. Thomas Ewing (R)
(Fifteenth District)
1317 Longworth House Office
  Building
Washington, D.C. 20515
Phone: 202-225-2371
FAX: 202-225-8071

Rep. Donald Manzullo (R)
(Sixteenth District)
506 Cannon House Office Building
Washington, D.C. 20515
Phone: 202-225-5676
FAX: 202-225-5284

Rep. Lane Evans (D)
(Seventeenth District)
2335 Rayburn House Office Building
Washington, D.C. 20515
Phone: 202-225-5905
FAX: 202-225-5396

Rep. Ray LaHood (R)
(Eighteenth District)
2112 Rayburn House Office Building
Washington, D.C. 20515
Phone: 202-225-6201
FAX: 202-225-9249

Rep. Glenn Poshard (D)
(Nineteenth District)
107 Cannon House Office Building
Washington, D.C. 20515
Phone: 202-225-5201
FAX: 202-225-1541

Rep. Richard J. Durbin (D)
(Twentieth District)
2463 Rayburn House Office Building
Washington, D.C. 20515
Phone: 202-225-5271
FAX: 202-225-0170

INDIANA

Senators
Senator Richard Green Lugar (R)
306 Hart Senate Office Building
Washington, D.C. 20510
Phone: 202-224-4814
FAX: 202-224-7877

Senator Daniel R. Coats (R)
404 Russell Senate Office Building
Washington, D.C. 20510
Phone: 202-224-5623
FAX: 202-224-1966

Representatives
Rep. Peter J. Visclosky (D)
(First District)
2464 Rayburn House Office Building
Washington, D.C. 20515
Phone: 202-225-2461
FAX: 202-225-2493

Rep. David McIntosh (R)
(Second District)
2217 Rayburn House Office Building
Washington, D.C. 20515
Phone: 202-225-3021
FAX: 202-225-8140

Rep. Tim Roemer (D)
(Third District)
415 Cannon House Office Building
Washington, D.C. 20515
Phone: 202-225-3915
FAX: 202-225-6798

Rep. Mark Souder (R)
(Fourth District)
1513 Longworth House Office
  Building
Washington, D.C. 20515
Phone: 202-225-4436
FAX: 202-225-8810

Rep. Steve Buyer (R)
(Fifth District)
1419 Longworth House Office
  Building
Washington, D.C. 20515
Phone: 202-225-5037
FAX: (Unlisted)

Rep. Dan Burton (R)
(Sixth District)
2411 Rayburn House Office Building
Washington, D.C. 20515
Phone: 202-225-2276
FAX: 202-225-0016

Rep. John T. Myers (R)
(Seventh District)
2372 Rayburn House Office Building
Washington, D.C. 20515
Phone: 202-225-5805
FAX: 202-225-1649

Rep. John Hostettler (R)
(Eighth District)
306 Cannon House Office Building
Washington, D.C. 20515
Phone: 202-225-4636
FAX: 202-225-4688

Rep. Lee H. Hamilton (D)
(Ninth District)
2187 Rayburn House Office Building
Washington, D.C. 20515
Phone: 202-225-5315
FAX: 202-225-1101

Rep. Andrew Jacobs, Jr. (D)
(Tenth District)
2313 Rayburn House Office Building
Washington, D.C. 20515
Phone: 202-225-4011
FAX: 202-226-4093

IOWA

Senators
Senator Charles E. Grassley (R)
135 Hart Senate Office Building
Washington, D.C. 20510
Phone: 202-224-3744
FAX: 202-224-6020

Senator Thomas R. Harkin (D)
531 Hart Senate Office Building
Washington, D.C. 20510
Phone: 202-224-3254
FAX: 202-224-9369

Representatives
Rep. James A. S. Leach (R)
(First District)
2186 Longworth House Office
  Building
Washington, D.C. 20515
Phone: 202-225-6576
FAX: 202-226-1278

Rep. Jim Nussle (R)
(Second District)
308 Cannon House Office Building
Washington, D.C. 20515
Phone: 202-225-2911
FAX: 202-225-9129

Rep. James R. Lightfoot (R)
(Third District)
2444 Rayburn House Office Building
Washington, D.C. 20515
Phone: 202-225-3806
FAX: 202-225-6973

Rep. Greg Ganske (R)
(Fourth District)
2373 Rayburn House Office Building
Washington, D.C. 20515
Phone: 202-225-4426
FAX: (Unlisted)

Rep. Tom Latham (R)
(Fifth District)
418 Cannon House Office Building
Washington, D.C. 20515
Phone: 202-225-5476
FAX: 202-225-5796

KANSAS

Senators
Senator Robert Dole (R)
141 Hart Senate Office Building
Washington, D.C. 20510
Phone: 202-224-6521
FAX: 202-224-8952

Senator Nancy Landon Kassebaum (R)
302 Russell Senate Office Building
Washington, D.C. 20510
Phone: 202-224-4774
FAX: 202-224-3514

Representatives
Rep. Charles P. Roberts (R)
(First District)
1125 Longworth House Office
    Building
Washington, D.C. 20515
Phone: 202-225-2715
FAX: 202-225-5375

Rep. Sam Brownback (R)
(Second District)
2243 Longworth House Office
    Building
Washington, D.C. 20515
Phone: 202-225-6601
FAX: 202-225-1445

Rep. Jan Meyers (R)
(Third District)
2338 Rayburn House Office Building
Washington, D.C. 20515
Phone: 202-225-2865
FAX: 202-225-0554

Rep. Todd Tiahrt (R)
(Fourth District)
2371 Rayburn House Office Building
Washington, D.C. 20515
Phone: 202-225-6216
FAX: 202-225-5398

KENTUCKY

Senators
Senator Wendell Hampton Ford (D)
173A Russell Senate Office Building
Washington, D.C. 20510
Phone: 202-224-4343
FAX: 202-224-1144

Senator Mitch McConnell (R)
120 Russell Senate Office Building
Washington, D.C. 20510
Phone: 202-224-2541
FAX: 202-224-2499

Representatives
Rep. Edward Whitfield (R)
(First District)
1533 Longworth House Office
    Building
Washington, D.C. 20515
Phone: 202-225-3115
FAX: 202-225-2169

Rep. Ron Lewis (R)
(Second District)
2333 Rayburn House Office Building
Washington, D.C. 20515
Phone: 202-225-3501
FAX: (Unlisted)

Rep. Mike Ward (D)
(Third District)
2246 Rayburn House Office Building
Washington, D.C. 20515
Phone: 202-225-5401
FAX: (unlisted)

Rep. Jim Bunning (R)
(Fourth District)
2437 Rayburn House Office Building
Washington, D.C. 20515
Phone: 202-225-3465
FAX: 202-225-0003

Rep. Harold D. Rogers (R)
(Fifth District)
2468 Cannon House Office Building
Washington, D.C. 20515
Phone: 202-225-4601
FAX: 202-225-0940

Rep. Scotty Baesler (D)
(Sixth District)
508 Cannon House Office Building
Washington, D.C. 20515
Phone: 202-225-4706
FAX: 202-225-2122

LOUISIANA

Senators

Senator J. Bennett Johnston, Jr. (D)
136 Hart Senate Office Building
Washington, D.C. 20510
Phone: 202-224-5824
FAX: 202-224-2952

Senator John B. Breaux (D)
516 Hart Senate Office Building
Washington, D.C. 20510
Phone: 202-224-4623
FAX: 202-224-2435

Representatives

Rep. Robert Livingston, Jr. (R)
(First District)
2368 Longworth House Office
  Building
Washington, D.C. 20515
Phone: 202-225-3015
FAX: 202-225-0739

Rep. William J. Jefferson (D)
(Second District)
428 Cannon House Office Building
Washington, D.C. 20515
Phone: 202-225-6636
FAX: 202-225-1988

Rep. W. J. "Billy" Tauzin (D)
(Third District)
2330 Rayburn House Office Building
Washington, D.C. 20515
Phone: 202-225-4031
FAX: 202-225-0563

Rep. Cleo Fields (D)
(Fourth District)
513 Cannon House Office Building
Washington, D.C. 20515
Phone: 202-225-8490
FAX: 202-225-8959

Rep. James O. McCrery, III (R)
(Fifth District)
225 Cannon House Office Building
Washington, D.C. 20515
Phone: 202-225-2777
FAX: 202-225-8039

Rep. Richard H. Baker (R)
(Sixth District)
434 Cannon House Office Building
Washington, D.C. 20515
Phone: 202-225-3901
FAX: 202-225-7313

Rep. James A. Hayes (D)
(Seventh District)
2432 Rayburn House Office Building
Washington, D.C. 20515
Phone: 202-225-2031
FAX: 202-225-1175

MAINE

Senators

Senator William S. Cohen (R)
322 Hart Senate Office Building
Washington, D.C. 20510
Phone: 202-224-2523
FAX: 202-224-2693

Senator Olympia Snow (R)
176 Russell Senate Office Building
Washington, D.C. 20510
Phone: 202-224-5344
FAX: 202-224-6853

Representatives

Rep. James Longley (R)
(First District)
1530 Longworth House Office
  Building
Washington, D.C. 20515
Phone: 202-225-6116
FAX: 202-225-9065

Rep. John Baldacci (D)
(Second District)
2268 Rayburn House Office Building
Washington, D.C. 20515
Phone: 202-225-6306
FAX: 202-225-8297

MARYLAND

Senators
Senator Paul S. Sarbanes (D)
309 Hart Senate Office Building
Washington, D.C. 20510
Phone: 202-224-4524
FAX: 202-224-1651

Senator Barbara A. Mikulski (D)
709 Hart Senate Office Building
Washington, D.C. 20510
Phone: 202-224-4654
FAX: 202-224-8858

Representatives
Rep. Wayne T. Gilchrest (R)
(First District)
412 Cannon House Office Building
Washington, D.C. 20515
Phone: 202-225-5311
FAX: 202-225-0254

Rep. Robert Erlich (R)
(Second District)
1610 Longworth House Office
   Building
Washington, D.C. 20515
Phone: 202-225-3061
FAX: 202-225-4251

Rep. Benjamin L. Cardin (D)
(Third District)
227 Cannon House Office Building
Washington, D.C. 20515
Phone: 202-225-4016
FAX: 202-225-9219

Rep. Albert R. Wynn (D)
(Fourth District)
423 Cannon House Office Building
Washington, D.C. 20515
Phone: 202-225-8699
FAX: 202-225-8714

Rep. Steny H. Hoyer (D)
(Fifth District)
1705 Longworth House Office
   Building
Washington, D.C. 20515
Phone: 202-225-4131
FAX: 202-225-4300

Rep. Roscoe Bartlett (R)
(Sixth District)
312 Cannon House Office Building
Washington, D.C. 20515
Phone: 202-225-2721
FAX: 202-225-2193

Rep. Kweisi Mfume (D)
(Seventh District)
2419 Rayburn House Office Building
Washington, D.C. 20515
Phone: 202-225-4741
FAX: 202-225-3178

Rep. Constance A. Morella (R)
(Eighth District)
223 Cannon House Office Building
Washington, D.C. 20515
Phone: 202-225-5341
FAX: 202-225-1389

MASSACHUSETTS

Senators
Senator Edward M. Kennedy (D)
315 Russell Senate Office Building
Washington, D.C. 20510
Phone: 202-224-4543
FAX: 202-224-2417

Senator John Kerry (D)
421 Russell Senate Office Building
Washington, D.C. 20510
Phone: 202-224-2742
FAX: 202-224-8525

Representatives
Rep. John W. Oliver (D)
(First District)
1323 Longworth House Office
  Building
Washington, D.C. 20515
Phone: 202-225-5335
FAX: 202-226-1224

Rep. Richard E. Neal (D)
(Second District)
131 Cannon House Office Building
Washington, D.C. 20515
Phone: 202-225-5601
FAX: 202-225-8112

Rep. Peter L. Blute (R)
(Third District)
1029 Longworth House Office
  Building
Washington, D.C. 20515
Phone: 202-225-6101
FAX: 202-225-2217

Rep. Barney Frank (D)
(Fourth District)
2404 Rayburn House Office Building
Washington, D.C. 20515
Phone: 202-225-5931
FAX: 202-225-0182

Rep. Martin T. Meehan (D)
(Fifth District)
1223 Longworth House Office
  Building
Washington, D.C. 20515
Phone: 202-225-3411
FAX: 202-225-0771

Rep. Peter G. Torkildsen (R)
(Sixth District)
120 Cannon House Office Building
Washington, D.C. 20515
Phone: 202-225-8020
FAX: 202-225-8037

Rep. Edward J. Markey (D)
(Seventh District)
2133 Rayburn House Office Building
Washington, D.C. 20515
Phone: 202-225-2836
FAX: 202-225-8689

Rep. Joseph P. Kennedy, II (D)
(Eighth District)
1210 Longworth House Office
  Building
Washington, D.C. 20515
Phone: 202-225-5111
FAX: 202-225-9322

Rep. John J. Moakley (D)
(Ninth District)
235 Cannon House Office Building
Washington, D.C. 20515
Phone: 202-225-8273
FAX: 202-225-3984

Rep. Gerry E. Studds (D)
(Tenth District)
237 Cannon House Office Building
Washington, D.C. 20515
Phone: 202-225-3111
FAX: 202-225-2212

MICHIGAN

Senators
Senator Spencer Abraham (R)
105 Dirksen Senate Office Building
Washington, D.C. 20510
Phone: 202-224-4822
FAX: 202-224-8834

Senator Carl M. Levin (D)
459 Russell Senate Office Building
Washington, D.C. 20510
Phone: 202-224-6221
FAX: 202-224-5908

Representatives
Rep. Bart Stupak (D)
(First District)
317 Cannon House Office Building
Washington, D.C. 20515
Phone: 202-225-4735
FAX: 202-225-4744

Rep. Peter Hoekstra (R)
(Second District)
1319 Longworth House Office
  Building
Washington, D.C. 20515
Phone: 202-225-4401
FAX: 202-226-0779

Rep. Vernon Ehlers (R)
(Third District)
1526 Longworth House Office
  Building
Washington, D.C. 20515
Phone: 202-225-3831
FAX: (Unlisted)

Rep. David Camp (R)
(Fourth District)
137 Cannon House Office Building
Washington, D.C. 20515
Phone: 202-225-3561
FAX: 202-225-9679

Rep. James A. Barcia (D)
(Fifth District)
1717 Longworth House Office
  Building
Washington, D.C. 20515
Phone: 202-225-8171
FAX: 202-225-2168

Rep. Frederick S. Upton (R)
(Sixth District)
2439 Longworth House Office
  Building
Washington, D.C. 20515
Phone: 202-225-3761
FAX: 202-225-4986

Rep. Nick Smith (R)
(Seventh District)
1708 Longworth House Office
  Building
Washington, D.C. 20515
Phone: 202-225-6276
FAX: 202-225-6281

Rep. Dick Chrysler (R)
(Eighth District)
2347 Rayburn House Office Building
Washington, D.C. 20515
Phone: 202-225-4872
FAX: 202-225-1260

Rep. Dale F. Kildee (D)
(Ninth District)
2239 Rayburn House Office Building
Washington, D.C. 20515
Phone: 202-225-3611
FAX: 202-225-6393

Rep. David E. Bonior (D)
(Tenth District)
2207 Rayburn House Office Building
Washington, D.C. 20515
Phone: 202-225-2106
FAX: 202-226-1169

Rep. Joe Knollenberg (R)
(Eleventh District)
1218 Longworth House Office
  Building
Washington, D.C. 20515
Phone: 202-225-5802
FAX: 202-226-2356

Rep. Sander Martin Levin (D)
(Twelfth District)
106 Cannon House Office Building
Washington, D.C. 20515
Phone: 202-225-4961
FAX: 202-226-1033

Rep. Lynn Rivers (D)
(Thirteenth District)
2107 Rayburn House Office Building
Washington, D.C. 20515
Phone: 202-225-6261
FAX: 202-225-0489

Rep. John Conyers, Jr. (D)
(Fourteenth District)
Rayburn House Office Building
Washington, D.C. 20515
Phone: 202-225-5126
FAX: 202-225-0072

Rep. Barbara-Rose Collins (D)
(Fifteenth District)
1108 Longworth House Office
  Building
Washington, D.C. 20515
Phone: 202-225-2261
FAX: 202-225-6645

Rep. John D. Dingell (D)
(Sixteenth District)
2328 Rayburn House Office Building
Washington, D.C. 20515
Phone: 202-225-4071
FAX: 202-225-7426

MINNESOTA

Senators
Senator Rod Grams (R)
154 Russell Senate Office Building
Washington, D.C. 20510
Phone: 202-224-3244
FAX: 202-224-9931

Senator Paul Wellstone (DFL)
717 Hart Senate Office Building
Washington, D.C. 20510
Phone: 202-224-5641
FAX: 202-224-8438

Representatives
Rep. Gil Gutknecht (DFL)
(First District)
436 Cannon House Office Building
Washington, D.C. 20515
Phone: 202-225-2472
FAX: 202-225-0051

Rep. David Minge (D)
(Second District)
1508 Longworth House Office
  Building
Washington, D.C. 20515
Phone: 202-225-2331
FAX: 202-226-0836

Rep. James Ramstad (R)
(Third District)
322 Cannon House Office Building
Washington, D.C. 20515
Phone: 202-225-2871
FAX: 202-225-6351

Rep. Bruce F. Vento (DFL)
(Fourth District)
2304 Rayburn House Office Building
Washington, D.C. 20515
Phone: 202-225-6631
FAX: 202-225-1968

Rep. Martin Olav Sabo (DFL)
(Fifth District)
2336 Rayburn House Office Building
Washington, D.C. 20515
Phone: 202-225-4755
FAX: 202-225-4886

Rep. William Luther (D)
(Sixth District)
1713 Longworth House Office
  Building
Washington, D.C. 20515
Phone: 202-225-2271
FAX: 202-225-9802

Rep. Collin C. Peterson (DFL)
(Seventh District)
1133 Longworth House Office
  Building
Washington, D.C. 20515
Phone: 202-225-2165
FAX: 202-225-1593

Rep. James L. Oberstar (DFL)
(Eighth District)
2366 Rayburn House Office Building
Washington, D.C. 20515
Phone: 202-225-6211
FAX: 202-225-0699

MISSISSIPPI

Senators
Senator Thad Cochran (R)
326 Russell Senate Office Building
Washington, D.C. 20510
Phone: 202-224-5054
FAX: 202-224-3576

Senator Trent Lott (R)
487 Russell Senate Office Building
Washington, D.C. 20510
Phone: 202-224-6253
FAX: 202-224-2262

Representatives
Rep. Roger Wicker (R)
(First District)
2314 Rayburn House Office Building
Washington, D.C. 20515
Phone: 202-225-4306
FAX: 202-225-4328

Rep. Bennie Thompson (D)
(Second District)
1408 Longworth House Office
  Building
Washington, D.C. 20515
Phone: 202-225-5876
FAX: 202-225-5898

Rep. G. V. "Sonny" Montgomery (D)
(Third District)
2184 Rayburn House Office Building
Washington, D.C. 20515
Phone: 202-225-5031
FAX: 202-225-3375

Rep. Mike Parker (D)
(Fourth District)
1410 Longworth House Office
  Building
Washington, D.C. 20515
Phone: 202-225-5865
FAX: 202-225-5886

Rep. Gene Taylor (D)
(Fifth District)
214 Cannon House Office Building
Washington, D.C. 20515
Phone: 202-225-5772
FAX: 202-225-7074

MISSOURI

Senators
Senator John Ashcroft (R)
249 Russell Senate Office Building
Washington, D.C. 20510
Phone: 202-224-6154
FAX: 202-224-7615

Senator Christopher Samuel "Kit"
  Bond (R)
293 Russell Senate Office Building
Washington, D.C. 20510
Phone: 202-224-5721
FAX: 202-224-7491

Representatives
Rep. William L. Clay (D)
(First District)
2306 Rayburn House Office Building
Washington, D.C. 20515
Phone: 202-225-2406
FAX: 202-225-1725

Rep. James M. Talent (R)
(Second District)
1022 Longworth House Office
  Building
Washington, D.C. 20515
Phone: 202-225-2561
FAX: 202-225-2563

Rep. Richard A. Gephardt (D)
(Third District)
1432 Longworth House Office
  Building
Washington, D.C. 20515
Phone: 202-225-2671
FAX: 202-225-7414

Rep. Isaac "Ike" Skelton, IV (D)
(Fourth District)
2227 Rayburn House Office Building
Washington, D.C. 20515
Phone: 202-225-2876
FAX: 202-225-2695

Rep. Karen McCarthy (D)
(Fifth District)
2334 Rayburn House Office Building
Washington, D.C. 20515
Phone: 202-225-4535
FAX: 202-225-5990

Rep. Pat Danner (D)
(Sixth District)
1217 Longworth House Office
  Building
Washington, D.C. 20515
Phone: 202-225-7041
FAX: 202-225-8221

Rep. Melton D. Hancock (R)
(Seventh District)
129 Cannon House Office Building
Washington, D.C. 20515
Phone: 202-225-6536
FAX: 202-225-7700

Rep. Bill Emerson (R)
(Eighth District)
2454 Cannon House Office Building
Washington, D.C. 20515
Phone: 202-225-4404
FAX: 202-225-9621

Rep. Harold L. Volkmer (D)
(Ninth District)
2409 Rayburn House Office Building
Washington, D.C. 20515
Phone: 202-225-2956
FAX: 202-225-7834

MONTANA

Senators
Senator Max Baucus (D)
511 Hart Senate Office Building
Washington, D.C. 20510
Phone: 202-224-2651
FAX: (Unavailable at T.O.P.)

Senator Conrad Burns (R)
183 Dirksen Senate Office Building
Washington, D.C. 20510
Phone: 202-224-2644
FAX: 202-224-8594

Representative At Large
Rep. Pat Williams (D)
2457 Rayburn House Office Building
Washington, D.C. 20515
Phone: 202-225-3211
FAX: 202-226-0244

NEBRASKA

Senators
Senator J. James Exon (D)
528 Hart Senate Office Building
Washington, D.C. 20510
Phone: 202-224-4224
FAX: 202-224-5213

Senator Joseph R. Kerrey (D)
303 Hart Senate Office Building
Washington, D.C. 20510
Phone: 202-224-6551
FAX: 202-224-7645

Representatives
Rep. Douglas K. Bereuter (R)
(First District)
2348 Rayburn House Office Building
Washington, D.C. 20515
Phone: 202-225-4806
FAX: 202-226-1148

Rep. Jon Christensen (R)
(Second District)
1113 Longworth House Office
  Building
Washington, D.C. 20515
Phone: 202-225-4155
FAX: 202-225-4684

Rep. William Barrett (R)
(Third District)
1213 Longworth House Office
  Building
Washington, D.C. 20515
Phone: 202-225-6435
FAX: 202-225-0207

NEVADA

Senators
Senator Harry M. Reid (D)
324 Hart Senate Office Building
Washington, D.C. 20510
Phone: 202-224-3542
FAX: 202-224-7327

Senator Richard H. Bryan (D)
364 Russell Senate Office Building
Washington, D.C. 20510
Phone: 202-224-6244
FAX: 202-224-1867

Representatives
Rep. John Ensign (D)
(First District)
2431 Rayburn House Office Building
Washington, D.C. 20515
Phone: 202-255-5965
FAX: 202-225-8808

Rep. Barbara F. Vucanovich (R)
(Second District)
2202 Rayburn House Office Building
Washington, D.C. 20515
Phone: 202-225-6155
FAX: 202-225-2319

NEW HAMPSHIRE

Senators
Senator Judd Gregg (R)
393 Russell Senate Office Building
Washington, D.C. 20510
Phone: 202-224-3324
FAX: 202-224-4952

Senator Robert C. Smith (R)
332 Dirksen Senate Office Building
Washington, D.C. 20510
Phone: 202-224-2841
FAX: 202-224-1353

Representatives
Rep. William Zeliff (R)
(First District)
224 Cannon House Office Building
Washington, D.C. 20515
Phone: 202-225-5456
FAX: 202-225-4370

Rep. Charles Bass (R)
(Second District)
230 Cannon House Office Building
Washington, D.C. 20515
Phone: 202-225-5206
FAX: 202-225-0046

NEW JERSEY

Senators
Senator Bill Bradley (D)
731 Hart Senate Office Building
Washington, D.C. 20510
Phone: 202-224-3224
FAX: 202-224-8567

Senator Frank R. Lautenberg (D)
506 Hart Senate Office Building
Washington, D.C. 20510
Phone: 202-224-4744
FAX: 202-224-9707

Representatives
Rep. Robert E. Andrews (D)
(First District)
1005 Longworth House Office
  Building
Washington, D.C. 20515
Phone: 202-225-6501
FAX: 202-225-6583

Rep. Frank Lobiondo (R)
(Second District)
241 Cannon House Office Building
Washington, D.C. 20515
Phone: 202-225-6572
FAX: 202-225-8530

Rep. H. James Saxton (R)
(Third District)
438 Cannon House Office Building
Washington, D.C. 20515
Phone: 202-225-4765
FAX: 202-225-0778

Rep. Christopher H. Smith (R)
(Fourth District)
2353 Rayburn House Office Building
Washington, D.C. 20515
Phone: 202-225-3765
FAX: 202-225-7768

Rep. Marge S. Roukema (R)
(Fifth District)
2244 Rayburn House Office Building
Washington, D.C. 20515
Phone: 202-225-4465
FAX: 202-225-9048

Rep. Frank J. Pallone, Jr. (D)
(Sixth District)
420 Cannon House Office Building
Washington, D.C. 20515
Phone: 202-225-4671
FAX: 202-225-9665

Rep. Bob Franks (R)
(Seventh District)
429 Cannon House Office Building
Washington, D.C. 20515
Phone: 202-225-5361
FAX: 202-225-9460

Rep. Bill Martini (R)
(Eighth District)
1728 Longworth House Office
  Building
Washington, D.C. 20515
Phone: 202-225-5751
FAX: 202-226-2273

Rep. Robert G. Torricelli (D)
(Ninth District)
2159 Rayburn House Office Building
Washington, D.C. 20515
Phone: 202-225-5061
FAX: 202-225-0843

Rep. Donald M. Payne (D)
(Tenth District)
417 Cannon House Office Building
Washington, D.C. 20515
Phone: 202-225-3436
FAX: 202-225-4160

Rep. Rodney Frelinghuysen (R)
(Eleventh District)
2447 Rayburn House Office Building
Washington, D.C. 20515
Phone: 202-225-5034
FAX: 202-225-0658

Rep. Richard Zimmer (R)
(Twelfth District)
228 Cannon House Office Building
Washington, D.C. 20515
Phone: 202-225-5801
FAX: 202-226-0792

Rep. Robert Menendez (D)
(Thirteenth District)
1531 Longworth House Office
   Building
Washington, D.C. 20515
Phone: 202-225-7919
FAX: 202-225-0792

NEW MEXICO

Senators
Senator Pete V. Domenici (R)
427 Dirksen Senate Office Building
Washington, D.C. 20510
Phone: 202-224-6621
FAX: 202-224-7371

Senator Jeff Bingaman (D)
524 Hart Senate Office Building
Washington, D.C. 20510
Phone: 202-224-5521
FAX: 202-224-1810

Representatives
Rep. Steven H. Schiff (R)
(First District)
1009 Longworth House Office
   Building
Washington, D.C. 20515
Phone: 202-225-6316
FAX: 202-225-4975

Rep. Joseph R. Skeen (R)
(Second District)
2367 Rayburn House Office Building
Washington, D.C. 20515
Phone: 202-225-2365
FAX: 202-225-9599

Rep. Bill Richardson (D)
(Third District)
2349 Rayburn House Office Building
Washington, D.C. 20515
Phone: 202-225-6190
FAX: 202-225-1950

NEW YORK

Senators
Senator Daniel Patrick Moynihan (D)
464 Russell Senate Office Building
Washington, D.C. 20510
Phone: 202-224-4451
FAX: 202-224-9293

Senator Alfonse M. D'Amato (R)
520 Hart Senate Office Building
Washington, D.C. 20510
Phone: 202-224-6542
FAX: 202-224-5871

Representatives
Rep. Michael Forbes (R)
(First District)
229 Cannon House Office Building
Washington, D.C. 20515
Phone: 202-225-3826
FAX: 202-225-0776

Rep. Rick Lazio (R)
(Second District)
314 Cannon House Office Building
Washington, D.C. 20515
Phone: 202-225-3335
FAX: 202-225-4669

Rep. Peter King (R)
(Third District)
118 Cannon House Office Building
Washington, D.C. 20515
Phone: 202-225-7896
FAX: 202-226-2279

Rep. Daniel Frisa (R)
(Fourth District)
116 Cannon House Office Building
Washington, D.C. 20515
Phone: 202-225-5516
FAX: 202-225-4672

Rep. Gary L. Ackerman (D)
(Fifth District)
2445 Rayburn House Office Building
Washington, D.C. 20515
Phone: 202-225-2601
FAX: 202-225-1589

Rep. Floyd H. Flake (D)
(Sixth District)
1035 Longworth House Office
  Building
Washington, D.C. 20515
Phone: 202-225-3461
FAX: 202-225-4169

Rep. Thomas J. Manton (D)
(Seventh District)
203 Cannon House Office Building
Washington, D.C. 20515
Phone: 202-225-3965
FAX: 202-225-1909

Rep. Jerrold Nadler (D)
(Eighth District)
424 Cannon House Office Building
Washington, D.C. 20515
Phone: 202-225-5635
FAX: 202-225-6923

Rep. Charles E. Schumer (D)
(Ninth District)
2412 Longworth House Office
  Building
Washington, D.C. 20515
Phone: 202-225-6616
FAX: 202-225-4183

Rep. Edolphus Towns (D)
(Tenth District)
2232 Rayburn House Office Building
Washington, D.C. 20515
Phone: 202-225-5936
FAX: 202-225-1018

Rep. Major R. Owens (D)
(Eleventh District)
2305 Rayburn House Office Building
Washington, D.C. 20515
Phone: 202-225-6231
FAX: 202-226-0112

Rep. Nydia Velazquez (D)
(Twelfth District)
132 Cannon House Office Building
Washington, D.C. 20515
Phone: 202-225-2361
FAX: 202-226-0327

Rep. Susan Molinari (R)
(Thirteenth District)
123 Cannon House Office Building
Washington, D.C. 20515
Phone: 202-225-3371
FAX: 202-225-1272

Rep. Carolyn Maloney (D)
(Fourteenth District)
1504 Longworth House Office
  Building
Washington, D.C. 20515
Phone: 202-225-7944
FAX: 202-225-4709

Rep. Charles Bernard Rangel (D)
(Fifteenth District)
2252 Rayburn House Office Building
Washington, D.C. 20515
Phone: 202-225-4365
FAX: 202-225-0816

Rep. Jose E. Serrano (D)
(Sixteenth District)
336 Cannon House Office Building
Washington, D.C. 20515
Phone: 202-225-4361
FAX: 202-225-6001

Rep. Eliot L. Engel (D)
(Seventeenth District)
1434 Longworth House Office
  Building
Washington, D.C. 20515
Phone: 202-225-2464
FAX: 202-225-5513

Rep. Nita M. Lowey (D)
(Eighteenth District)
1424 Longworth House Office
  Building
Washington, D.C. 20515
Phone: 202-225-6506
FAX: 202-225-0546

Rep. Sue Kelly (R)
(Nineteenth District)
2354 Rayburn House Office Building
Washington, D.C. 20515
Phone: 202-225-5441
FAX: 202-225-0962

Rep. Benjamin A. Gilman (R)
(Twentieth District)
2185 Rayburn House Office Building
Washington, D.C. 20515
Phone: 202-225-3776
FAX: 202-225-2541

Rep. Michael R. McNulty (D)
(Twenty-First District)
217 Cannon House Office Building
Washington, D.C. 20515
Phone: 202-225-5076
FAX: 202-225-5077

Rep. Gerald B. H. Solomon (R)
(Twenty-Second District)
2265 Rayburn House Office Building
Washington, D.C. 20515
Phone: 202-225-5614
FAX: 202-225-5234

Rep. Sherwood L. Boehlert (R)
(Twenty-Third District)
1127 Longworth House Office
  Building
Washington, D.C. 20515
Phone: 202-225-3665
FAX: 202-225-1891

Rep. John McHugh (R)
(Twenth-Fourth District)
416 Cannon House Office Building
Washington, D.C. 20515
Phone: 202-225-4611
FAX: 202-226-0621

Rep. James T. Walsh (R)
(Twenty-Fifth District)
1330 Longworth House Office
  Building
Washington, D.C. 20515
Phone: 202-225-3701
FAX: 202-225-4042

Rep. Maurice Hinchey (D)
(Twenty-Sixth District)
1313 Longworth House Office
  Building
Washington, D.C. 20515
Phone: 202-225-6335
FAX: 202-226-0774

Rep. L. William Paxon (R)
(Twenty-Seventh District)
1314 Longworth House Office
  Building
Washington, D.C. 20515
Phone: 202-225-5265
FAX: 202-225-5910

Rep. Louise M. Slaughter (D)
(Twenty-Eighth District)
2421 Rayburn House Office Building
Washington, D.C. 20515
Phone: 202-225-3615
FAX: 202-225-7822

Rep. John J. Lafalce (D)
(Twenty-Ninth District)
2310 Rayburn House Office Building
Washington, D.C. 20515
Phone: 202-225-3231
FAX: 202-225-8693

Rep. Jack Quinn (R)
(Thirtieth District)
331 Cannon House Office Building
Washington, D.C. 20515
Phone: 202-225-3306
FAX: 202-226-0347

Rep. Amory "Amo" Houghton, Jr. (R)
(Thirty-First District)
1110 Longworth House Office
   Building
Washington, D.C. 20515
Phone: 202-225-3161
FAX: 202-225-5574

NORTH CAROLINA

Senators
Senator Jesse A. Helms (R)
403 Dirksen Senate Office Building
Washington, D.C. 20510
Phone: 202-224-6342
FAX: 202-224-7588

Senator Lauch Faircloth (R)
702 Hart Senate Office Building
Washington, D.C. 20510
Phone: 202-224-3154
FAX: 202-224-7406

Representatives
Rep. Eva Clayton (D)
(First District)
222 Cannon House Office Building
Washington, D.C. 20515
Phone: 202-225-3101
FAX: 202-225-3354

Rep. Walter Jones (D)
(Second District)
2229 Rayburn House Office Building
Washington, D.C. 20515
Phone: 202-225-4531
FAX: 202-225-1539

Rep. Walter Jones (R)
(Third District)
2436 Rayburn House Office Building
Washington, D.C. 20515
Phone: 202-225-3415
FAX: 202-225-0666

Rep. Fred Heineman (D)
(Fourth District)
2458 Rayburn House Office Building
Washington, D.C. 20515
Phone: 202-225-1784
FAX: 202-225-6314

Rep. Richard Burr (D)
(Fifth District)
2469 Rayburn House Office Building
Washington, D.C. 20515
Phone: 202-225-2071
FAX: 202-225-4060

Rep. John Howard Coble (R)
(Sixth District)
403 Cannon House Office Building
Washington, D.C. 20515
Phone: 202-225-3065
FAX: 202-225-8611

Rep. Charles G. Rose, III (D)
(Seventh District)
2230 Rayburn House Office Building
Washington, D.C. 20515
Phone: 202-225-2731
FAX: 202-225-2470

Rep. W. B. "Bill" Hefner (D)
(Eighth District)
2470 Rayburn House Office Building
Washington, D.C. 20515
Phone: 202-225-3715
FAX: 202-225-4036

Rep. Sue Myrick (R)
(Ninth District)
401 Cannon House Office Building
Washington, D.C. 20515
Phone: 202-225-1976
FAX: 202-225-8995

Rep. David Funderburk (R)
(Tenth District)
2238 Rayburn House Office Building
Washington, D.C. 20515
Phone: 202-225-2576
FAX: 202-225-0316

Rep. Charles H. Taylor (R)
(Eleventh District)
516 Cannon House Office Building
Washington, D.C. 20515
Phone: 202-225-6401
FAX: 202-225-0519

Rep. Melvin Watt (D)
(Twelfth District)
1232 Longworth House Office
  Building
Washington, D.C. 20515
Phone: 202-225-1510
FAX: 202-225-1512

NORTH DAKOTA

Senators
Senator Byron L. Dorgan (D)
713 Hart Senate Office Building
Washington, D.C. 20510
Phone: 202-224-2551
FAX: 202-224-1193

Senator Kent Conrad (D)
724 Hart Senate Office Building
Washington, D.C. 20510
Phone: 202-224-2043
FAX: 202-224-7776

Representative At Large
Rep. Earl Pomeroy (D)
318 Cannon House Office Building
Washington, D.C. 20515
Phone: 202-225-2611
FAX: 202-226-0893

OHIO

Senators
Senator John H. Glenn, Jr. (D)
503 Hart Senate Office Building
Washington, D.C. 20510
Phone: 202-224-3353
FAX: 202-224-7983

Senator Mike DeWine (R)
140 Russell Senate Office Building
Washington, D.C. 20510
Phone: 202-224-2315
FAX: 202-224-6519

Representatives
Rep. Steve Chabot (D)
(First District)
503 Cannon House Office Building
Washington, D.C. 20515
Phone: 202-225-2216
FAX: 202-225-4732

Rep. Rob Portman (R)
(Second District)
238 Cannon House Office Building
Washington, D.C. 20515
Phone: 202-225-3164
FAX: 202-225-1992

Rep. Tony P. Hall (D)
(Third District)
2264 Rayburn House Office Building
Washington, D.C. 20515
Phone: 202-225-6465
FAX: 202-225-6766

Rep. Michael G. Oxley (R)
(Fourth District)
2233 Rayburn House Office Building
Washington, D.C. 20515
Phone: 202-225-2676
FAX: 202-226-1160

Rep. Paul E. Gillmor (R)
(Fifth District)
1203 Longworth House Office
  Building
Washington, D.C. 20515
Phone: 202-225-6405
FAX: 202-225-1985

Rep. Frank Cremeans (R)
(Sixth District)
1429 Longworth House Office
  Building
Washington, D.C. 20515
Phone: 202-225-5705
FAX: 202-226-0331

Rep. David L. Hobson (R)
(Seventh District)
1507 Longworth House Office
  Building
Washington, D.C. 20515
Phone: 202-225-4324
FAX: 202-225-1984

Rep. John A. Boehner (R)
(Eighth District)
1020 Longworth House Office
  Building
Washington, D.C. 20515
Phone: 202-225-6205
FAX: 202-225-0704

Rep. Marcy Kaptur (D)
(Ninth District)
2104 Rayburn House Office Building
Washington, D.C. 20515
Phone: 202-225-4146
FAX: 202-225-7711

Rep. Martin R. Hoke (R)
(Tenth District)
212 Cannon House Office Building
Washington, D.C. 20515
Phone: 202-225-5871
FAX: 202-226-0994

Rep. Louis Stokes (D)
(Eleventh District)
2365 Rayburn House Office Building
Washington, D.C. 20515
Phone: 202-225-7032
FAX: 202-225-1339

Rep. John R. Kasich (R)
(Twelfth District)
1131 Longworth House Office
  Building
Washington, D.C. 20515
Phone: 202-225-5355
FAX: (Unlisted)

Rep. Sherrod Brown (D)
(Thirteenth District)
1407 Longworth House Office
  Building
Washington, D.C. 20515
Phone: 202-225-3401
FAX: 202-225-2266

Rep. Thomas C. Sawyer (D)
(Fourteenth District)
1414 Longworth House Office
  Building
Washington, D.C. 20515
Phone: 202-225-5231
FAX: 202-225-5278

Rep. Deborah Pryce (R)
(Fifteenth District)
128 Cannon House Office Building
Washington, D.C. 20515
Phone: 202-225-2015
FAX: 202-226-0986

Rep. Ralph S. Regula (R)
(Sixteenth District)
2309 Rayburn House Office Building
Washington, D.C. 20515
Phone: 202-225-3876
FAX: 202-225-3059

Rep. James A. Traficant, Jr. (D)
(Seventeenth District)
2446 Rayburn House Office Building
Washington, D.C. 20515
Phone: 202-225-5261
FAX: 202-225-3719

Rep. E. Bob Ney (R)
(Eighteenth District)
2183 Rayburn House Office Building
Washington, D.C. 20515
Phone: 202-225-6265
FAX: 202-225-3087

Rep. Steven LaTourette (D)
(Nineteenth District)
431 Cannon House Office Building
Washington, D.C. 20515
Phone: 202-225-5731
FAX: 202-225-9114

OKLAHOMA

Senators
Senator James Inhofe (R)
453 Russell Senate Office Building
Washington, D.C. 20510
Phone: 202-224-4721
FAX: (Unlisted)

Senator Donald L. Nickles (R)
133 Hart Senate Office Building
Washington, D.C. 20510
Phone: 202-224-5754
FAX: 202-224-6008

Representatives
Rep. Steve Largent (R)
(First District)
442 Cannon House Office Building
Washington, D.C. 20515
Phone: 202-225-2211
FAX: 202-225-9187

Rep. Tom Coburn (R)
(Second District)
2329 Rayburn House Office Building
Washington, D.C. 20515
Phone: 202-225-2701
FAX: 202-225-2796

Rep. William Brewster (D)
(Third District)
1727 Longworth House Office
  Building
Washington, D.C. 20515
Phone: 202-225-4565
FAX: 202-225-9029

Rep. J. C. Watts (R)
(Fourth District)
2344 Rayburn House Office Building
Washington, D.C. 20515
Phone: 202-225-6165
FAX: 202-225-9746

Rep. Ernest J. Istook, Jr. (R)
(Fifth District)
1116 Longworth House Office
  Building
Washington, D.C. 20515
Phone: 202-225-2132
FAX: 202-226-1463

Rep. Frank Lucas (R)
(Sixth District)
2206 Rayburn House Office Building
Washington, D.C. 20515
Phone: 202-225-5565
FAX: 202-225-8698

OREGON

Senator
Senator Mark O. Hatfield (R)
711 Hart Senate Office Building
Washington, D.C. 20510
Phone: 202-224-3753
FAX: 202-224-0276

(other Oregon senator's office vacant
  at time of publication)

Representatives
Rep. Elizabeth Furse (D)
(First District)
316 Cannon House Office Building
Washington, D.C. 20515
Phone: 202-225-0855
FAX: 202-225-9497

Rep. Wes Cooley (R)
(Second District)
118 Cannon House Office Building
Washington, D.C. 20515
Phone: 202-225-6730
FAX: 202-225-3129

Rep. Ron Wyden (D)
(Third District)
1111 Longworth House Office
Building
Washington, D.C. 20515
Phone: 202-225-4811
FAX: 202-225-8941

Rep. Peter A. DeFazio (D)
(Fourth District)
1233 Longworth House Office
Building
Washington, D.C. 20515
Phone: 202-225-6416
FAX: 202-225-0694

Rep. Catherine Webber (D)
(Fifth District)
218 Cannon House Office Building
Washington, D.C. 20510
Phone: 202-225-5711
FAX: 202-225-9477

PENNSYLVANIA

Senators
Senator Rick Santorum (R)
521 Dirksen Senate Office Building
Washington, D.C. 20510
Phone: 202-224-6324
FAX: 202-224-4161

Senator Arlen Specter (R)
530 Hart Senate Office Building
Washington, D.C. 20510
Phone: 202-224-4254
FAX: 202-224-1893

Representatives
Rep. Thomas M. Foglietta (D)
(First District)
341 Cannon House Office Building
Washington, D.C. 20515
Phone: 202-225-4731
FAX: 202-225-0088

Rep. Chaka Fattah (D)
(Second District)
410 Cannon House Office Building
Washington, D.C. 20515
Phone: 202-225-4001
FAX: 202-225-7362

Rep. Robert A. Borski (D)
(Third District)
2161 Rayburn House Office Building
Washington, D.C. 20515
Phone: 202-225-8251
FAX: 202-225-4628

Rep. Ron Klink (D)
(Fourth District)
1130 Longworth House Office
Building
Washington, D.C. 20515
Phone: 202-225-2565
FAX: 202-226-2274

Rep. William F. Clinger, Jr. (R)
(Fifth District)
2160 Rayburn House Office Building
Washington, D.C. 20515
Phone: 202-225-5121
FAX: 202-225-4681

Rep. Tim Holden (D)
(Sixth District)
1421 Longworth House Office
   Building
Washington, D.C. 20515
Phone: 202-225-5546
FAX: 202-226-0996

Rep. Wayne C. Weldon (R)
(Seventh District)
2452 Cannon House Office Building
Washington, D.C. 20515
Phone: 202-225-2011
FAX: 202-225-8137

Rep. Jim Greenwood (R)
(Eighth District)
515 Cannon House Office Building
Washington, D.C. 20515
Phone: 202-225-4276
FAX: 202-225-9511

Rep. R. G. "Bud" Shuster (R)
(Ninth District)
2188 Rayburn House Office Building
Washington, D.C. 20515
Phone: 202-225-2431
FAX: 202-225-2486

Rep. Joseph M. McDade (R)
(Tenth District)
2370 Rayburn House Office Building
Washington, D.C. 20515
Phone: 202-225-3731
FAX: 202-225-9594

Rep. Paul E. Kanjorski (D)
(Eleventh District)
2429 Cannon House Office Building
Washington, D.C. 20515
Phone: 202-225-6511
FAX: 202-225-9024

Rep. John P. Murtha (D)
(Twelfth District)
2423 Rayburn House Office Building
Washington, D.C. 20515
Phone: 202-225-2065
FAX: 202-225-5709

Rep. Jon Fox (R)
(Thirteenth District)
1516 Rayburn House Office Building
Washington, D.C. 20515
Phone: 202-225-6111
FAX: 202-226-0798

Rep. William J. Coyne (D)
(Fourteenth District)
2455 Rayburn House Office Building
Washington, D.C. 20515
Phone: 202-225-2301
FAX: 202-225-1844

Rep. Paul McHale (D)
(Fifteenth District)
511 Rayburn House Office Building
Washington, D.C. 20515
Phone: 202-225-6411
FAX: 202-225-5320

Rep. Robert S. Walker (R)
(Sixteenth District)
2369 Rayburn House Office Building
Washington, D.C. 20515
Phone: 202-225-2411
FAX: 202-225-2484

Rep. George W. Gekas (R)
(Seventeenth District)
2410 Longworth House Office
   Building
Washington, D.C. 20515
Phone: 202-225-4315
FAX: 202-225-8440

Rep. Michael Doyle (D)
(Eighteenth District)
1222 Longworth House Office
   Building
Washington, D.C. 20515
Phone: 202-225-2135
FAX: 202-225-7747

Rep. William F. Goodling (R)
(Nineteenth District)
2263 Rayburn House Office Building
Washington, D.C. 20515
Phone: 202-225-5836
FAX: 202-226-1000

Rep. Frank Mascara (D)
(Twentieth District)
2210 Rayburn House Office Building
Washington, D.C. 20515
Phone: 202-225-4665
FAX: 202-225-4772

Rep. Philip English (R)
(Twenty-First District)
1714 Longworth House Office
  Building
Washington, D.C. 20515
Phone: 202-225-5406
FAX: 202-225-1081

RHODE ISLAND

Senators

Senator Claiborne Pell (D)
335 Russell Senate Office Building
Washington, D.C. 20510
Phone: 202-224-4642
FAX: 202-224-4680

Senator John H. Chafee (R)
567 Dirksen Senate Office Building
Washington, D.C. 20510
Phone: 202-224-2921
FAX: 202-224-7472

Representatives

Rep. Patrick Kennedy (D)
(First District)
326 Cannon House Office Building
Washington, D.C. 20515
Phone: 202-225-4911
FAX: 202-225-4417

Rep. John F. Reed (R)
(Second District)
1510 Longworth House Office
  Building
Washington, D.C. 20515
Phone: 202-225-2735
FAX: 202-225-9580

SOUTH CAROLINA

Senators

Senator James Strom Thurmond (R)
217 Russell Senate Office Building
Washington, D.C. 20510
Phone: 202-224-5972
FAX: 202-224-1300

Senator Ernest F. Hollings (D)
125 Russell Senate Office Building
Washington, D.C. 20510
Phone: 202-224-6121
FAX: 202-224-3573

Representatives

Rep. Mark Sanford (R)
(First District)
231 Cannon House Office Building
Washington, D.C. 20515
Phone: 202-225-3176
FAX: 202-225-4340

Rep. Floyd D. Spence (R)
(Second District)
2405 Rayburn House Office Building
Washington, D.C. 20515
Phone: 202-225-2452
FAX: 202-225-2455

Rep. Lindsey Graham (R)
(Third District)
221 Cannon House Office Building
Washington, D.C. 20515
Phone: 202-225-5301
FAX: 202-225-5383

Rep. Bob Inglis (R)
(Fourth District)
1237 Longworth House Office
  Building
Washington, D.C. 20515
Phone: 202-225-6030
FAX: 202-226-1177

Rep. John M. Spratt, Jr. (D)
(Fifth District)
1536 Longworth House Office
  Building
Washington, D.C. 20515
Phone: 202-225-5501
FAX: 202-225-0464

Rep. James E. Clyburn (D)
(Sixth District)
319 Cannon House Office Building
Washington, D.C. 20515
Phone: 202-225-3315
FAX: 202-225-2313

SOUTH DAKOTA

Senators
Senator Larry Pressler (R)
283 Rayburn House Office Building
Washington, D.C. 20510
Phone: 202-224-5842
FAX: 202-224-1630

Senator Thomas Andrew Daschle (D)
317 Hart Senate Office Building
Washington, D.C. 20510
Phone: 202-224-2321
FAX: 202-224-2047

Representative At Large
Rep. Timothy P. Johnson (D)
2438 Rayburn House Office Building
Washington, D.C. 20515
Phone: 202-225-2801
FAX: 202-225-2427

TENNESSEE

Senators
Senator Fred Thompson (R)
363 Russell Senate Office Building
Washington, D.C. 20510
Phone: 202-224-3344
FAX: 202-224-8062

Senator Bill Frist (R)
506 Dirksen Senate Office Building
Washington, D.C. 20510
Phone: 202-224-1036
FAX: 202-228-3679

Representatives
Rep. James H. Quillen (R)
(First District)
102 Cannon House Office Building
Washington, D.C. 20515
Phone: 202-225-6356
FAX: 202-225-7812

Rep. John J. Duncan, Jr. (R)
(Second District)
115 Cannon House Office Building
Washington, D.C. 20515
Phone: 202-225-5435
FAX: 202-225-6440

Rep. Zach Wamp (R)
(Third District)
2406 Rayburn House Office Building
Washington, D.C. 20515
Phone: 202-225-3271
FAX: 202-225-6974

Rep. Van Hilleary (R)
(Fourth District)
125 Cannon House Office Building
Washington, D.C. 20515
Phone: 202-225-6831
FAX: 202-225-4520

Rep. Bob Clement (D)
(Fifth District)
1230 Cannon House Office Building
Washington, D.C. 20515
Phone: 202-225-4311
FAX: 202-225-1035

Rep. Barton J. Gordon (D)
(Sixth District)
103 Cannon House Office Building
Washington, D.C. 20515
Phone: 202-225-4231
FAX: 202-225-6887

Rep. Ed Bryant (R)
(Seventh District)
339 Cannon House Office Building
Washington, D.C. 20515
Phone: 202-225-2811
FAX: 202-225-2814

Rep. John S. Tanner (D)
(Eighth District)
1427 Longworth House Office
   Building
Washington, D.C. 20515
Phone: 202-225-4714
FAX: 202-225-1765

Rep. Harold Eugene Ford (D)
(Ninth District)
3211 Rayburn House Office Building
Washington, D.C. 20515
Phone: 202-225-3265
FAX: 202-225-9215

TEXAS

Senators
Senator Phil Gramm (R)
370 Russell Senate Office Building
Washington, D.C. 20510
Phone: 202-224-2934
FAX: 202-228-2856

Senator Kathyrn "Kay" Bailey
   Hutchison (R)
703 Hart Senate Office Building
Washington, D.C. 20510
Phone: 202-224-5922
FAX: 202-224-0776

Representatives
Rep. Jim Chapman (D)
(First District)
2417 Rayburn House Office Building
Washington, D.C. 20515
Phone: 202-225-3035
FAX: 202-225-7265

Rep. Charles N. Wilson (D)
(Second District)
2256 Rayburn House Office Building
Washington, D.C. 20515
Phone: 202-225-2401
FAX: 202-225-1764

Rep. Sam Johnson (R)
(Third District)
1030 Longworth House Office
   Building
Washington, D.C. 20515
Phone: 202-225-4201
FAX: 202-225-1485

Rep. Ralph M. Hall (D)
(Fourth District)
2236 Rayburn House Office Building
Washington, D.C. 20515
Phone: 202-225-6673
FAX: 202-225-3332

Rep. John Wiley Bryant (D)
(Fifth District)
205 Cannon House Office Building
Washington, D.C. 20515
Phone: 202-225-2231
FAX: 202-225-9721

Rep. Joe Linus Barton (R)
(Sixth District)
1514 Longworth House Office
   Building
Washington, D.C. 20515
Phone: 202-225-2002
FAX: 202-225-3052

Rep. Bill Archer (R)
(Seventh District)
1236 Longworth House Office
   Building
Washington, D.C. 20515
Phone: 202-225-2571
FAX: 202-225-4381

Rep. Jack Fields (R)
(Eighth District)
2228 Rayburn House Office Building
Washington, D.C. 20515
Phone: 202-225-4901
FAX: 202-225-2772

Rep. Steve Stockman (R)
(Ninth District)
2449 Rayburn House Office Building
Washington, D.C. 20515
Phone: 202-225-6565
FAX: 202-225-1584

Rep. Lloyd Doggett (D)
(Tenth District)
242 Cannon House Office Building
Washington, D.C. 20515
Phone: 202-225-4865
FAX: 202-225-3018

Rep. Chet Edwards (D)
(Eleventh District)
328 Cannon House Office Building
Washington, D.C. 20515
Phone: 202-225-6105
FAX: 202-225-0350

Rep. Preston M. "Pete" Geren (D)
(Twelfth District)
1730 Longworth House Office
   Building
Washington, D.C. 20515
Phone: 202-225-5071
FAX: 202-225-2786

Rep. William Thornberry (R)
(Thirteenth District)
126 Cannon House Office Building
Washington, D.C. 20515
Phone: 202-225-3706
FAX: 202-225-6142

Rep. Greg Laughlin (D)
(Fourteenth District)
236 Cannon House Office Building
Washington, D.C. 20515
Phone: 202-225-2831
FAX: 202-225-1108

Rep. E. "Kika" de la Garza (D)
(Fifteenth District)
1401 Longworth House Office
   Building
Washington, D.C. 20515
Phone: 202-225-2531
FAX: 202-225-2534

Rep. Ronald D'Emory Coleman (D)
(Sixteenth District)
440 Cannon House Office Building
Washington, D.C. 20515
Phone: 202-225-4831
FAX: 202-225-4831

Rep. Charles W. Stenholm (D)
(Seventeenth District)
1211 Longworth House Office
   Building
Washington, D.C. 20515
Phone: 202-225-6605
FAX: 202-225-2234

Rep. Sheila Lee (D)
(Eighteenth District)
1711 Longworth House Office
   Building
Washington, D.C. 20515
Phone: 202-225-3816
FAX: 202-225-6186

Rep. Larry Ed Combest (R)
(Nineteenth District)
1511 Longworth House Office
   Building
Washington, D.C. 20515
Phone: 202-225-4005
FAX: 202-225-9615

Rep. Henry B. Gonzalez (D)
(Twentieth District)
2413 Rayburn House Office Building
Washington, D.C. 20515
Phone: 202-225-3236
FAX: 202-225-1915

Rep. Lamar S. Smith (R)
(Twenty-First District)
2443 Rayburn House Office Building
Washington, D.C. 20515
Phone: 202-225-4236
FAX: 202-225-8628

Rep. Tom DeLay (R)
(Twenty-Second District)
407 Cannon House Office Building
Washington, D.C. 20515
Phone: 202-225-5951
FAX: 202-225-5241

Rep. Henry Bonilla (R)
(Twenty-Third District)
1529 Longworth House Office
   Building
Washington, D.C. 20515
Phone: 202-225-4511
FAX: 202-225-2237

Rep. Martin Frost (D)
(Twenty-Fourth District)
2459 Rayburn House Office Building
Washington, D.C. 20515
Phone: 202-225-3605
FAX: 202-225-4951

Rep. Ken Bentsen (D)
(Twenty-Fifth District)
303 Cannon House Office Building
Washington, D.C. 20515
Phone: 202-225-7508
FAX: 202-225-4210

Rep. Richard K. Armey (R)
(Twenty-Sixth District)
301 Cannon House Office Building
Washington, D.C. 20515
Phone: 202-225-7772
FAX: 202-225-7614

Rep. Solomon P. Ortiz (D)
(Twenty-Seventh District)
2136 Rayburn House Office Building
Washington, D.C. 20515
Phone: 202-225-7742
FAX: 202-226-1134

Rep. Frank Tejeda (D)
(Twenty-Eighth District)
323 Cannon House Office Building
Washington, D.C. 20515
Phone: 202-225-1640
FAX: 202-225-1641

Rep. Gene Green (D)
(Twenty-Ninth District)
1004 Longworth House Office
   Building
Washington, D.C. 20515
Phone: 202-225-1688
FAX: 202-225-9903

Rep. Eddie B. Johnson (D)
(Thirtieth District)
1721 Longworth House Office
   Building
Washington, D.C. 20515
Phone: 202-225-8885
FAX: 202-226-1477

UTAH

Senators
Senator Robert Bennett (R)
241 Dirksen Senate Office Building
Washington, D.C. 20510
Phone: 202-224-5444
FAX: 202-224-6717

Senator Orrin G. Hatch (R)
135 Russell Senate Office Building
Washington, D.C. 20510
Phone: 202-224-5251
FAX: 202-224-6331

Representatives
Rep. James V. Hansen (R)
(First District)
2466 Rayburn House Office Building
Washington, D.C. 20515
Phone: 202-225-0453
FAX: 202-225-5857

Rep. Karen Shepherd (D)
(Second District)
414 Cannon House Office Building
Washington, D.C. 20515
Phone: 202-225-3011
FAX: 202-226-0354

Rep. William Orton (D)
(Third District)
1122 Longworth House Office
  Building
Washington, D.C. 20515
Phone: 202-225-7751
FAX: 202-226-1223

VERMONT

Senators
Senator Patrick Leahy (D)
433 Russell Senate Office Building
Washington, D.C. 20510
Phone: 202-224-4242
FAX: 202-224-3595

Senator James M. Jeffords (R)
513 Hart Senate Office Building
Washington, D.C. 20510
Phone: 202-224-5141
FAX: 202-224-8330

Representative At Large
Rep. Bernard Sanders (Soc)
213 Cannon House Office Building
Washington, D.C. 20515
Phone: 202-225-4115
FAX: 202-225-6790

VIRGINIA

Senators
Senator John W. Warner (R)
225 Russell Senate Office Building
Washington, D.C. 20510
Phone: 202-224-2023
FAX: 202-224-6295

Senator Charles S. Robb (D)
493 Russell Senate Office Building
Washington, D.C. 20510
Phone: 202-224-4024
FAX: 202-224-8689

Representatives
Rep. Herbert H. Bateman (R)
(First District)
2350 Rayburn House Office Building
Washington, D.C. 20515
Phone: 202-225-4261
FAX: 202-225-4382

Rep. Owen B. Pickett (D)
(Second District)
2430 Rayburn House Office Building
Washington, D.C. 20515
Phone: 202-225-4215
FAX: 202-225-4218

Rep. Robert C. Scott (D)
(Third District)
501 Cannon House Office Building
Washington, D.C. 20515
Phone: 202-225-8351
FAX: 202-225-8354

Rep. Norman Sisisky (D)
(Fourth District)
2352 Cannon House Office Building
Washington, D.C. 20515
Phone: 202-225-6365
FAX: 202-226-1170

Rep. Lewis F. Payne, Jr. (D)
(Fifth District)
1119 Longworth House Office
  Building
Washington, D.C. 20515
Phone: 202-225-4711
FAX: 202-226-1147

Rep. Robert W. Goodlatte (R)
(Sixth District)
214 Cannon House Office Building
Washington, D.C. 20515
Phone: 202-225-5431
FAX: 202-225-9681

Rep. Thomas J. Bliley, Jr. (R)
(Seventh District)
2241 Rayburn House Office Building
Washington, D.C. 20515
Phone: 202-225-2815
FAX: 202-225-0011

Rep. James P. Moran, Jr. (D)
(Eighth District)
430 Cannon House Office Building
Washington, D.C. 20515
Phone: 202-225-4376
FAX: 202-225-0017

Rep. Rick Boacher (D)
(Ninth District)
2245 Rayburn House Office Building
Washington, D.C. 20515
Phone: 202-225-3861
FAX: 202-225-0442

Rep. Frank R. Wolf (R)
(Tenth District)
104 Cannon House Office Building
Washington, D.C. 20515
Phone: 202-225-5136
FAX: 202-225-0437

Rep. Thomas Davis (R)
(Eleventh District)
1609 Longworth House Office
  Building
Washington, D.C. 20515
Phone: 202-225-1492
FAX: 202-225-2274

WASHINGTON

Senators
Senator Patty Murray (D)
302 Hart Senate Office Building
Washington, D.C. 20510
Phone: 202-224-2621
FAX: 202-224-0238

Senator Slade Gorton (R)
730 Hart Senate Office Building
Washington, D.C. 20510
Phone: 202-224-3441
FAX: 202-224-9393

Representatives
Rep. Rick White (R)
(First District)
1520 Longworth House Office
  Building
Washington, D.C. 20515
Phone: 202-225-6311
FAX: 202-225-3286

Rep. Jack Metcalf (R)
(Second District)
1503 Longworth House Office
  Building
Washington, D.C. 20515
Phone: 202-225-2605
FAX: 202-225-2608

Rep. Linda Smith (R)
(Third District)
1527 Longworth House Office
  Building
Washington, D.C. 20515
Phone: 202-225-3536
FAX: 202-225-9095

Rep. Doc Hastings (R)
(Fourth District)
1431 Longworth House Office
  Building
Washington, D.C. 20515
Phone: 202-225-5816
FAX: 202-226-1137

Rep. George Nethercutt (R)
(Fifth District)
1201 Longworth House Office
  Building
Washington, D.C. 20515
Phone: 202-225-2006
FAX: 202-225-7181

Rep. Norman D. Dicks (D)
(Sixth District)
2467 Rayburn House Office Building
Washington, D.C. 20515
Phone: 202-225-5916
FAX: 202-226-1176

Rep. James A. McDermott (D)
(Seventh District)
1707 Longworth House Office
  Building
Washington, D.C. 20515
Phone: 202-225-3106
FAX: 202-225-9212

Rep. Jennifer Dunn (R)
(Eighth District)
1641 Longworth House Office
  Building
Washington, D.C. 20515
Phone: 202-225-7761
FAX: 202-225-8673

Rep. Randy Tate (R)
(Ninth District)
1535 Longworth House Office
  Building
Washington, D.C. 20515
Phone: 202-225-8901
FAX: 202-226-2361

WEST VIRGINIA

Senators
Senator Robert C. Byrd (D)
311 Hart Senate Office Building
Washington, D.C. 20510
Phone: 202-224-3954
FAX: 202-224-4025

Senator John D. Rockefeller, IV (D)
109 Hart Senate Office Building
Washington, D.C. 20510
Phone: 202-224-6472
FAX: 202-224-7665

Representatives
Rep. Alan B. Mollohan (D)
(First District)
2242 Rayburn House Office Building
Washington, D.C. 20515
Phone: 202-225-4172
FAX: 202-225-7564

Rep. Robert W. Wise (D)
(Second District)
2434 Rayburn House Office Building
Washington, D.C. 20515
Phone: 202-225-2711
FAX: 202-225-7856

Rep. Nick Joe Rahall, II (D)
(Third District)
2269 Rayburn House Office Building
Washington, D.C. 20515
Phone: 202-225-3452
FAX: 202-225-9061

WISCONSIN

Senators
Senator Russell Feingold (D)
502 Hart Senate Office Building
Washington, D.C. 20510
Phone: 202-224-5323
FAX: 202-224-2725

Senator Herb Kohl (D)
330 Hart Senate Office Building
Washington, D.C. 20510
Phone: 202-224-5653
FAX: 202-224-9787

Representatives
Rep. Mark Neumann (R)
(First District)
1719 Longworth House Office
  Building
Washington, D.C. 20515
Phone: 202-225-3031
FAX: 202-225-9820

Rep. Scott L. Klug (R)
(Second District)
1224 Longworth House Office
  Building
Washington, D.C. 20515
Phone: 202-225-2906
FAX: 202-225-6942

Rep. Steven C. Gunderson (R)
(Third District)
2235 Rayburn House Office Building
Washington, D.C. 20515
Phone: 202-225-5506
FAX: 202-225-6195

Rep. Gerald D. Kleczka (D)
(Fourth District)
2301 Rayburn House Office Building
Washington, D.C. 20515
Phone: 202-225-4572
FAX: 202-225-0719

Rep. Thomas M. Barrett (D)
(Fifth District)
313 Cannon House Office Building
Washington, D.C. 20515
Phone: 202-225-3571
FAX: 202-225-2185

Rep. Thomas E. Petri (R)
(Sixth District)
2262 Rayburn House Office Building
Washington, D.C. 20515
Phone: 202-225-2476
FAX: 202-225-2356

Rep. David R. Obey (D)
(Seventh District)
2462 Rayburn House Office Building
Washington, D.C. 20515
Phone: 202-225-3365
FAX: 202-225-0561

Rep. Toby Roth (R)
(Eighth District)
2234 Rayburn House Office Building
Washington, D.C. 20515
Phone: 202-225-5665
FAX: 202-225-0087

Rep. E. James Sensenbrenner, Jr. (R)
(Ninth District)
2332 Rayburn House Office Building
Washington, D.C. 20515
Phone: 202-225-5101
FAX: 202-225-3190

WYOMING

Senators
Senator Craig Thomas (R)
237 Russell Senate Office Building
Washington, D.C. 20510
Phone: 202-224-6441
FAX: 202-224-3230

Senator Alan K. Simpson (R)
261 Dirksen Senate Office Building
Washington, D.C. 20510
Phone: 202-224-3424
FAX: 202-224-1315

Representative At Large
Rep. Barbara Cubin (R)
1019 Longworth House Office
  Building
Washington, D.C. 20515
Phone: 202-225-2311
FAX: 202-225-0726

NOTES

Chapter One

1. The figure $22,950 was computed by dividing the 1984 federal debt of $1.836 trillion by the 80 million taxpayers in the United States in 1984. Similarly, the 1995 figure on page 4 of $43,500 was computed by dividing the 1995 federal debt of $5 trillion by the 115 million taxpayers in the United States in 1995.
2. Estimate of the National Taxpayers Union, based on U.S. Treasury, *Statement of Liabilities and Other Financial Commitments of the U.S. Government* and NTUF staff calculations and estimates of actuarial liabilities from government data.
3. Quoted in Milton and Rose Friedman, *Tyranny of the Status Quo* (New York: Harcourt, 1983-84), 35.
4. Harry E. Figgie, Jr., and Gerald J. Swanson, *Bankruptcy 1995: The Coming Collapse of America and How to Stop It* (Boston: Little, Brown, 1992).
5. Robert M. Dunn, Jr., "Deficit: Interest Threatens to Outpace Growth," *Los Angeles Times,* September 2, 1984, sec. 1, 7.
6. From an interview with John Templeton, who cites "The Historical Statistics of the United States, Colonial Times to 1970" (Washington, D.C.: U.S. Department of Commerce, 1976).
7. "Reducing the Deficit: Spending and Revenue Options" (Washington, D.C.: U.S. Government Printing Office, 1984), 1-5.

Chapter Two
1. J. Peter Grace, *War on Waste* (New York: Macmillan, 1984), v.
2. Ibid., v.
3. Ibid., v.
4. George Herbert Mead, *Mind, Self, and Society,* vol. 1 (Chicago: University of Chicago Press, 1934), ll.
5. *Financial Times of London,* June 7, 1995

Chapter Three
1. For a more thorough treatment of the destructive force of a large national debt, see Debt Shock: *The Full Story of the World Credit Crisis* by Darrell Delamaide (Garden City, N.Y.: Doubleday, 1984).
2. Ibid., 157.

Chapter Four
1. Friedman, *Tyranny*, 12.
2. John F. Kennedy, Inaugural Address, January 20, 1961.
3. Summarized in *Business Week,* June 18, 1984, 15.
4. "Messiah of the Market," *Time,* August 27, 1984, 43.

Chapter Five
1. Information about South Bronx from Horowitz, Craig, "A South Bronx Renaissance," *New York,* November 21, 1994, 54-59.
2. Philip K. Howard, *The Death of Common Sense* (New York: Random House, 1994), 33, 37, 156-157.
3. John B. O'Donnell and Jim Haner, "Welfare Gone Haywire," *Reader's Digest* (condensed from the *Baltimore Sun*), May, 1995, 92-96.
4. "Welfare Reform: A Priority for Clinton Administration," *Children Today 1993,* Vol. 22, Issue 2, 4-6.
5. Brian Dumaine, "Blacks on Blacks," *Fortune,* November 2, 1992, 118-132.
6. Carlton Stowers, "Healing Spirit," *People*, May 15, 1995, 103.
7. Dan Fisher and friends, "Angels of Mercy," *Successful Farming,* December, 1993, 20

Chapter Seven
1. "Manville's Big Concern As It Files in Chapter 11 is Litigation, Not Debt," *Wall Street Journal,* August 27, 1982, 1, 8.
2. Barry Newman, "Banker's Delight," Wall Street Journal, September 20, 1984, 1, 22.

Chapter Eight
1. J. Peter Grace, *Burning Money* (New York: Macmillan, 1984), 3.
2. Ibid., 88-89.

Chapter Nine
1. Here is how one of the early proposed amendments to the Constitution reads (next page).

Article

Section 1. Prior to each fiscal year, the Congress shall adopt a statement of receipts and outlays for that year in which total outlays are not greater than total receipts. The Congress may amend such statement provided revised outlays are not greater than revised receipts. Whenever three-fifths of the whole number of both Houses shall deem it necessary, Congress in such statement may provide for a specific excess of outlays over receipts by a vote directed solely to that subject. The Congress and the President shall, pursuant to legislation or through exercise of their powers under the first and second articles, ensure that actual outlays do not exceed the outlays set forth in such statement.

Section 2. Total receipts for any fiscal year set forth in the statement adopted pursuant to this article shall not increase by a rate greater than the rate of increase in national income in the year or years ending not less than six months nor more than twelve months before such fiscal year, unless a majority of the whole number of both Houses of Congress shall have passed a bill directed solely to approving specific additional receipts and such bill has become law.

Section 3. The Congress may waive the provisions of this article for any fiscal year in which a declaration of war is in effect.

Section 4. Total receipts shall include all receipts of the United States except those derived from borrowing and total outlays shall include all outlays of the United States except those for repayment of debt principal.

Section 5. The Congress shall enforce and implement this article by appropriate legislation.

Section 6. On and after the date this article takes effect, the amount of Federal public debt limit as of such date shall become permanent and there shall be no increase in such amount unless three-fifths of the whole number of both Houses of Congress shall have passed a bill approving such increase and such bill has become law.

Section 7. This article shall take effect for the second fiscal year beginning after its ratification.

2. Friedman, *Tyranny,* 65.

Chapter Ten
1. The Council of Economic Advisers' "Economic Report to the President," February, 1984 (Washington, D.C.: U.S. Government Printing Office, 1984), 220-223.

Chapter Eleven
1. Clarence W. Hall, "The Country That Saved Itself," *Reader's Digest,* November, 1964, 143.
2. Ibid., 147.